The U.S. Coast Guard's War on Human Smuggling

New Perspectives on Maritime History and Nautical Archaeology

UNIVERSITY PRESS OF FLORIDA
Florida A&M University, Tallahassee
Florida Atlantic University, Boca Raton
Florida Gulf Coast University, Ft. Myers
Florida International University, Miami
Florida State University, Tallahassee
New College of Florida, Sarasota
University of Central Florida, Orlando
University of Florida, Gainesville
University of North Florida, Jacksonville
University of South Florida, Tampa
University of West Florida, Pensacola

The U.S. Coast Guard's War on Human Smuggling

Dennis L. Noble

James C. Bradford
and Gene Allen Smith
Series Editors

University Press of Florida

Gainesville · Tallahassee · Tampa
Boca Raton · Pensacola ·Orlando · Miami
Jacksonville · Ft. Myers · Sarasota

Copyright 2011 by Dennis L. Noble

Printed in the United States of America. This book is printed on Glatfelter Natures Book, a paper certified under the standards of the Forestry Stewardship Council (FSC). It is a recycled stock that contains 30 percent post-consumer waste and is acid-free.

All rights reserved

Portions of chapter 1 appeared in a different form in Dennis L. Noble, "Lessons Unlearned: The Camarioca Boatlift," *Naval History* 23, no. 4 (August 2009): 44–49.

Portions of chapter 7 appeared in a different form in Dennis L. Noble, "The *Golden Venture*: Where Migrant Interdiction and Search and Rescue Collided," *Wreck & Rescue*, 11, no. 3 (2006): 21–23.

Frontispiece: A Haitian child being handed up to a crewman on a U.S. Coast Guard cutter.

All photographs unless otherwise noted are courtesy of the U.S. Coast Guard.

16 15 14 13 12 11 6 5 4 3 2 1

Library of Congress Cataloging-in-Publication Data
Noble, Dennis L.
The U.S. Coast Guard's war on human smuggling / Dennis L. Noble.
p. cm.—(New perspectives on maritime history and nautical archaeology)
Includes bibliographical references and index.
ISBN 978-0-8130-3606-9 (alk. paper)
1. Illegal aliens—United States. 2. Human smuggling—United States—Prevention—History—20th century. 3. Human smuggling—United States—Prevention—History—21st century. 4. United States. Coast Guard—History—20th century. 5. United States. Coast Guard—History—21st century. 6. United States—Emigration and immigration—History—20th century. 7. United States—Emigration and immigration—History—21st century.
I. Title.
JV6455.N63 2011
364.1'370973—dc22 2010054026

The University Press of Florida is the scholarly publishing agency for the State University System of Florida, comprising Florida A&M University, Florida Atlantic University, Florida Gulf Coast University, Florida International University, Florida State University, New College of Florida, University of Central Florida, University of Florida, University of North Florida, University of South Florida, and University of West Florida.

University Press of Florida
15 Northwest 15th Street
Gainesville, FL 32611-2079
http://www.upf.com

This is for Charles W. "Skip" Bowen,
who started me on this voyage,
and
for all the U.S. Coast Guard personnel
who know the hard mission of dealing
with undocumented migrants.

The story of migrant work is more than an account of legal policies, politics or tactics. It is a human story both from the migrants involved and the men and women charged with stopping them.

MCPOCG Charles W. Bowen

You can't do migrant operations without having your heart broken.

Rear Adm. Arthur E. Brooks, USCG

Contents

Preface

A continuing "hot button" domestic issue in the United States centers on the flow of undocumented migrants into America. Most of the attention of the general public and decision makers focuses on the Southwestern border between Mexico and the United States. Unbeknownst to many, there are people from all nations who try to enter the United States without documents by a maritime route.

Those who study the movement of undocumented migrants into the United States may rightfully point out the numbers from the sea are much smaller than those crossing at the Southwestern border. A common thread in the story of undocumented migrants using the maritime route is how quickly human smugglers change their tactics to counter law enforcement agencies. This also applies to those crossing by land. Should the United States decide to take greater control of its Southwestern border, then there is no doubt that those who deal in human trafficking will turn more to the sea. Therefore, it is important to know what took place in the past and continues today.

To examine all aspects of this subject would take a volume many times larger than the present. To bring the problem into better focus, I have chosen to center the study on the U.S. Coast Guard's role in intercepting undocumented migrants. In the service's lexicon, I am examining their role in alien migrant interdiction operations (AMIO). While this book focuses on the U.S. Coast Guard, this is not to slight other law enforcement agencies in their duties to intercept undocumented migrants. I have chosen the U.S. Coast Guard because of its unique maritime law enforcement powers not given to the other four armed forces and for the simple fact that it is the lead federal service in dealing with undocumented migrants from the sea route.

The U.S. Coast Guard has intercepted undocumented migrants from many nations. Instead of showing all the various nationalities, I have further narrowed the work to three groups of people: Cuban, Haitian, and Chinese. These three ethnic groups present a wide range of the problems faced and show the worldwide aspect of human trafficking from the sea.

My journey on this project began with a conversation with Master Chief Petty Officer (MCPO) Charles W. Bowen, USCG, who was at the time officer-in-charge of Station Marathon in the Florida Keys. Master Chief Bowen has extensive experience in working with undocumented migrants in the Caribbean basin. He pointed out that the story of the service's work in AMIO is not just about law enforcement but a "human story." Bowen's comment and the research involved in the study caused me to focus largely on two aspects, with one major exception. The main thrust of this book is to put a human face on the enforcers—the U.S. Coast Guard people doing the work—and, as much as possible, the undocumented migrants. The leadership of the U.S. Coast Guard has failed to show that the men and women who work with undocumented migrants are human. This failure is not the focus of this work but does help explain why crews have not received the attention they deserve. For example, Vincent C. Thomas Jr., a contributing editor for *Sea Power* magazine, in 1984 derided the "ineffective way in which the Coast Guard communicates to the media and general public the accomplishments of its people. Heroics at sea by Coast Guard personnel are an everyday occurrence; those accomplishments should be communicated routinely to higher authority as a matter of practice, so that the information is at least available for release to the public. That simply is not happening now; as a result, a horrendous vacuum of newsworthy information exists." Thomas's comments continue to be true twenty-five years later. Those who expect to see long discussions on the pros and cons of immigration policy will not find them in this work. Again, the focus is on the people who enforce the policies. However, perhaps the changing policies say much about the struggles for a clear immigration policy.

The second thrust of this book deals with an overview of the major machinations concerning undocumented migrants that took place over the years. The U.S. Coast Guard does not set the policies and laws governing undocumented migrants. In our system of government, the service must follow the policies that are set by civilian decision makers. As will be seen throughout this book, many of the decisions can be described charitably as confused. Constantly changing policies makes enforcement all that more complicated. The political background helps to understand an additional burden of confusing policies placed upon the men and women of the service in carrying out their mission.

The one exception to the major thrusts of this book is put forth in chapter 1. Operación Pedro Pan (Operation Peter Pan) is not connected with the sea. It is used to graphically illustrate one desperate reason why many Cubans later chose to enter rafts to escape their country. Furthermore, most who sent their children away felt it was a temporary measure. Surely Fidel Castro would never remain in power. This feeling of a short-lived Castro takeover is an important aspect of the Cuban–U.S. relationship.

To give the reader some knowledge of Cuba, Haiti, and the People's Republic of China, there is only a brief discussion of each country. Readers should consult standard histories on each of these interesting countries.

Readers will note that a number of chapters are devoted to Cuba. Cuba marked a major change in the U.S. Coast Guard's mission dealing with undocumented migrants and represents great difficulties with decision makers to come to grip with Fidel Castro's government, so it is only natural that more space is devoted to the subject.

There is no examination of the incursion into Haiti during President William J. Clinton's administration although the root cause can be traced to increased migration from Haiti. There are also no detailed examinations of rioting in camps in Guantánamo or in the United States by undocumented migrants. Again, the focus of this work is that undertaken by the service at sea.

I use the term undocumented migrants—for that is what the Cuban, Haitian, and Chinese of this work are—rather than the loaded words "illegal alien" or "illegal migrant." The word "illegal" is used only in direct quotes from other sources.

After the establishment of the Department of Homeland Security, many agencies dealing with the enforcement of undocumented migrants found themselves reorganized. Instead of explaining each change in the organizations, I use the most common names during most of the period of the study: the Immigration and Naturalization Service (INS), the Border Patrol, and the Customs Service.

I have visited U.S. Coast Guard units and interviewed service people, either in person or via e-mail, in my attempt to put a human face on the enforcers. In some cases U.S. Coast Guard people wished to remain anonymous, and I have honored their request.

The reader will note there are few detailed accounts of the tactics used by the U.S. Coast Guard in capturing human smugglers from the period after 1994. Only general information is given in order not to provide operational tactics that might hinder the work of the service.

If this study brings out the difficulties in enforcing the policies of stopping undocumented migrants from the maritime route and puts a human face on the enforcers and the undocumented migrants, then the book has accomplished its mission.

The U.S. Coast Guard's War on Human Smuggling

Introduction

A U.S. Coast Guard petty officer received orders for a permanent transfer to a station in Florida. The first night on board his new unit, he found himself on a speeding boat in pursuit of a human smuggler with a load of Cuban undocumented migrants. As the U.S. Coast Guard boat drew near, the smugglers grabbed a child and put the toddler over the gunwale of the boat, trying to keep the pursuing boat from coming alongside. "The people in the smuggler's boat were screaming at the smugglers. I wondered, 'What is going on down here?'"[1]

This book is an attempt to show "what is going on" down in Florida and other locations during the U.S. Coast Guard's mission of intercepting undocumented migrants. Most Americans picture the U.S. Coast Guard as a rescue service. This perception is not without foundation. The number of people saved yearly numbers into the hundreds. Then why is the service chasing after undocumented migrants off Florida and other locations?

Since 1789, the U.S. Coast Guard and its many predecessors have not only saved lives but have also carried out polar operations, manned lighthouses, inspected merchant vessels for safety, participated in combat alongside the other armed forces of the United States, and enforced the federal laws of the United States. One of the predecessors of the U.S. Coast Guard, the Revenue Marine, later the U.S. Revenue Cutter Service, came into being as a maritime law enforcement force to protect U.S. customs. This traditional federal law enforcement mission is what makes the U.S. Coast Guard unique compared to the other active and reserve armed forces. The other branches of the U.S. military are usually prohibited from taking part in active law enforcement activities within the United States under federal law (18 U.S.C. § 1385), passed on June 16, 1878, and known as the Posse Comitatus Act. Passed to prevent a military police force within the United States, it has undergone many changes over the years but still is in effect. In the case of undocumented migrant operations, a U.S. Navy ship cannot on its own enforce the law concerning undocumented migrants but can take part in such operations only if a U.S. Coast Guard law enforcement detachment is on board the ship.[2]

One of the traditional law enforcement duties of the service focuses on preventing undocumented migrants from entering the United States. From 1794 until the U.S. Civil War this largely meant actions against the slave trade.

On February 19, 1862, reacting to a fear of the "yellow peril," the U.S. Congress prohibited the importation of Chinese laborers—in the West called "coolies"—and forbade U.S.-flagged vessels and citizens from participating in that trade. Eventually this led to the Chinese Exclusion Act of 1882, which remained in effect until 1943. The act caused human trafficking into the United States. One estimate places the number of Chinese smuggled into America during the last years of the nineteenth century at twenty thousand people.[3]

In 1914 the U.S. Revenue Cutter Service, noted for maritime law enforcement, and the U.S. Life-Saving Service, known for saving lives from shore-based stations, combined to form the U.S. Coast Guard. In trying to stop human smuggling, nothing much changed for the newly named service until 1929, when the great social experiment of Prohibition, the stopping of the sale of alcoholic beverages, began. During Prohibition, running booze and undocumented migrants proved lucrative enterprises. Ernest Hemingway's 1937 novel *To Have and Have Not* has Henry Morgan running both liquor and Chinese from Havana, Cuba, to Florida.

A steady trickle of undocumented Chinese migrants entered the United States until World War II. The numbers slowly increased after the war until 1949, when Mao Zedong's ascendancy to power in the People's Republic of China virtually stopped the flow. The tide began again shortly after Mao's death, and in 1980 the numbers of people rapidly increased.

From 1794 until 1980, the known numbers of undocumented migrants trying to reach the United States via the sea remained relatively small, so policing the traffic of undocumented migrants was never a primary mission of the service. (The number of people who actually succeeded in entering the United States without being stopped is likely much larger than those caught.) Intercepting undocumented migrants continued as a "tack on" mission to other duties of the U.S. Coast Guard. During Prohibition, for instance, stopping the flow of unlawful liquor into the United States proved the main mission of the service. If the cuttermen found smuggled Chinese on a rumrunner, so much the better for the leadership to put before Congress during budget hearings. The problem with this type of part-time operation is that crews did not receive adequate training in the tactics of stopping human smuggling.

With two major exceptions, cases concerning undocumented migrants from 1914 to 1980 generated very little interest, if any, both inside and outside the service. The first exception began in 1965. On September 28, 1965, Fidel Castro opened the port of Camarioca, Cuba, to any Cuban who wished to leave the country, if a Cuban exile living in the United States brought a boat south to transport those who wished to leave. Known as the Camarioca Boatlift, at least 2,979 Cubans took this opportunity to leave their country.

The second exception began on November 23, 1970, off the coast of Massachusetts. On that date, Simas Kudirka, a seaman from an anchored Soviet fishing vessel, came on board a nearby anchored U.S. Coast Guard cutter and asked for asylum. Due to a series of bad decisions, and perhaps little knowledge on the part of the senior leadership of the service of what constitutes a political refugee, the Soviets were allowed to come on board the cutter and forcibly take Kudirka back to the Soviet ship.

While the Kudirka case did not rebound to the U.S. Coast Guard's credit, it did show the need for its leadership and crews to understand the legal issues of refugees, asylum, and undocumented migrants. This became clear after 1980.

Most people in the United States feel their country is based on openness to those escaping persecution, no matter their race, nationality, or creed. President Ronald Reagan said, "Can we doubt that only a divine Providence placed this land, this land of freedom, here as a refuge for all those people in the world who yearn to breathe free? Jews and Christians enduring persecution behind the Iron Curtain, the boat people of Southeast Asia, Cuba, and Haiti."[4] Despite President Reagan's words, decision makers of both political parties have found themselves at odds with this perception over the years. The executive and legislative branches from time to time have moved away from the concept, citing national security, economic and social concerns, foreign policy, limited resources, and an intolerant and resentful public. While it is not the intent of this book to detail all the legal ramifications of international and domestic law concerning refugees and undocumented migrants, part of the story of the U.S. Coast Guard's efforts at stemming the tide of undocumented migrants from the sea is the changing policies that govern those who must enforce the law.

Fidel Castro's overthrow of the Cuban government of Fulgencio Batista in 1959 is one of the defining moments in the story of the U.S. Coast Guard's efforts to stop human smuggling into the United States. Castro at first hinted at his democratic leanings and then openly announced that his would be a Communist government. Some Cubans began to flee the country, first in an orderly manner, using scheduled airlines. Then, in 1965, the trickle became larger. In 1980 the trickle turned into a tidal wave, during what became known as the Mariel Boatlift (see chapters 2–4).

Words such as "overwhelm" and "inundate" do not adequately convey the effect that the Mariel Boatlift had upon local, state, and federal governmental agencies, or on the people of Cuba and Florida. For a very short period from April to September of 1980, approximately 125,000 Cubans successfully made the ninety-mile sea passage from their island country to the United States. Mariel changed the U.S. Coast Guard's part-time mission of intercepting undocumented migrants to a full-time mission.

In 1994 large numbers of Cubans again took to the sea in literally anything that floated to escape their country; this caused the U.S. Coast Guard to mount a special operation. Operation Able Vigil proved the service's "largest peacetime operation since the Vietnam War." Cutters, already engaged in Haitian operations, now faced a mass migration from Cuba. The operation also caused President Bill Clinton's announcement of what is now popularly known as the "wet foot/dry foot" policy. This policy changed the automatic entry of undocumented Cuban migrants into the United States. During this period, General (Gen.) John M. Shalikashvili, the chairman of the Joint Chiefs of Staff, ordered Department of Defense forces to assist the U.S. Coast Guard. All of the other four United States armed forces participated in Operation Able Vigil. The work of the U.S. Coast Guard in the Caribbean basin during the period from 1965 through Operation Able Vigil is the first time in U.S. military history that the other four larger military forces all supported the U.S. Coast Guard. Cuban undocumented migrants continued their dangerous voyage across the Florida Straits.

In 1988 Captain (Capt.) Alex Larzeller, USCG, wrote, "We must consider how to deal with another massive migration by sea—for I have little doubt that this nation will face such an event again sometime in the future."[5] Even as Larzeller's work rolled off the press, the U.S. Coast Guard began feeling the impact of the captain's prophetic words. The largest numbers did not come from Cuba, however. From 1982 through 1989, a total of 609 Cubans were intercepted by the service while 21,588 Haitians were brought aboard cutters and small boats. Clearly, the service seemed on the brink of another mass migration from yet another Caribbean island nation.

The voyages of the undocumented Haitian migrants remind one of a line from the novelist Ford Madox Ford's, *The Good Soldier*: "This is the saddest story I have ever heard."[6] Immigration from Haiti, both documented and undocumented, rose steadily soon after François "Papa Doc" Duvalier took over the government in 1957. Duvalier's reign—and that of his son, Jean-Claude "Baby Doc" Duvalier—began a long period of political oppression combined with economic hardship. The overthrow of Baby Doc's regime in 1986 ushered in another period of unrest, which generated more people wishing to flee from their island home.

Like the Cubans, the Haitians suffered greatly during their voyage in deplorable craft. The Haitians, however, had disadvantages not encountered by the Cubans. Geography made their voyage longer, thus more dangerous. Until 1994 U.S. policy dictated that Cubans, because they were fleeing from a communist country, were immediately welcomed with open arms and citizenship. In other words, according to U.S. policy, they could claim refugee status because they were fleeing from the political oppression of a communist government. Haitians, on the other hand, because they came from a supposedly "free" country, were generally looked upon as economic refugees, and this did not entitle them to the welcome that the Cubans received.

This policy remains in effect. Also mitigating against the fleeing Haitians, but not officially mentioned by U.S. policymakers, Haitians had darker skin than most Cuban refugees, and the practice of voodoo by some Haitians caused many in America to remark that they "were not even Christian." Adding yet another problem for the Haitians, information began circulating in the media that most Haitians had human immunodeficiency virus (HIV).

From January 1993 until September 1994, the U.S. Coast Guard faced two mass migrations at the same time. The number of Haitians that crossed the decks of cutters during this period more than tripled from 1990. These large numbers in the Caribbean Basin caused the establishment of two major operations, Operation Able Vigil, discussed above, and Operation Able Manner.

Operation Able Manner began on January 15, 1993, and ended on November 26, 1994. The work centered largely in the Windward Passage, the stretch of the sea between Cuba and Haiti. At its height, the operation used seventeen cutters, nine aircraft, and five U.S. Navy ships. This operation continued until a new government in Haiti was in place by November 1994.

Beginning in 1991 another migrant group, albeit a group the service had a long experience with, began adding to the U.S. Coast Guard's statistics. That year the service first recorded 138 undocumented migrants from the People's Republic of China (PRC). Two years later this had ballooned to 2,511.

A quick glance at a map of the world reveals that any undocumented migrant trying to enter the United States from the PRC via the sea has an immense voyage to consider. It is 6,492 miles (10,447 kilometers) from the Chinese southeastern coastal city of Fuzhou to San Francisco, for example. Yet many Chinese willingly attempted the voyage to what is known in China as the "Golden Mountain," or *Meiguo*, the "beautiful country."

In the period from 1990 to 1993, the U.S. Coast Guard faced a tsunami of smuggled Chinese on ships. A 1993 internal Department of Justice report concerning this smuggling declared it an "immigration emergency." By April of 1993 James Hayes, the assistant director for investigations of the Immigration and Naturalization Service (INS), said, "The way these boats have been coming in, I wouldn't be surprised if I saw one land in Topeka,

Kansas. They seem to have the ability to show up anywhere."[7] Shortly thereafter, the ship *Golden Venture* ran aground at Queens, New York, and became the most important case of smuggling Chinese into this country.

As with the Cubans and Haitians, the human trafficking of Chinese has slackened a little since 1994, but undocumented migrants from all three ethnic groups continue to attempt to enter the United States, and the U.S. Coast Guard continues to intercept—in the service's lexicon, interdict—them.

The story of the U.S. Coast Guard's role in preventing the entry into the United States can be told through examining policies, strategy, and tactics. It can be told through an administrative or operational history. MCPO Charles W. Bowen, USCG, officer-in-charge of Station Marathon in the Florida Keys said, "The story of migrant work is more than an account of legal policies, politics or tactics. It is a human story both from the migrants involved and the men and women charged with stopping them."[8]

What Master Chief Bowen did not mention, however, is how few Americans understand what the people of the U.S. Coast Guard go through to accomplish the important mission of intercepting undocumented migrants. Nor do they know about the migrants themselves. The undocumented migrants and those attempting to enforce the law are not humanized. This book attempts to give general backgrounds to the laws, policies, and some tactics used to stop human smuggling by the U.S. Coast Guard, but the main focus is to give a human face to those undertaking this important and often dangerous mission. One way to show the human side is to see how the enforcers feel about the duty they are called upon to perform. In other words, this study relies more on humans than laws or policies. It is an attempt to tell the story of a small group of men and women trying to carry out a difficult mission.

PART I

1959–1992

1 From Operación Pedro Pan to "Machine Gun Alley"

> Don't let anyone tell you there isn't plenty of water between Havana and Key West.
>
> Ernest Hemingway, *To Have and Have Not*

On January 2, 1959, part of Fidel Castro's revolutionary army triumphantly entered Havana, Cuba. Greeted "by tens of thousands of jubilant, cheering 'Habaneros,'" tourists in the Hilton Hotel "threw confetti from the windows as the rebel convoy passed below."[1] Many in the United States felt the overthrow of Fulgencio Batista's regime was a move toward a better democratic and social order in the island country. Within two years, however, Castro declared himself a "Marxist-Leninist until the last day of my life."[2] In this short time, an amazing number of political machinations took place.

The United States' relationship with Cuba is as complicated as the Caribbean nation's history. Christopher Columbus landed on Cuba on October 28, 1492. The next year he returned with seventeen ships and fifteen hundred men. The first Spanish governor of the island, Diego Velázquez, divided the native people of the island, the Ciboney and Taíno Arawak, among the colonists as slaves for gold mines and sugar plantations. Within fifty years of the Spanish conquest of the island, the native peoples were virtually extinct.[3]

By 1523 the Spanish began bringing African slaves to take over the work in the mines and fields. By 1830 at least fourteen thousand Africans arrived each year in this cruel trade.

Other Europeans began coveting the island. French and English raiders began striking Cuba. The Dutch arrived in the early 1600s. Soon both raiding and commerce swept the island. England occupied Cuba for seven months in 1762 but restored it to Spain after the Seven Years' War in 1763 in exchange for the colony of Florida. When Spain lost most of its American empire, it retained and tightened control of Cuba.

During the first quarter of the nineteenth century, the island country's economy flourished. Sugar dominated the Cuban economy, which demanded more slaves. Tobacco also proved an important crop. By the middle of the century, Cuba provided at least a quarter of Spain's revenues, largely through sugar. The sugar crop continued to demand more and more slaves until the slave trade was outlawed internationally.

By the 1840s and 1850s the island saw repeated invasions as some in the United States began to think that Cuba should be annexed by the United States. Spain then increased their military presence on the island. From 1868 to 1878 Cubans began their long struggle for independence from Spain. The period ended in a treaty that Spain did not enforce. The 1890s again saw Cubans demand freedom. José Martí established the Cuban Revolutionary Party in 1892 in the United States; he returned to Cuba in 1895 and died in the struggle for independence.[4]

The year of Martí's death saw a growing fervor in the United States for war with Spain. The 1898 explosion and sinking of the USS *Maine* in Havana's harbor became the catalyst for war between Spain and the United States. Some in the United States saw this as the perfect time to annex the island. However, Congress inserted the Teller Amendment into the declaration of war. Named for Sen. Henry Moore Teller of Colorado, the amendment stated that the United States would not exercise jurisdiction or control over Cuba, except for a brief period of pacification, and would leave as soon as the war was over. War was declared on April 25, 1898, and the Treaty of Peace was signed in Paris on December 10, 1898. Spain ceded Puerto Rico and Guam to United States and allowed the United States to purchase the Philippine Islands from Spain for 20 million dollars. The peace treaty established the independence of Cuba.

In 1900 Cuba had a Constituent Assembly and elections took place. Despite the Teller Amendment, U.S. troops remained in Cuba.

On March 2, 1901, as the U.S. Congress debated the army's appropriation, another amendment that impacted Cuba—and continues to impact Cuba—entered the diplomatic history of the two countries. Known as the Platt Amendment and named for Sen. Orville Platt but largely drafted by the secretary of war, Elihu Root, the amendment contained eight conditions to which the Cuban government had to agree to before the United States would withdraw its troops from the country. It also provided for the United States naval base at Guantánamo Bay. Another condition stated the Cuban government had to make a treaty with the United States to incorporate the terms of the amendment into their constitution. Although recognizing the amendment limited their sovereignty, the Cubans agreed.[5]

In 1934, under President Franklin D. Roosevelt's "Good Neighbor Policy," the Treaty of Relations between Cuba and the United States abrogated the Platt Amendment, except for giving up the base at Guantánamo. By this time Cuba had become a playground for many from the United States and a lucrative source of wealth for many others.[6]

Just prior to the Treaty of Relations, a young soldier, Fulgencio Batista y Zaldívar, led the successful "Sergeant's Revolt" in 1933. The unrest in Cuba caused concern within the U.S. government.[7] "With practically the entire Navy on the West Coast," the U.S. Coast Guard received orders to proceed to Cuba. The service sent a large force made up of eight destroyers—on loan from the navy (manned by U.S. Coast Guardsmen) for use during Prohibition to help stop smugglers of liquor into the United States—and four cutters. Known as the Cuban Expedition, the U.S. Coast Guard crews served in Cuban waters from "the first half of September 1933, and terminated 6 November 1933."[8]

As a result of the revolt, Batista gained the position of Army chief of staff. In 1940 he won election as president but was voted out of office in 1944. In a bloodless coup, Batista again seized power in 1952. Because his coup followed a series of corrupt administrations, Batista at first gained acceptance, but he soon lost favor when he temporarily suspended voting and the constitution. From then on until the end of his regime, he received strong opposition. On July 26, 1953, Fidel Castro led an attack on the Moncada Barracks near Santiago de Cuba and thus began his rise to power.

Concerned about the reaction of the United States to his successful revolution, Castro performed a whirlwind public relations trip to his northern neighbor in April 1959. He assured Americans that his "heart" resided "with the democracies" and he did "not agree with communism."[9] In a speech delivered to the National Press Club in Washington, D.C., Castro said, "We are against all kinds of dictators, whether of a man, or a country, or a class, or an oligarchy, or by the military. That is why we are against communism."[10]

Shortly after Castro's takeover, he began tweaking Uncle Sam by condemning the United States for training the former dictator's soldiers. He warned President Dwight D. Eisenhower that "200,000 gringos will die" if the United States sent Marines to Cuba.[11] Castro, still denying any communist sympathy, began to expropriate American companies, especially those of the United Fruit Company. All American-owned sugar plantations were seized, which totaled some 8,310,000 acres. Castro also started social reforms. For example, he passed the rent law, which stated that those who paid less than one hundred pesos a month had their rents cut in half; those with rents higher than one hundred pesos had their payment reduced 30 to 40 percent. This cut into the earnings of the upper class who invested in rental property.[12]

Castro took over the U.S.-owned Texaco and ESSO (Standard Oil) and the British-Dutch Shell oil industries. Goaded by the expropriations of American companies, the U.S. Congress authorized the president to cancel the U.S. bonus pay to Cuba for sugar imports. Castro countered with a comment that Cuba "would keep taking over gringo assets 'until not even the nails in their shoes are left.'"[13]

Castro's barbed comments continued. When the French merchant ship *La Coubre* exploded in Havana's harbor on March 4, 1960, Castro blamed the explosion and resulting deaths on the United States. President Eisenhower countered by "virtually wiping out the U.S. market for sugar." Eventually, on October 19, 1960, the president imposed an embargo, with the exception of medicines, medical supplies, and many food products. Castro, in a speech on January 2, 1961, then demanded the immediate reduction of the U.S. embassy in Havana to eleven people. President Eisenhower followed this with severing diplomatic and consular relations with Cuba the next day. As these actions played out, Castro began courting the Soviet Union.[14]

At the height of the Cold War, the specter of a hostile communist government so close to the United States' mainland worried many. Reacting to this fear, President Eisenhower on March 17, 1960, authorized the Central Intelligence Agency (CIA) to begin recruiting and training Cuban exiles to overthrow Castro's government. This led to the ill-starred Bay of Pigs invasion on April 17, 1961. The crushing of the invasion by Castro's forces had an even stronger effect on U.S.–Cuban relations. It proved to the people of the island that Castro's constant warnings of a U.S.-planned invasion of their country proved correct. Just as importantly, the invasion caused Castro to implement even stronger repressive controls on the population. Some have pointed out that the Bay of Pigs made it impossible for any armed resistance against Castro to succeed. Furthermore, it led Castro to demand missiles from the Soviet Union. This in turn led to the Cuban Missile Crisis of October 1962, bringing the United States to the brink of nuclear war. One of the agreements worked out to resolve this major incident stated that the United States "would pledge publicly not to invade Cuba." Just as the Bay of Pigs helped Castro prevent a revolt from within the country, the "Cuban missile crisis provided a guarantee against attack from without, ensuring a Cuban communist government for decades to come."[15]

The 1980 Cuban Mariel Boatlift is usually pointed to as the defining moment in dealing with Cuban mass migration into the United States. For the U.S. Coast Guard, Mariel meant a major change in one of their missions. Unbeknownst to many, however, Mariel was the second of three mass movements of people trying to flee Cuba via the sea. Scholars point out that Cubans actually began leaving shortly after Castro assumed power. Many professionals and skilled workers left via regular commercial flights from Havana to Miami prior to the clampdowns invoked after the Bay of Pigs invasion. "According to Castro, Cuba lost more than 50 percent of its doctors and teachers to the United States during the first two years of the revolution." Some attempted to make it to the United States via the sea.[16]

During the more than four decades of Fidel Castro's power, it is difficult to recall that until after the Bay of Pigs, an underground movement existed. The underground and the government spewed forth a steady stream of propaganda. Not long after the successful revolution, the underground began circulating rumors that Castro intended to pass a law that would take away parents' rights over their children—*la patria potestad*. Actions of the government soon gave parents good reason to believe this rumor. In February 1961, "the government announced that all schools would be closed and made it clear there would be no private education."[17] Before the revolution, private schools remained almost exclusively for those with money.

The government claimed that the educated children would be used to help those in the countryside who could not read and write. The children would remain in camps and then be sent out to teach. Many Cubans saw this as a thinly veiled effort to propagandize the children while they remained in camp.

As the government fought back against the underground, those in the resistance naturally worried about their families. This fear led to Operaçion Pedro Pan (Operation Peter Pan). The operation involved the granting of waivers of visas and pointed out how the United States, for the first time, became a country of first asylum. Previously, those seeking refugee status in the United States underwent interviews and investigations in another country. The country where the refugee made the first application was considered the first country of asylum.[18] Therefore, if the refugee were denied the status or visa, that ended the United States' problem. Castro's Cuba changed this procedure.

As more and more Cubans sought to leave their country for the United States, the bureaucracy involved in the application for a visa slowed or stopped the applicants. A 1960 State Department memorandum dealing with actions against Castro stated that many Cubans in the United States did not want to speak out against the new government because of families still in the island country. The document went on to point out that "it was frequently of great operational interest to expedite visas for family members," but the work required obtaining visas "was usually very difficult if not impossible to arrange."[19]

The U.S. government decided to enact a visa waiver program. This action made the United States the country of first asylum. In other words, Cubans could now enter the United States without a visa investigation and then claim refugee status while already within the country.

All of these factors concerning the underground's fears for their families and obtaining visas led to the children's program that became known as

Operaçion Pedro Pan. The plan began when James Baker, director of the Ruston Academy in Havana, pointed out that parents involved in the underground wanted safe conduct out of Cuba for their families. The heads of the families usually told their government that their children had student visas to study in the United States, a logical cover story for those who could afford to send their children away from Cuba for a higher education. Once the United States broke relations with Cuba in 1960, the visas could not be processed. Then things became complicated.[20]

The U.S. State Department gave Father Bryan Walsh, the head of Miami's Catholic Welfare Bureau, authority to issue visa waivers to children between the ages of six and sixteen without any security clearances; those from ages sixteen to eighteen needed a clearance. "This marked the first time in U.S. history that a private individual had been given such authority."[21] Church liaisons and resistance groups working for the CIA smuggled the waivers into Cuba.

Before Baker left Cuba, he organized a committee to help in forwarding the children's names to the United States and arranging all the required visa waivers and transportation to the United States. The group also supplied information to the CIA on missions in Cuba.[22]

Penny Powers, a nurse at the British embassy in Cuba, worked within the group. During World War II, Powers had helped transport ten thousand Jewish children from Germany to England. She arranged for British visas for the Cuban children and flights to Jamaica, then a colony of Great Britain. Because this was too complicated, the U.S. visa waiver program continued. Only children received the waivers, but the resistance hatched an elaborate plan in which the children, once in the United States, might claim their parents. Everyone in the program expected this complicated arrangement to be a temporary one: Castro surely would not remain in power much longer. Obviously, Castro did. The Cuban Missile Crisis ended the program.

Just before the October crisis, Cuba stopped all U.S. flights entering or leaving the island. Afterward, Cuba wished to resume the flights, but the United States refused. This left many in the island country with waivers but no means of escape. It also left the children already in the United States without their parents. Many of the children eventually ended up in foster homes, orphanages, and other locations. At the end of the operation, "there were about 6,000 children in the United States waiting for their parents." On October 10, 1965, Castro opened the port of Camarioca. Cuba and the United States signed an agreement establishing two flights a day between Varadero and the United States. "Many children were reunited with their parents at this time, but others never were."[23]

These stark statistics and facts cover the wrenching affects of the operation on families. Michael Musa, a ten-year-old in 1961, left via Havana's airport. "Just before I got on the plane, I saw my father walk away to hide, so I couldn't see him. But I did see him. He was crying."[24]

Musa and his six-year-old sister, Maria, eventually ended up in Indiana. "I remember a man in Miami drawing a sketch on paper of the United States, and showing me Indiana. I had never heard of Indiana. But he pointed at it and told me, 'That's where you are going.'"[25]

Placed in a foster home in Indianapolis, Michael and Maria found no one spoke Spanish. Michael never completely unpacked his suitcase. "His mother had folded his clothes, and he did not want to disturb any lasting touch of her hands on the fabric."[26] Within six months, the family was reunited and lived in Indianapolis.

Rafael Pavelo's fate differed from Michael Musa's. Rafael, at thirteen, found himself sent from Miami to a seminary in Costa Rica. His parents were not able to join him. Rafael remembered a letter he received from his mother. "The stationary was stained with her tears. And the envelope held a lock of her hair. 'I remember holding the hair in my hand and crying,' said Mr. Pavelo. 'I missed my family so much.'"[27]

Rafael's mother and father entered into bitter arguments about who was to blame for sending him away. They were divorced within two years of his departure. In 2000 Mr. Pavelo lived in Chicago and was employed as a social worker.[28]

Between 1960 and 1962, more than 14,048 children were brought out of Cuba to the United States through this complicated secret plan. It was the largest unaccompanied "child refugee movement in the recorded history of the Western Hemisphere."[29]

In Cuba "the myth holds that the Central Intelligence Agency robbed the nation of its children. The exile community claims that the program saved those children from communism." As with most things dealing with

Cuba and the United States since 1959, the truth is more complicated than these simple statements.[30]

Six years after taking power, Castro faced growing unrest among the island population. Many, especially the middle class, became disillusioned with the economy and the turn to communism. Castro needed a way to defuse any potential internal problems. Speaking in Havana's Plaza de la Revolución (Revolution Plaza) on September 28, 1965, he announced that Cubans whose American relatives requested it would be allowed to leave beginning October 10, 1965, with certain provisos. Cubans would have to be picked up by the relatives in the United States at the small port of Camarioca. Located on the north coast of Cuba, to the east of Havana, the port lies almost directly across the Straits of Florida from Key West, Florida. Cuban men of military age—fourteen to twenty-seven years old—and necessary workers would not be allowed to leave.[31]

In effect, Castro used refugees as a way to relieve pressure on his government and as a way to gain a propaganda coup. If the United States welcomed the Cubans, it might put a strain on state and federal facilities in Florida, which might cause unrest, thus helping Castro's government. If the United States refused entry to the people, Castro might well point out that the United States did not really welcome foreigners to its shore, which again rebounded to his propaganda. The U.S. government, conversely, might also use the fleeing refugees for their own uses against Castro. Many of the news releases and newspaper articles during what would become known as the Camarioca Boatlift described as people "disenchanted," "longing for freedom," "oppressed," and having "ideals betrayed." The American press generally showed sympathy for those who made the treacherous passage "to escape communism." In short, refugees now found themselves pawns in the machinations of governments and in foreign policy.[32]

The U.S. Coast Guard had for many years operated patrols in the waters off Florida. After the 1959 Cuban Revolution, cutter crews began rescuing Cubans in deplorable craft drifting helplessly in the Straits of Florida.

By 1961 one of the routes taken by some Cubans attempting to flee to Florida ran from the northern coast of Cuba to Cay Sal Banks. Located approximately sixty nautical miles southeast of the Florida Keys, the Banks, in Bahamian waters, lie between Andros Island, Bahamas, and Cuba. Cubans who chose this route waited at Cay Sal Banks until spotted by U.S. Coast Guard fixed-wing aircraft. The aircraft then vectored cutters to the area and the white ships transported the Cubans to Key West. The intelligence service of the Cuban government, however, monitored the radio transmissions. At one point, Cubans in Soviet-made helicopters landed at Anguilla Cay to capture seventeen men and women. To counter the capture of the refugees, U.S. Coast Guard aircraft began flying away from the point where they spotted the Cubans. At a certain location, the aircraft crew sent a message in code to the U.S. Coast Guard Rescue Coordination Center (RCC) in Miami, which then dispatched a cutter to the proper position. After the Bay of Pigs invasion of 1961, the rescue work at sea continued, but now the service also patrolled for exiled Cubans who started from the United States and wanted to conduct operations against Castro's forces.[33]

As mentioned previously, one of the outcomes of the Missile Crisis of 1962 was the U.S. government's announcement that "it would take every step" to prevent attempts against Cuba from the United States and would prevent exiles from being trained in U.S. territory. This caused the U.S. Coast Guard to put out a patrol line close to Cuba. Aerial patrols, usually made by HU-16E *Albatross* amphibious aircraft along with HH-52A helicopters, and larger cutters worked at this "outer patrol." The patrol needed larger cutters for at-sea endurance rather than the 82- and 95-foot patrol boats. Previously the service maintained patrols near the U.S. shoreline with 40-foot boats and other small craft, with 82- and 95-foot patrol boats at ranges between the outer patrol and near shore.[34]

By the time that Castro announced the opening of Camarioca, on September 28, 1965, the service's patrols centered chiefly on law enforcement. This changed.

Upon learning of Castro's new policy, a few Cubans tentatively made their way to Camarioca. Castro, to show his sincerity, built quarters for people awaiting boats, even providing playgrounds for children. Soon the trickle of refugees became a torrent.[35]

Two critical factors figured prominently into the U.S. Coast Guard's operations for this first of the Cuban mass migrations via the sea. One factor focused on the craft used to bring the refugees to Key West. Most of the private boats used to transport those wishing to leave their country were better than those first used after 1959, but most still remained unsuitable for crossing the Straits of Florida. The second important factor was the weather. October is within hurricane season. Unseaworthy craft combined with weather that even old salts fear had all the ingredients for the possibility of a major loss of life at sea. If this happened, Castro again stood to gain from such a catastrophe: the United States let Cubans die in the straits.

In 1965 Rear Admiral (Rear Adm.) Irvin J. Stevens, USCG, commanded the service's District 7, which encompasses Florida and much of the Caribbean. Admiral Stevens pointed out that the work dealing with the Cuban situation could not be neatly pigeonholed. "It's an operation in which search and rescue, law enforcement and observation are all bound together and it is practically impossible to foretell which phase will be uppermost at a given time. What looks like search and rescue may turn out to be law enforcement or vice versa."[36] Forty-seven years later, in 2007, Rear Adm. David W. Kunkel, commanding District 7, pointed out that Admiral Stevens's comment still remained true.[37]

As the numbers of Cubans found at sea swelled, it "placed a heavy burden" on the crews of the U.S. Coast Guard stationed in Florida. The service's air station at Miami, for example, flew an estimated 1 million miles on patrol.[38]

Those flying the aircraft patrols felt frustrated at times. "There's no way to guess how many refugees have been lost before we could get to them," said one pilot. Lieutenant (junior grade) (Lt. [jg]) Tom Osborn, for example, recalled the case of the "voices in the night." Osborn said the air station had received "a call from the district Rescue Coordination Center, that a seaman had overheard faint voices as his ship cruised through the Caribbean night." The ship dropped a buoy in the location and circled until a U.S. Coast Guard aircraft could reach the area and drop an electronic data marker.[39]

Early the next morning, Lieutenant Osborn and his aircrew departed in their *Albatross* aircraft to continue the search. They searched "until our fuel was nearly exhausted." As fate would have it, on their final leg of the search, a crew member reported spotting something. There, "wallowing in eight to 10 [foot seas and] troughs was a small boat. A Cuban kneeled inside, thrashing a red cloth in the air. If we hadn't spotted him that last time, he might have never been found."[40]

Those serving on larger cutters, patrol boats, and small craft also worked long hours. H. R. Kaplan, a civilian writer employed by the U.S. Coast Guard, described the scene he observed while on board the 210-foot cutter *Diligence* (WMEC-616). The cutter came alongside a "pathetically inadequate" craft with "two haggard men, aged 34 and 24." They had departed Tampa, Florida, on Florida's west coast, en route to Camarioca. Their outboard motor broke down and they had drifted for two days, their only food "sugared water and crackers which they dipped into the water." While an engineer from the cutter worked on the Cuban's engine, the cook sent down sandwiches and fresh water for the two men. Then the executive officer, Lieutenant Commander (Lt. Cdr.) John Fuechsel, explained that the novice sailors could proceed on their way to Cuba, but if they entered their waters and picked up Cubans, they risked legal action upon their return to Florida. Because these two men had not entered Cuban waters, their boat would not be seized.[41]

Two hours later, the lookout on board the *Diligence* spotted a sailboat crowded with refugees "standing shoulder to shoulder." Sailing without difficulties, the boat proceeded to Key West. Shortly thereafter a desperate call came over the radio: a Cuban boat was taking on water and needed immediate help. A helicopter from the cutter flew a pump to the boat.[42]

Even later, the *Diligence* came upon the motorboat *Loretta*, out of Fort Lauderdale, Florida, on Florida's east coast. Three men and two women made up the crew, with navigation duties performed by the women. Apparently the navigators needed more practice because they felt they had reached Cuba. Instead they touched at Cay Sal Banks. The choppy straits discouraged the motorboat's crew and, requesting additional fuel, they told the cutter's crew they planned to return to Key West. Many on the *Diligence*, however, felt that as soon as the cutter sailed far enough away, the *Loretta*'s crew planned to continue its voyage.[43]

During the Camarioca Boatlift, the U.S. Coast Guard established a receiving center at their Key West base to process the Cuban refugees. At the center, the Cubans received examinations by the Public Health Service and questioning by the Immigration and Naturalization Service (INS) and the Customs Service. The U.S. Coast Guard Wives Club and the U.S. Navy Wives Club prepared packets for the Cuban families that arrived with children. The families received the packets as they were processed at the receiving center and then were placed on buses and transported to Miami.[44]

The Camarioca Boatlift officially ended on November 15, 1965, due to political changes in both the United States and Cuba. Somewhere between 2,979 and 5,000 Cubans escaped their homeland by boat during this short period.[45] Fearing a massive loss of life, President Lyndon B. Johnson arranged a memorandum of understanding with Fidel Castro to shift the movement of refugees from the sea to commercial air transportation. The aircraft movement became known as the "Freedom Flight" program. The United States agreed to provide the aircraft between Miami and Varadero, Cuba, about 87 miles (140 km) east of Havana, "with such frequency and capacity as to permit the movement of between 3,000 and 4,000 persons per month." Castro applied the same restrictions on this program as he did on the boatlift—that is, men of military age and necessary workers were not allowed to leave. During the first year, the flights brought more than forty-five thousand Cubans to Florida.[46]

This caused an uneasiness or fear on the part of officials in Florida's local and state governments concerning the financial drain this wave of undocumented migrants made upon their budgets. Furthermore, many in low-skilled jobs grew angry at the possibility of noncitizens receiving preferential treatment. The U.S. Congress, reacting to the fears and the number of Cubans entering Florida, passed the Cuban Adjustment Act of 1966. Briefly, the act allowed those Cubans who arrived after Castro's takeover, January 1, 1959, to become permanent resident aliens, a step in the procedure to become a citizen. It also allowed the Cubans access to monetary aid. More than forty years later, the act is still hotly debated in Cuba and the United States.

The Freedom Flights ran from 1965 to 1973, when Castro closed the program. One estimate of the number of people brought into the United States on the flights totaled a quarter of a million people. Another seventy thousand Cubans made the journey first to Spain and then the United States. Another thirty-eight thousand came in through third countries.[47]

Both presidents Johnson and Richard M. Nixon looked upon the Camarioca Boatlift and the Freedom Flights as "undertaken in the absence of a clear immigration policy for refugees from Cuba. Both were perceived as emergencies and handled as such. Neither Johnson nor Nixon tried to normalize the immigration policy during the airlift's seven years."[48]

The ending of the Camarioca Boatlift and Freedom Flights did not put an end to Cubans trying to escape their homeland via the sea. In some cases, reports appeared in Florida newspapers of Cuban gunboats allegedly firing upon the refugees. The *Miami Herald*, for example, in 1968 pointed out the gunboat's practice "earned the Florida Straits the nickname of 'Machinegun Alley' since 1959." Commander (Cdr.) J.W.E. Ward, USCG, told a U.S. Senate judiciary committee that the service "on numerous occasions," found drifting boats and rafts and makeshift craft of various sorts, "some with bullet holes [in them]." Yet another newspaper account revealed the discovery of fourteen bodies on Anguilla Cay in the early 1960s.[49]

Located in the National Archives are long-forgotten reports of the service's work in the 1960s. On September 20, 1966, for example, Capt. Robert C. Tischler, flying for Mackey Airlines, observed "1 small open boat loaded with Cubans and rowing. Towing raft which also was loaded. . . . Rowing to the north. Waving and flashing mirrors." The U.S. Coast Guard dispatched a helicopter and the 210-foot medium-endurance cutter *Diligence* to the scene, which brought thirteen Cubans to safety. In a letter of commendation to Captain Tischler, Rear Adm. L. M. Thayer, the commander of U.S. Coast Guard District 7, said that from "the description of the boat and raft obtained from the on scene units it is doubtful whether they would have succeeded in reaching Florida had they encountered any adverse weather." Further, Tischler had relayed the information to the U.S. Coast Guard in a manner that did not attract the Cuban authorities, and Admiral Thayer felt this "materially contributed to their safe evacuation."[50]

In August 1967 Ramon Donestevez laid plans "to lead a flotilla of boats . . . from Marathon in the Keys to Cuba" during the first week in September. An editorial by Channel 4, Miami, called such a plan "a foolhardy sea venture." To meet this "venture," the U.S. Coast Guard District 7 issued Operation Order 22-63 on September 7. The plan called for a picket line of cutters and small craft offshore north and south from Marathon to stop the flotilla. This show of determination to arrest those in flotilla appeared to have successfully stopped the boats when all U.S. Coast Guard units received orders to return to their normal duties on September 8, 1967. Thirty-two years later, the U.S. Coast Guard again had to issue orders dealing with a flotilla bound for Cuban waters.[51] (See chapters 13 and 14.)

Bernard B. Fall, in his classic work on the Vietnam War, *Street without Joy*, wrote, "Sometimes, there occurs an almost irrelevant incident which, in the light of later developments, seems to have been a sign of the gods, a dream-like warning which, if heeded, could have changed fate—or so it seems."[52]

At two o'clock in the morning of February 27, 1968, the 292-foot Cuban cattle ship *26 de Julio* (26th of July) in international waters off Virginia, communicated that the crew sought political asylum. Returning the radio call, the U.S. Coast Guard RCC at Portsmouth, Virginia, directed the ship to proceed to Hampton Roads, Virginia, and anchor there. The RCC then ordered Master Chief Boatswain's Mate (BMCM) Paul W. Caviness, the officer-in-charge of the 82-foot patrol boat *Point Brown* (WPB-82362), to the anchored position of the ship.[53]

BMCM Caviness's orders directed him to stay "well clear" of the vessel and circle it. The Cuban ship remained anchored ten miles east-northeast of Cape Henry, Virginia, still not in U.S. waters—at the time the United States observed a three-mile limit. Nearing the Cuban ship, Caviness radioed RCC that he observed a Jacob's ladder (a rope ladder) rigged over the side of the *26 de Julio*. Later in the day the master chief "saw three men [on board the ship] lower a lifeboat, climb into it and start rowing away."

Caviness relayed the new situation to RCC, which brought back orders to remain at least one-half mile ahead of the small boat and act as a guide into U.S. waters. All accounts, both official and in newspapers, state that the orders kept the cutter too far away to do anything about the coming drama.

At 1:58 p.m., Caviness now watched as the Cuban ship got under way and made for the lifeboat. BMCM Caviness logically thought the *26 de Julio* might be coming alongside the lifeboat to pick it up. Seven minutes later, the Cuban ship made another pass at the boat and Caviness now recognized that the vessel intended to ram the craft with the three men on board. As he watched, the ship "did push the small boat," throwing the Cubans into the sea. The RCC received the stark report: "heard small arms fire from the vessel." Later newspaper accounts claimed "machine gun" fire in their stories. In any event, a message to BMCM Caviness directed him to "take action required [to] prevent vessel [from] running down small boat." Caviness later reported that he then "uncovered" his deck gun.

When later asked by a television reporter why he did not take immediate action, BMCM Caviness said he was awaiting orders and "wasn't prepared to go out there and take action that might involve the whole nation and might be over my head." He later readily admitted, however, that he "went through a lot watching those three men in the water."

At just about this time, the U.S. Coast Guard tug *Chock* (WYTL-65602) arrived on scene, with Lt. Cdr. R. H. Elkins, the executive officer of U.S. Coast Guard Group Norfolk, Virginia, on board. Lieutenant Commander Elkins, speaking through an interpreter, questioned the master of the *26 de Julio*, Richard Puri.

Captain Puri told Elkins that the four crewmen had taken over the ship at gunpoint and locked the remaining crew in a compartment. One of the alleged gunmen backed out of the plot just before the lowering of the lifeboat and then unlocked the compartment. Puri claimed that the three men did not want political asylum but were "escaping to Canada with money."

The master of the Cuban cattle ship stated to Lieutenant Commander Elkins that he had picked up the three men in the water. With the *26 de Julio* between the men and the *Point Brown* and *Chock*, the U.S. Coast Guard crews could not confirm this claim. A television reporter on a nearby chartered boat, however, felt the men had drowned. Much like Captain Puri, the reporter could offer no proof for his interpretation. Eventually, Captain Puri sent a radio message to the U.S. Coast Guard: "The trouble is settled. We go back to Cuba." The ship hoisted the damaged lifeboat and proceeded on course to their home port.

Later, Rear Adm. Edward C. Allen Jr., commander of U.S. Coast Guard District 5, which encompasses the Norfolk area, praised BMCM Paul Caviness's actions. "He did precisely what he should have done," said Admiral Allen. "There [was] no question of the possibility of an international incident."

Master Chief Caviness did follow orders correctly, but the incident, given the nature of Cuban American relations at the time, naturally caused a great deal of anger among many. In a letter to the commandant of the U.S. Coast Guard, an executive vice president of a Miami bank who had fled Cuba in 1960 with his family wrote, "How can a vessel representing the United States Government turn its back on those who were murdered simply because they were seeking the shores of liberty and freedom? . . . Avoid a possible international incident? Do Communist[s] avoid international incidents?"

The letter seems like a mild rebuke when compared to a news wire account. Sources confirmed the stopping of an 18-foot boat with Cuban exiles just before they left the waters of Miami on February 29. In addition to four Cubans jammed into the craft, authorities uncovered a 20 mm cannon and an automatic rifle. The exiles planned to attack the *26 de Julio*. The Cubans in the small boat received jail sentences on charges of illegally exporting arms.

The reaction to the *26 de Julio* incident took an almost predictable turn: Rep. Paul Rogers (D-FL) called for a probe of the case. Representative Rogers said the situation smacked of a *Pueblo* incident, the case in which the North Koreans seized a U.S. spy ship and there appeared no plans to cope with the incident.

Again, almost predictably, Rep. Thomas N. Downing (D-VA) replied to Rogers: "I see no reason to imply at this point that any criticism is due as far as our Coast Guard personnel are concerned. I see no reason at this time for an investigation." One of Rogers's comments, however, is important: "There should be some standing orders on what to do when people are trying to flee to this country. It's time this government took strong action. We ought to know what to do and not be afraid to stand up for freedom."

Not recognized at the time, the incident with the *26 de Julio* proved a portent of what the U.S. Coast Guard would face over the coming forty years. On November 23, 1970, for example, in the waters near Martha's Vineyard, Massachusetts, Simas Kudirka, a Lithuanian seaman from the Soviet fishing vessel *Sovietskaya Litva*, leaped on board the 210-foot U.S. Coast Guard cutter *Vigilant* (WMEC-617) while it remained alongside the Soviet vessel at a meeting of officials concerning fishing issues. Kudirka, upon making it on board the cutter, declared that he wished political asylum. In a Byzantine series of events, Soviet seamen were allowed to come on board the *Vigilant* and, in full view of the U.S. Coast Guard, forcibly return the Lithuanian seaman back to the *Sovietskaya Litva*. The ensuing investigation proved, among many other findings, that the service and the

Department of State had a confusing line of communications at best. Furthermore, the senior leadership of the U.S. Coast Guard appeared to have a dim understanding of what constituted political asylum and how to handle those claiming it. The investigation recommended that the service "explore those areas in which the Coast Guard would benefit by having detailed guidelines on current State Department policy and procedures." Another obvious solution centered on better lines of communication.[54]

Two years later, in 1972, Lt. Cdr. James J. Meade, USCG, wrote that it "would be [a] tragedy if we [the U.S. Coast Guard] all did not learn some fundamental lessons from the mistakes involved in the VIGILANT case. Ideally, the report of the formal board of investigation should have been read by every officer [of the service]." Lieutenant Commander Meade pointed out that most of the report contained dull bureaucratic language, couched in lengthy technical terms. "What is needed," wrote Meade, "is a short, readable treatment of the affair, which can touch on the *fundamental* considerations involved without encumbering the reader with unnecessary detail" (emphasis by Meade). Apparently, like most people in the U.S. Coast Guard, Lieutenant Commander Meade did not know of an easy way to grasp a situation that does touch "on the fundamental considerations:" the *26 de Julio* case.[55]

Over the coming years, the Camarioca Boatlift and the *26 de Julio* incident did not remain in the U.S. Coast Guard's corporate memory. There is no doubt that decision makers in the service did not recognize the importance of Camarioca. Yet the boatlift clearly pointed to what Castro might do if faced with domestic pressure. The coming years proved this fact. Both the boatlift and the *26 de Julio* incident indicated that if clear, understandable policies dealing with refugees were not in place and completely understood by both U.S. Coast Guard decision makers and the people at the working level, someone paid the price for this lapse or confusion. The *26 de Julio* incident clearly pointed to what might happen if the mass media in the United States reported on the work of the service without understanding the complete picture. This, too, would be proven in the coming years.

One wonders what might have happened if someone in the U.S. Coast Guard's hierarchy had heeded the "dreamlike warning" that Fall mentioned. Would it have, indeed, changed fate?

In 1965 H. R. Kaplan, the U.S. Coast Guard writer who sailed in the cutter *Diligence* during the Camarioca Boatlift, remarked that near the entrance to the U.S. Coast Guard base at Key West lay a pier facing the Straits. It was "always filled with Cubans waiting anxiously to see a friend or loved one on one of the incoming boats. . . . It is a place where hope and despair intermingle."[56] After more than four decades, Key West remains a place of "hope and despair" for Cubans.

2 Opening the Floodgates

> If your government wants people in small boats, we can give you more than you bargained for.
>
> Rafael Rodriguez, vice president of Cuba

From 1965 through 1979, charge and countercharge continued between the United States and Cuba. In September 1968, for example, Cuba announced "the capture of 18 CIA agents who were attempting an espionage raid."[1] On September 16, 1968, Cuban exiles in the United States fired a bazooka at a Polish freighter moored at the Port of Miami. The exiles attacked the ship because Poland traded with Cuba.[2] On February 24, 1971, the U.S. Coast Guard seized four Cuban vessels in U.S. territorial waters. Cuba denied this charge. On March 2, the fishing crews received fines and returned to Cuba. The captains and forty-seven crewmen claimed "they were interrogated and incited to defect."[3] To say that relations between the two countries, for the most part, remained strained is a master understatement. The years between 1968 and 1980 are like a gathering storm. When the storm finally broke, it came over an incident not related to the sea, but for six months in 1980 the results, like a tsunami, overwhelmed everything in its path, both at sea and ashore.

The causes of much of the brewing storm came from a poor Cuban economy. In 1961, for example, a mere two years after the revolution, Ernesto "Che" Guevara announced at an August meeting of the Organization of American States (OAS) that Cuba expected by 1980 to have a net per capita income of US$3,000, "or more than the actual per capita of the United States." He went on to say that "if you let us develop [in peace] and in 20 years let us come back, we shall see if the chant of the siren was that of revolutionary Cuba or not."[4] Four years later, Fidel Castro, already facing problems, initiated the Camarioca Boatlift and the Freedom Flights as a way to relieve pressure from those who were dissatisfied with the continuing economic and social conditions in Cuba.

Eight years after Che's speech, Castro, speaking in the Plaza de la Revolución, announced his goal of a 10 million ton sugar harvest in 1970, believing this might improve economic conditions. At the time of the 1970 harvest—known as the *zafra* in Cuba—Castro went into the fields followed by many photographers to make sure the country viewed him at work. Cuban newspapers and information agencies made much of the help in the harvest from outside sources, including Venceremos ("We will win") Brigades from the United States and ten Vietnamese "fighters straight from battles with U.S. forces."[5] Despite the much-touted *La Gran Zafra*, Castro admitted failure. He called for "revolutionary fortitude to turn setback into victory." Those sympathetic to the regime pointed out, however, that the 8.5-million-ton harvest proved to be "the largest in Cuban history."[6] Castro stated he would resign because of not meeting his goal, but his resignation was refused. The outcome of the *La Gran Zafra* drove Cuba to depend more on the Soviet Union, which also caused more disaffection among many Cubans and eventually led to even greater economic problems.

Another of the elements leading to the boatlift in 1980 centered on hijacking. Beginning in the 1960s, newspapers in the United States reported on what seemed like the daily seizing of some type of transportation—usually commercial airliners—and the person, or persons, demanding to be flown to Cuba. In November 1972, the United States and Cuba, showing at last some cooperation, entered into talks to end the hijacking by making it a crime. Those sympathetic to the Castro government pointed out that Cubans hijacked boats to come to the United States, but the U.S. government did nothing to alleviate the problem.[7] Nevertheless, a formal agreement to end hijacking of aircraft was signed on February 15, 1973.

Another of the large issues that caused the events of 1980 centered on how some in Cuba felt about their life under Fidel Castro's government. The government became repressive. Newspapers that did not praise the revolution found themselves shut down. Committees for the Defense of the Revolution (CDR) were formed. The committees, made up of millions of citizens, watched their neighborhoods. Individual members reported on anything they considered politically wrong. Their reports not only concerned political matters but also social activities. This put a great deal of power into the hands of those reporting for the neighborhood, and the committees became the conduit for the government to control all facets of life in Cuba. As one Cuban put it, "The CDR [could not] do anything for anyone, but it could 'sink' anyone."[8]

Castro used the schools to help support his revolutionary government. Mirta Ojito, who left Cuba in 1980, said her school record contained not only information about her grades but also information about her family's political views. Her record noted that "this student still goes to church" and that Ojito had "excellent grades but needs to become more involved in revolutionary activities."[9]

Some who left Cuba reported that by the 1970s Cubans faced a shortage in housing, consumer goods, and food. "Houses and apartments were in such short supply in Havana that even divorced couples were forced to remain together in the same residence."[10]

Even though some workers had secure employment, many saw no reason to work. Although they earned a wage, the constant shortage of consumer goods and food caused no incentive to work. Even if some consumer goods were obtainable, the price remained almost impossible, plus the purchasing of certain items seemed Byzantine. To buy a television set, for example, a person who wished to make the purchase had to first be approved by a committee that reported if the person was a hard worker and deserved such a luxury. If turned down, the only alternative was the black market, with inflated prices and the chance of arrest from the police. Ojito recalled that for her family to obtain a television set they needed a government coupon. First her mother and father skimped for years to obtain extra money. Then her father took two hundred pesos, which amounted to one and a half times his monthly salary as a truck driver, and purchased a coupon that stated "he had donated an old American TV to the government." With the fake coupon and another seven hundred pesos, "a fortune for us," he purchased a Russian-made television set. Ojito realized the transaction was "all sort of illegal, but my father was confident he wouldn't get caught." Without the coupon, the family could not have bought the television set.[11]

Castro's international military actions also led many to question the government. He committed his army to the African nations of Angola and Ethiopia. At least 20 percent of his forces remained in Africa, which forced him to use his reserves. "Reserves made up 80 percent of overseas personnel." This caused shortages in skilled workers, causing difficulties throughout Cuba.[12]

In 1977, according to Mirta Ojito, many Cubans welcomed the election of President James "Jimmy" Carter and thought it heralded the beginning of a new era between the two countries.[13] Ojito felt that Castro saw in President Carter someone who would finally recognize his government. It seemed that Carter did want to change the relationship between the two countries. Officials from both nations exchanged talks on a wide variety of subjects. President Carter sanctioned talks between Cuban exiles with the Cuban government about the release of political prisoners in Cuba, and many were released as a result.

Fidel Castro willingly entered into one of President Carter's seemingly humanitarian efforts. On March 18, 1977, President Carter lifted the bans on American citizens visiting relatives in Cuba and spending U.S. dollars in that nation. Castro felt this might again make his government look good. Furthermore, such a move would bring in more money to Cuba and Castro agreed on various points, one of which allowed separated Cuban families to reunite in the United States. The actions of Carter meant the first relaxation of the trade embargo in at least fourteen years.

More than one hundred thousand Cuban exiles visited Cuba during the next year and a half. Wayne S. Smith, the former chief of the U.S. Special Interest Section in Havana, wrote that Castro's plan to gain U.S. dollars proved successful as the country "earned over 100 million from exile visits from 1979 and 1980."[14] An observer remembered: "The exiles arrived decked out in their best clothes, carrying radios, television sets, and toasters, smoking cigars, and talking about how the streets of Miami were paved with gold. Watching some of these meetings, I could see how upsetting it was for the people who still lived in Havana."[15] Some "even brought parts for old American automobiles on their flights to Cuba."[16] Instead of solidifying Castro's hold on Cuba, the visits made many Cubans question their lives under the present government. As Smith noted, at a time when Cubans "were asked to tighten their belts" and face years of little return, in came the exiles giving their former countrymen a vision of the easy life in the United States. "More and more Cuban citizens began to yearn for a piece of that vision."[17]

The decade of the 1970s ended with a movement toward seemingly better relations between Cuba and the United States. True, some problems continued. On August 30, 1979, for example, Carter demanded the removal of reported Soviet ground combat troops. On October 11, Castro again criticized the United States for the continued U.S. embargo and its presence at Guantánamo Bay. These issues aside, the two countries seemed to have at least a limited dialogue in progress. A few people in the U.S. government, however, could see that the social forces building within Cuba combined with the visits of the returning visitors had a potential for deep unrest in Cuba.

The 1980s began with the first glimpse of the coming tsunami. On the night of January 31, 1980, some sixty-five Cubans crept aboard the Cuban government's 110-foot dredge *Fifth of December* docked in the Port of Cárdenas. Brandishing pistols, six of the group took the dredge's crew prisoner. Arriving in the Florida Keys on February 1, the U.S. government granted the hijackers and two of the dredge's crew political asylum. The *Fifth of December* and its remaining crew returned to Cuba.

On the day of the hijacking of the dredge, the Cuban Analytic Center of the CIA ominously reported that the "Castro regime may again resort to large-scale emigration to reduce discontent caused by Cuba's deteriorating economic condition. . . . The revival of such a policy could reduce discontent."[18] No one heeded this prophetic warning.

Two weeks after the hijacking of the *Fifth of December*, eight Cubans took over the Liberian freighter *Lissette* in Havana's harbor. The Cubans stated they had placed a bomb on the ship and demanded to be taken to Florida. Also hijacked in February was the 45-foot Cuban fishing boat *Lucero*; its twenty-six hijackers received political asylum in the United States. The U.S. media covered all the hijackings extensively; the Cuban Americans in Florida greeted the hijackers as heroes.

The hijackings angered the Castro government. Carlos Rafael Rodriguez, Cuba's vice president, called upon the chief of the U.S. Interest Section in Havana, Wayne S. Smith, and informed him that Cuba continued to cooperate in aerial hijackings while the United States did not want to cooperate with hijackings at sea. Rodriguez warned that Cuba might open a new Camarioca. "If your government wants people in small boats," said Rodriguez, "we can give you more than you bargained for." President Castro, in a speech on March 8, reiterated the threat. Smith felt the Cubans did not so much want the hijackers returned, but they did want them punished, as the Cubans punished air hijackers.[19]

Another sticking point was the amount of time it took released political prisoners to receive visas. Castro also felt the number of people accepted for immigration remained smaller than the United States had agreed upon. In short, the improved relations now deteriorated. Anyone researching Cuban American relationships in 1980 quickly recognizes one incident that began the tidal wave of events that eventually led to the Mariel Boatlift.

Hector Sanyunstiz, born September 27, 1949, in La Torcaza, a small rural town in eastern Cuba, came to the conclusion he had to leave his country. The school dropout had run afoul of the authorities, and he saw no future for himself in Cuba. He dismissed trying to make the dangerous voyage across the Straits of Florida. During the first months of 1980, Sanyunstiz's thoughts turned to seeking asylum in the Peruvian Embassy. Earlier a group of twelve Cubans had tried to run a bus past the Cuban guards and through the embassy's gates. They made it within the embassy, but unfortunately the Peruvian ambassador was sympathetic to Castro's government and, against all international conventions, returned the asylum seekers back to the Cubans. For this, the Peruvian government recalled him. Ernesto Pinto, the chargé d'affaires, in effect ran the embassy until another experienced diplomat joined the embassy. The Peruvian government demanded that the Cubans who had made it into the grounds of the embassy be returned to them; Cuba complied. Word of this quickly circulated throughout Havana. Sanyunstiz, as did other Habaneros, also heard rumors that the Peruvians planned to send the Cubans to Lima on Wednesday, April 2.

On March 30 Sanyunstiz and a friend, Radames Gomez, began thinking of a way to break into the Peruvian embassy grounds before April 2 so that they could leave with the other Cubans. Sanyunstiz felt that the loosely guarded embassy provided an easy portal of escape. A former bus driver, Sanyunstiz enlisted another bus driver, Francisco Raul Diaz Molina, whose route took him by the embassy, to help the two men. Eventually, the three hit upon a plan that featured Molina's bus crashing the gate to the embassy. Three other Cubans, one a woman with a child, joined the trio.

On Tuesday, April 1, Sanyunstiz, the more experienced driver, relieved Gomez at the wheel. He drove along Fifth Avenue in the Miramar section of Havana. As he neared the location of the Peruvian Embassy, between Ninety-sixth and Seventy-second streets, he pressed down on the gas pedal. The bus reached forty miles an hour. At the given location, Sanyunstiz turned the wheel and aimed the vehicle at the gate. The bus roared toward the barrier. Cuban guards opened fire. The bus stopped more than a third of the way into the grounds. Gomez bled from the head and back. Sanyunstiz suffered a leg injury. A mortally wounded Cuban guard lay on the ground, struck by the gunfire of the other guards.

Upon learning of problems at his embassy, Ernesto Pinto rushed back from a meeting. He arrived shortly after the bus crashed through the gate. Pinto directed his security detail to bring the Cubans from the bus into the embassy. Soon thereafter, Pinto faced Cuba's head of state security, Gen. José Abrantes. General Abrantes demanded the return of the Cubans. If they were not returned, Abrantes threatened action on his own. Pinto refused. General Abrantes backed off when Pinto pointed out the political nature of the incident. Pinto then ordered embassy staff to take the injured Cubans to a military hospital for treatment. He advised his staff to keep the Cubans under close observation, as they now were under the protection of international treaties.[20]

On the same day that Sanyunstiz rammed his bus through the gate of the Peruvian Embassy, the Refugee Act of 1980 came into being. Seen by some as a relief valve for Castro, the act called for, among other items, the United States to accept as many as one thousand former political prisoners each month for six months.[21]

Two days later, on Thursday, April 3, reacting to persistent rumors in Miami of an impending boatlift, the Refugee Program Bureau of the U.S. State Department chaired an interagency meeting in Washington, D.C. Meeting "in a conference room of the fourth floor of the State Department Annex were representatives of the Justice Department, Coast Guard, Immigration and Naturalization Service, and Department of Health and Human Services, and three State Department experts on Cuban affairs and refugees." The subject of the meeting focused on what would happen if Castro opened a port for mass migration as happened during the Camarioca Boatlift. The consensus of the meeting recognized that everything happening in Cuba, the economy, the recent spate of hijackings, the CIA's warning and Castro's speech of March 8, all pointed to a situation that required concern. The head of the committee reported that they did not think any boatlift imminent. There was "not enough concrete evidence . . . to justify sounding an alarm." Furthermore, some expressed "concern that overt preparations for a migration might help to precipitate one." However, the members did agree to start the preliminary work on a contingency plan.[22]

In Cuba the day after the interagency meeting convened in Washington, D.C., another part of the drama at the Peruvian Embassy in Havana began. Over the days since the Cubans' crashing into the embassy, Ernesto Pinto continued meeting with officials of the Cuban government about the rights of the six Cubans at the embassy.

At 8:00 a.m. of Good Friday, April 4, Pinto heard heavy construction equipment outside the embassy. With curious Cuban onlookers watching, two bulldozers quickly set about leveling the cement guard posts outside of the embassy. The Cuban guards walked away. The Peruvian grounds now lay open. Pinto feared an armed assault on the embassy. Earlier, in *Granma*, the Cuban government's newspaper, Pinto read that the Cuban government had decided not to protect the embassy from those who wished to leave the country, that from "now on, the embassy's officials will be solely responsible for what occurs in their embassy." Furthermore, "not one of the people who had tried to obtain a visa by breaking into an embassy would ever be allowed to leave Cuba."[23]

Pinto began a series of diplomatic moves with other Latin American embassies in Havana to gain their support in protecting those seeking refuge within embassies in Havana. While he made his round of the embassies, Habaneros watched the events unfold at the Peruvian embassy. Recognizing an unguarded opening to the embassy, Cubans began slowly moving into the embassy's grounds. By the time Pinto returned, "dozens of Cubans" stood "quietly on the lawn, in small groups."[24] The embassy's security staff determined what members in the groups belonged to Castro's state security agents and quickly separated them from the other citizens. As word spread, thousands began crowding onto the grounds. "All of Fifth Avenue seemed to be a never-ending parade leading to one final destination: the Peruvian embassy."[25] Pinto had two meetings with Castro, which took place in the president's car.

Smith wrote in 1987 that no matter what one thought of him, "Castro's political instincts [were] usually pretty good." The situation at the Peruvian Embassy, however, broke this mold. According to Smith's Cuban sources, the death of the Cuban guard "drove him up the wall." A Cuban official told Smith that when he informed "the *comandante* of the policeman's death, his face turned deep red. I have never seen him so angry." Smith felt that one of the reasons for the strange act of removing the guards from the embassy came about because of the death on January 11, 1980, of Celia Sánchez, his long-time secretary and confidant. She "was probably the only person in the world [Castro] fully trusted." Cubans, according to Smith, felt Celia Sánchez "was Castro's gyroscope. After she died, he lost his equilibrium for a time, until he could walk without her." This may have been the root cause of his "gross miscalculation" concerning the embassy.[26]

By April 5, an estimated ten thousand to eleven thousand Cubans jammed into the Peruvian Embassy's grounds and Cuban guards again patrolled the entrance. Mirta Ojito noted that less "than twenty-four hours after Castro had for the first time in twenty-one years relinquished his hold over his people, he'd had to seize it back."[27] The Cuban government struck back by saying the people inside the embassy were social outcasts.

Stung by the poor international reaction to the situation in the Peruvian Embassy, Castro appeared at the embassy on April 7 and announced he would allow those Cubans inside the embassy to leave their country. Later Cuban government officials offered the Cubans inside the embassy safe conduct passes to their homes until transportation for them could be arranged. Only two thousand to three thousand accepted this offer. The others feared that even under the passes they might incur violence from neighbors and others. According to many who used the passes, there was good reason for this apprehension. Some were not allowed to leave their homes to purchase food; it had to be smuggled in by family and friends. One refugee who received poor treatment from his neighbors realized that the people he lived near for more than twenty years treated him badly "out of fear."[28]

Unable to take the large number of refugees into their country, the Peruvian government appealed to the international community for help. The United States replied that it was willing to take "some," as long as they went to Peru first. The United States eventually said the problem was a Latin American one and the "entire matter is up to the Peruvian government."[29] Cuba refused to accept any help from the international community in the care of the refugees.

As the conditions in the embassy worsened, President Carter issued Presidential Determination Number 80-16 on April 14, 1980, which decreed that up to thirty-five hundred refugees from the Peruvian embassy could enter the United States even though they were still in Cuba. In the past, only those who applied for refugee status to the United States did so in a second country. The Cuban government, however, said the matter concerned only Peru and Cuba. Eventually, Castro decreed air evacuations to Peru could begin. However, the Cuban government shortly thereafter complained about the long flight. The government of Costa Rica said it would provide an intermediate stop. The refugees arriving in Costa Rica told stories of the violence they underwent at the Havana airport before they were allowed to leave.

Castro now decided to use a stop-and-go strategy. He stopped the flights to Costa Rica, saying those who wanted to travel to the United States should go there directly. No one in Cuba pointed out that it was his own idea to break up the journey. Part of his strategy was to have a large number of people inside the embassy so that he could stage a mass demonstration against those who wished to leave. A highly organized march, estimated by the Cuban government at a million people, provided "the largest display of pro-government support in Cuba since Castro came to power."[30]

By April 12, 1980, Castro knew he needed something to relieve the pressures on his government. Camarioca had worked. At the time of the Peruvian embassy incident, Napoleon Vilaboa, on the executive committee of a Cuban exile group known as the Committee of 75, was in Havana negotiating for the release of political prisoners and for visas for exiles to visit family. Vilaboa received word on April 12 that Castro had no objection to the refugees in the Peruvian embassy leaving. Vilaboa pointed out the obvious, that most wanted to go to the United States. There seemed no objection. He learned that Castro planned to open the port of Mariel for boats to bring out the embassy refugees and their families.

When Vilaboa returned to Miami and reported to the committee, they agreed that the refugees needed to be brought out quickly. Calls went out for boats, and within twenty-four hours, forty-two privately owned boats made ready to sail for Cuba.

In the meanwhile, two lobster boats from Key West, the *Dos Hermanos* and *Blanche II* became the first two boats to reach Cuba on Monday, April 21. Vilaboa's flotilla sailed on Saturday, April 19, and quickly ran into bad weather and rough seas. One boat sank without loss of life. The scattered boats managed to straggle into Mariel.

Vilaboa received a warm welcome from Rene Rodriguez of the Cuban Communist Party Committee. Rodriguez said that members of the families who brought the boats could also leave. Vilaboa pointed out that an estimated 250,000 Cubans had applied for exit visas. Rodriquez replied, "If a million want to go, then a million could leave."[31] The *Dos Hermanos* and *Blanche II* left Mariel on Tuesday, April 22, marking the beginning of the largest mass migration by sea in the history of the western hemisphere.

3 It's a Zoo Out There

Mariel, April 1980

> One refugee is a novelty,
> ten refugees are boring,
> and a hundred refugees
> are a menace.

After Fidel Castro opened the port of Mariel, the first Cubans from the port arrived in Key West, Florida, on April 12, 1980, thus beginning the Mariel Boatlift. Lasting only 168 days, the number of people involved staggers the imagination. In the heaviest months, May and June, an estimated five thousand people a day landed at Key West. Three years after the event, Ronald Copeland pointed out the lack of preparation on the part of the federal government and President Jimmy Carter's "inability to react quickly to the unforeseen event was painfully obvious. . . . No one has argued that the Carter administration handled the boatlift crisis satisfactorily."[1] The United States sea services, led by the U.S. Coast Guard, proved a shining exception to this condemnation. Interestingly, nine days before the Mariel Boatlift began the senior leadership of the U.S. Coast Guard read a General Accounting Office's (GAO) conclusion about their service. The GAO felt the service might have problems "effectively carrying out its responsibilities" because their budget had not grown to meet the continuing duties put upon them by Congress.[2] However, by September 26, 1980, the official ending of the boatlift, the U.S. Coast Guard's actions in helping to save 125,000 Cubans during Mariel laid to rest the doubts.[3]

No one in the U.S. Coast Guard's District 7 leadership saw the impending mass migration. Like most in Miami, they did notice the rumors circulating in the city about a possible repetition of the Camarioca Boatlift of 1965. Furthermore, as the standoff in the Peruvian embassy continued, rumors began circulating that some in the Florida Cuban community might be making plans to take private boats to the edge of Cuba's territorial waters as a means of attracting international attention to the plight of those in the embassy. The Miami Cubans, the rumor stated, also wanted to see if the Cuban Border Guard would allow them to pass food to the crowded refugee-seekers. Heeding all the rumors, the district leadership began "largely informal" contingency planning that focused mainly on reviewing the number of forces within the district to meet any Camarioca-type of operation. The leadership of the district also consulted with their next higher command, Commander, U.S. Coast Guard Atlantic Area, as to the possibility of obtaining additional units, should they be needed.[4]

On Tuesday, April 22, 1980, the first operational reaction of the leadership of District 7 to the rumors circulating throughout the Miami area came in the form of an air patrol by a HC-131A *Samaritan* launched from U.S. Coast Guard Air Station Miami to survey the seas between Cuba and Key West. The flights changed to a routine mission as the boatlift intensified.[5]

On Wednesday morning, April 23, Lt. Cdr. Samuel Dennis served as the commander, U.S. Coast Guard Group, Key West. His area of responsibility stretched through the Florida Keys and included three shore-based rescue stations, the 95-foot patrol boats *Cape York* (WPB-95332), *Cape Shoalwater* (WPB-95324), and an 82-foot patrol boat, the *Point Thatcher* (WPB-82314), detailed from St. Petersburg, Florida, plus two 41-foot boats for rescue work at Key West, other boats at stations Marathon and Islamorada, and an operations center and administrative offices. Dennis commanded 140 people.

As Lieutenant Commander Dennis sat down to breakfast, he looked out his window and noticed a long line of cars and boat trailers at a nearby civilian boat launch site. He grew concerned as the number of trailered boats grew. Dennis contacted his duty officer and asked if he had any information. The duty officer informed Dennis that he had contacted the Monroe County sheriff's department—Monroe County encompasses the Florida

Keys. The sheriff reported "a stream" of trailered boats southbound on U.S. 1, which ends at Key West. Lieutenant Commander Dennis immediately called U.S. Coast Guard District 7 headquarters in Miami. He then headed for his command. Dennis's and the U.S. Coast Guard's work had just begun.[6]

The Cuban community in Miami had finally decided to act on the rumors of Castro's offer to have the same rules as Camarioca, with some modifications. The boatlift began, however, with the efforts to transport the people in the Peruvian Embassy and their families. The Cuban government then modified this to include anyone who wanted to leave. Castro also added something extra, which was not learned until later.[7]

On the day that Lieutenant Commander Dennis hurried to his command, at least 280 refugees landed in Key West and 68 in Miami. The numbers increased and so did the number of craft of all types requesting assistance from the U.S. Coast Guard for all manner of difficulties at sea. The rising number of refugees caused U.S. Coast Guard headquarters in Washington, D.C., to meet with agencies in the National Security Council, which included the departments of State, Justice, Treasury, and the White House.[8]

Meanwhile, back at Mariel the Cuban government had organized the port area for the boatlift. In an area known as Mosquito, some two and a half miles from Mariel's harbor, high chain-link fences surrounded three compounds. One compound contained families, another single men, and the third former prisoners and other "undesirables." Guards with dogs patrolled each of the compounds.

The Cuban government set into motion a regimen for leaving. First, people reported to a given central location. Many of these people received physical and verbal abuse on their way to a gathering point. Once accounted for, they took a bus to Mosquito and underwent questioning and were relieved of most of their personal possessions. Officials and guards moved people to their respective compound where those leaving found primitive living conditions.

Most of those who made the voyage later reported that loudspeakers kept up a steady stream of information day and night about whose turn it was to be transported to the harbor. If someone did not respond to their name or the boat they were to take, they would not be allowed to leave. Most spent many sleepless nights in the compound.

At the beginning of the boatlift, the procedures in Mariel harbor seemed well organized. A Cuban patrol boat met the arriving boats and escorted them to the dock. Once tied up, soldiers searched the operators and the boat and then assigned a number to the boat. When ready, the Cubans called the boat number. The operators of the boat then handed over to the guards or officials the names of the people they were to pick up. Castro added an element to the organized procedure not recognized until later. For every family member taken by the boats, Cuba required the boat owner to take four other passengers chosen by the government. If the boat owner refused, the boat did not sail. Once officials received the names, they either announced them in the compound or called Havana. Again, if the people called did not respond in time, they lost their chance to leave.

One source reported that Cuban soldiers put the people through yet another event. Everyone had to brush Cuban soil from their shoes as they left. Some, after safely away from the dock, threw their shoes into the bay.[9]

Back in the United States, the U.S. Coast Guard's operation center began receiving hundreds of calls about sailing to Cuba. The center advised the callers that they should have seaworthy craft, plenty of life preservers, a radio, and emergency equipment, and they should not overload their boat. The center also advised the Cubans to tell family or friends the type of boat used and their planned route.

Another Miami office also bore the brunt of inquiries from anxious boaters. Many called the U.S. Customs Service about clearance for leaving the United States. The service granted clearances for leaving the country only, not for bringing in undocumented Cubans.

The calls to the U.S. Coast Guard and Customs Service quite naturally came from excited people with only one thought in minds: to get their family members into the United States. They either misunderstood or did not understand that the information given to them did not mean they could bring back undocumented people. As it turned out, many felt the U.S. government gave permission to bring their families into Florida. Both services may not have clearly stated the fact that the information the anxious people received did not mean endorsement for a trip to Cuba. In the days and months ahead, the misunderstandings and confused reports increased.[10]

Early on Wednesday, April 24, the teenaged Mirta Ojito awoke in her Havana home. Later her aunt and mother informed her that the immediate family was going to *el norte* (the north). For years her father had wanted to leave Cuba, and now the chance appeared. He managed to telephone his brother, Oswaldo, in the United States and asked if he would try to come for them. He learned Oswaldo had already departed to find transportation. The Ojito family felt they might leave quickly.

As Mirta later wrote in her memoir, the Mariel Boatlift was the first time that Cuba "turned against itself since the beginning of Castro's regime in 1959." The government sanctioned violence against those who wished to leave. Angry crowds attacked those suspected of leaving. She reported hearing of people killed and others dragged through the streets. Ojito described the situation within Cuba at the time a "de facto civil war." The family kept as low a profile as possible and waited.[11]

Meanwhile, Oswaldo learned of a neighbor who also wished to get his family out of Cuba and who had a contact with someone on a boat moored in the Miami River. The two men left to find the boat. Arriving at the docks, the two found Cubans "desperately waving wads of cash at anybody who had anything resembling a boat." Oswaldo, his neighbor, and ten others, paid for transportation on board the 60-foot, twenty-three-year-old shrimper *Valley Chief*. They departed for Mariel on the evening of Wednesday, April 23.[12]

During Thursday, April 24, eleven vessels safely arrived from Cuba at Key West or Miami with more than seven hundred Cubans. Both the U.S. Coast Guard headquarters in Washington, D.C., and the district headquarters now realized that they had a major situation close to getting out of hand.

Small craft not suited for the open sea and piloted by people with little seamanship abilities made up the first wave of boats attempting the passage from Key West to Mariel. Lines of fifty to one hundred trailered boats backed up at launching sites. At least one thousand small craft started for Mariel, most between twenty and forty feet in length. Many carried extra fuel in containers on their deck. One report had a person in an outbound boat come alongside another boat near the Key West entrance buoy and yell, "Which way to Cuba?"[13]

It is no hyperbole to state that the media also appeared as confused as everyone else. On April 23, for example, the *Miami Herald* reported that the U.S. State Department had issued a formal statement that anyone bringing Cuban refugees directly into the United States faced felony charges "punishable by six months in jail and a $2,000 fine." This statement was quickly withdrawn. Asked why, "one official said, 'Policy . . . no, politics.'" It appeared that no one wanted to antagonize the Cuban American community. At the same time, the *Miami News* reported that Customs seemed to look the other way on people departing Florida for Cuba. Furthermore, the newspaper, citing a federal official who asked not to be identified, informed readers there was "very little chance the Cuban boat people would be deported."[14]

Events continued escalating. By Friday, April 25, a second wave of boats mustered for the transit to Mariel. The lengths of the boats ranged from 18 to 90 feet. Many who did not own boats came to Key West with a large amount of money in the hope of buying boats or having someone take them to Mariel. Again, the seamanship of those on board the craft continued to be poor at best. About the only thing most boaters knew about navigation can be summed up in a saying, "210 for Mariel." That is, go to the Key West sea buoy and turn to compass heading 210 degrees. Most, however, knew nothing of deviation, variation, and currents and thus found themselves lost. The boaters expected to make thirty knots, but seas slowed the boats while engines gulped fuel. This wave of boaters tried to go in groups of ten to twenty at a time. Soon Lieutenant Commander Dennis's command found themselves "deluged" with requests for assistance. They conducted a twenty-four-hour-a-day towing service. The group at times had a waiting list of up to thirty boats that had broken down and needed assistance. Twelve cases needed medical evacuation or immediate assistance for sinking boats.[15]

The senior leadership of the U.S. Coast Guard began mustering additional forces to meet this unprecedented situation. Commander, U.S. Coast Guard Atlantic Area, dispatched two high-endurance cutters, the 378-foot *Dallas* (WHEC-716) and the 327-foot *Ingham* (WHEC-35), plus two additional 210-foot medium-endurance cutters and three additional 82-foot patrol boats to operate under the control of District 7. Additional aircraft and extra aircrews from other locations received orders to Florida.

District 7 began to organize a surface and air task force for the Straits of Florida and issued the first operational order for the boatlift. It stressed that the main "enemy forces" were "adverse weather, unseaworthy and overloaded boats and persons intent on violating U.S. law." Listed as the two main missions: "to provide maximum protection for refugee vessels . . . transiting between Florida and Cuba for an extended period of time."[16]

On this same Friday, Capt. W. J. Brogdon, USCG, a twenty-four-year veteran, commanded the 378-foot high-endurance cutter *Dallas*. His cutter had just moored at the U.S. Navy Base Guantánamo, Cuba, after finishing a portion of his refresher training with the Navy. The crew looked forward to a quick departure and some liberty ashore in Jamaica. Shortly after mooring, a U.S. Coast Guard officer hastily boarded the cutter "with a wild tale: the Seventh District had a SAR [Search and Rescue] case developing in Florida Straits, and we might be sent to help." Captain Brogdon replied, "That's two days away. What kind of SAR do they know about that will wait two days?" Later, Brogdon admitted that the pressures of underway training had made it impossible for him to concentrate on the events in the straits. Shortly after the officer passed on his "wild tale," Captain Brogdon received a message from the Commander, U.S. Coast Guard Atlantic Area to proceed to the Straits of Florida and operate under the control of District 7. At about the same time, the 327-foot high-endurance cutter *Ingham* also left Guantánamo for the same area. The cuttermen on both ships had no inkling of what lay ahead of them.[17]

The aviation branch of the U.S. Coast Guard had felt the crunch as much as those on the surface did. They, unlike Captain Brogdon, knew something of the situation developing within the Straits of Florida. Take, for example, one patrol by a flight on Sunday, April 26, 1980. Lt. Cdr. Gordon Kampert, USCG, flew over a mass of boats scattered between Cuba and Key West. He "pounded his fist on the armrest of the pilot's seat in frustration. 'My God, this is a zoo,' he said."

One skipper of a pleasure craft with Cubans on board jammed the airways with obscenities in his frustration at being lost. "I'm lost at sea, you f——g jerks," the skipper screamed. Another radio transmission cut in: "Mayday, Mayday. We are totally lost out here in these swells. This boat is going to break apart." At the same time, "a refugee boat somewhere off the coast of Cuba called for a surgeon. A girl passenger had been mangled when a tow rope broke under tension and snapped into her neck."

People trying to direct operations spoke in English. "The pleas and threats simply added to the noise. The confusion was in English, Spanish, mixtures of the two, and sometimes in Russian."

In the midst of all this, Lieutenant Commander Kampert spotted three very fast boats heading toward a waiting coastal freighter. "'We've got some druggers,' said Kampert. 'That's the mother ship.'"[18]

On Saturday, April 26, Vice President Walter Mondale presided over a meeting in the White House concerning Mariel. Attending were the chief of operations of the U.S. Coast Guard; the attorney general; the secretary of state; the secretary of health, education and welfare; a deputy director of the CIA; and other high officials of the Carter administration.

According to Mirta Ojito, the "rambling meeting" of several hours focused on two objectives: trying to get Miami Cubans to stop the charter boats and discussing legal actions that might stop the boatlift. The attendees quickly concluded that they could recommend very little to the president. No law prevented Americans from leaving the country, but it was unlawful to bring in undocumented people. The government could stop the Cubans from entering, but the stopping of people in overloaded boats and sending them back to sea meant certain death, plus the publicity of sending people back to a communist country seemed not only unpalatable but the political ramifications in an election year might also prove disastrous to the administration.

The U.S. Coast Guard at Key West felt the only way to stop the boatlift "would be to use force, and they told the White House officials just that." No one in the administration cared to think about the political repercussions of this option. Washington continued to insist that anyone bringing a boat from the United States to Cuba would be arrested and fined, although there was no way to accomplish this without the use of force. "The meeting ended inconclusively."[19]

The recognition of the approach of the bad weather season and the possibility of loss of life helped end the Camarioca Boatlift. The cutter *Dallas* arrived at its assigned area just before the "weather went to hell" on Sunday, April 27. An unexpected strong cold front passed through the area bringing gale force winds in its wake. Captain Brogdon recalled that the storm caused the "biggest mess of small boats you have ever seen. It was chaotic just trying to keep the people from killing themselves."[20]

Brogdon later wrote, "We saw them drifting, waving shirts, shooting flares or shining lights. We found boats capsized, in tow of other boats, abandoned, or sinking." Shouting voices jammed the radio frequencies. Normally, larger cutters in their day-to-day operations do very little SAR work with small craft. In this instance the "cutters found more SAR in a day than they usually handled in a year." The *Ingham* "at one time had five vessels in tow and an estimated fourteen persons on board, taken from four or five swamped boats."[21] As the weather passed, helicopters on board the cutters made the work somewhat easier. Commanding officers of the ships could immediately launch the aircraft and locate those in trouble, or could pluck many from immediate danger.

Even as cutters and helicopters fought to save those foundering in the rough seas, a meeting of the Customs Service, INS, and U.S. Coast Guard convened in the Miami Customs Building to discuss plans and procedures concerning the boatlift. Those attending learned of the probability of a forthcoming announcement from Washington, D.C., "which would help clarify the procedures to be employed by agencies of the U.S. Government." The attendees and many others would be caught completely off guard by President Carter.[22]

Meanwhile, the aftermath of the storm did little to slow the boatlift. The number of boats increased. People continued to bring large amounts of money to Key West to buy boats or to have someone else take them to Mariel. At this time, the U.S. Coast Guard Auxiliary, Division 13, made up of volunteer civilian boat owners, began assisting the service by taking care of routine SAR work around Key West.

Captain Brogdon, now commander of Coast Guard Squadron Southeast, later labeled the volume of boats as "staggering." By regulations, Brogdon should have coordinated everything as the on-scene commander. He found this an almost impossible task, so he decided to divide the ocean into sectors for the various cutters. Each of the commanding officers of the cutters received an order, "Handle whatever comes up in your area, and don't bother me with the minor details. If you need help, yell, or if things get slack in your area, let me know." Captain Brogdon also eliminated much of the paperwork involved in assistance cases, only requiring the essential data. "I always tried to be available in case one of the [commanding officers] wanted advice, but tried to refrain from giving it unless it was requested."[23]

Aboard the bridges of the squadron's cutters, crews busily worked radios, received sighting reports, and searched for boats in distress. Brogdon's cutter *Dallas*, as command ship for the squadron, used its Combat Information Center as a coordination center.

Brogdon began holding an evening meeting by radio of his commanders. This kept him informed of any problems so he could sort out any details and make new assignments. Most importantly, it allowed the commanding officers of the cutters to keep in touch with any changing policies.

Towing operations became critical. Brogdon later wrote that he had each of the cutters in their sectors tow disabled boats to one location and then one cutter would take the craft to Key West. Because the various types of vessels each required a different type of towing line (rope), the cutters soon began judging the size of the boats by the circumferences of tow line needed, that is, trawlers were "4-inch boats," the majority of yachts "3-inch boats," and the smallest "2-inch boats."[24]

By this time, Coast Guard District 7 had divided the waters from Key West to Cuba into stations, or sectors, numbered 0 to 3, 0 at Key West and 3 near the Cuban territorial waters. In April, Group Key West had control of sector 0 while the cutters worked all the sectors. Sector 3 had the important job of handling intelligence on the northbound boats and their numbers, along with whether they were overloaded.[25]

Captain Brogdon recalled that at first most of their work focused on the southbound craft. The U.S. Coast Guard crews tried to "discourage" these boats, "but this became more and more difficult farther south from Key West. These people were extremely determined to get their relatives." Brogdon commented, "Our primary task was to keep them alive while they were trying to cross the Straits in small, unseaworthy boats. We relied upon persuasion more than the law. They were knowingly breaking the law in any case, just making the trip."[26]

At first there was little traffic northbound, but then the tempo increased to "several thousand" refugees under way at a time. Most had not eaten in days and some suffered from medical problems. Almost all suffered from seasickness.

Many of the boats were so overloaded the weight threatened their stability, especially in any kind of sea. The commanding officers of the cutters that intercepted the dangerously jammed craft had some tough decisions to make. They had to determine which craft could make the trip, which people needed to come off an overloaded boat and whether that boat could safely proceed northward, and which people needed medical evacuation. Cdr. Martin J. Moynihan, commanding the cutter *Ingham*, pointed out one of the large problems of figuring out who would be removed to a cutter. "They all wanted to come aboard the ship and ride to Key West in luxury, instead of in their boats."[27]

By this time any carefully organized plan at Mariel crumbled and had almost broken down. The pressure of so many boats stopped the Cubans from checking each craft carefully; they could scarcely keep up with the number of boats. Officials put most of the boats at anchor in the harbor. The boat crews then awaited the call to the dock. The waiting period seemed interminable. Crews became bored and fearful at the same time. Nearing the end of April, more and more of a military presence grew in Mariel. When provisions ran low, Cubans charged those on the waiting boats high prices for any needed item. In other words, boat owners and those attempting escape spent many tension-filled days.

On Tuesday, April 29, Rear Adm. Benedict L. Stabile, commander of Coast Guard District 7, fearing a massive loss of life, sent a teletype message to the Cuban Border Guard requesting they send the names of vessels departing Mariel and the number of people on board each vessel. This would help the U.S. Coast Guard try to keep "some semblance of order." While no immediate reply was received, the district received unconfirmed reports that Cuban Border Guard patrol boats would escort vessels to the halfway point between Mariel and Key West. The cutter *Ingham* sighted two Cuban Border Guard patrol boats escorting at least eight boats from Mariel.

The next day, Wednesday, April 30, Admiral Stabile sent another teletype message to Cuba asking if they intended to continue the escorts and suggesting that the Border Guard escorts and U.S. Coast Guard cutters meet at a prearranged location for a turn-over procedure. Along with sending messages to Cuba, Coast Guard District 7 transmitted daily reports of their operations to other agencies.[28]

On the last day of April, Wednesday, the first potentially serious incident between Cuba and the United States happened. While twenty miles from Cuba, the pilots of a U.S. Coast Guard HC-131A *Samaritan* had two Cuban MiG fighters approach and make an identification pass of the aircraft. The fighters then returned and circled the unarmed U.S. Coast Guard aircraft until the HC-131A turned north. The same night, cutter *Dallas* watched as a Cuban patrol boat chased the 502-foot Greek freighter *Euro Champion*. When the cutter arrived in the area, the patrol boat fired a flare and turned toward Cuba.[29]

The Ojito family, on the last day of April, anxiously waited in their apartment, wondering whether Oswaldo had arrived to take them away from Cuba. Oswaldo, just as nervously, awaited the Cuban authorities to clear the Ojito family.

At the end of April, the situation in the Straits of Florida remained hectic for the U.S. Coast Guard at sea and for other federal agencies ashore. At least 7,665 Cubans had arrived in either Key West or Miami. (The numbers provided can only be estimated. No one knows how many died in the attempt.) These numbers proved only a prelude of what loomed on the horizon.[30]

4 A Liking for These People

> We'll continue to provide an open heart and open arms to refugees seeking freedom from Communist domination and from economic deprivation, brought about primarily by Fidel Castro and his government.
>
> President Jimmy Carter

The U.S. Coast Guard claimed that saving lives headed their priorities concerning the Cuban exodus in the Straits of Florida. Within fifteen days in May, however, President Jimmy Carter made two speeches that pushed law enforcement to at least an equal priority. The two speeches illustrate the confusion coming from the White House.

On Thursday, May 1, forty-nine vessels arrived in Key West from Mariel with 916 Cubans aboard. Of the forty-nine vessels, almost half did not carry passengers. News reports now spoke of "terrible" conditions in the Cuban harbor, with at least two thousand vessels and between fifteen thousand to twenty thousand "people from the U.S." The U.S. Coast Guard's official message report on the day's activities related that Cuban officials charged "exorbitant prices" on everything from fuel to food. Other comments detailed in the message spoke of a thirty-day delay in processing people who wanted to leave. Furthermore, some reported that Cuban officials were forcing boats taking relatives to the United States to also accept criminals as passengers.[1]

Four days later, on Monday, May 5, U.S. Navy ships and aircraft joined with the U.S. Coast Guard in trying to bring some order to the exodus. The initial naval force consisted of two amphibious warfare ships, the USS *Saipan* (LHA-2) and the USS *Boulder* (LST-1190), along with patrol aircraft from Naval Air Station Jacksonville, Florida.[2]

This larger force came under the tactical control of the Commander, U.S. Coast Guard District 7. The operational areas for the forces remained much the same as in April; that is, three commanders worked three sectors beginning at Key West. The commander of Group Key West's responsibility extended from the shore of the Keys out to thirty miles. He had under his command patrol boats, small craft, the U.S. Coast Guard helicopters brought to Key West, U.S. Coast Guard Auxiliary units, three stations within the Keys, and other resources. The waters closest to Cuba fell under the command of the commanding officer of the cutter *Dallas*, who controlled two high-endurance cutters, a 378- or 327-foot cutter, and from two to four medium-endurance cutters of usually 210 feet. To prevent any problems with warships of the Navy running up against Cuban patrol boats, the middle sector came under the command of Rear Adm. Warren Hamm, USN. Admiral Hamm controlled the two amphibious warfare ships and the helicopters attached to the ships.[3]

On the same day the U.S. Navy added their forces to the growing armada in the Straits of Florida, President Carter spoke to the Biennial National Convention of the League of Woman Voters. After brief remarks on a series of topics, none of which covered the large influx of Cubans leaving Mariel, the president asked for questions. Marian Shapiro from Hayes, Kansas, asked that in "light of thousands of illegal and legal immigrants arriving daily, a problem which is reaching critical proportions [in Florida,] what does your administration intend to do about enforcing current immigration laws and providing funds and programs for dealing with these newcomers, who are presently a great burden on local communities?"[4]

Carter said that the entire issue of the "Cuban refugees" came about because of the "inhumane approach by Fidel Castro." He went on to point out that he would enforce the law but that "we are the most generous nation on earth in receiving refugees, and I feel very deeply that this commitment should be maintained." Carter related that he had a special assistant, Jack Watson, working on the situation and staging areas for the refugees at Eglin Air Force Base in Florida. The president also went on to praise the local and state authorities in Florida and said he would go to Congress for additional funds. Carter closed with "we'll continue to provide an open heart and open arms to refugees seeking freedom from Communist domination and from economic deprivation, brought about primarily by Fidel Castro and his government." This became known as the "open heart and open arms" speech that many thought implied that the president felt he approved of the boatlift.[5]

On the same day that President Carter responded to Marian Shapiro, the U.S. Coast Guard worked two major cases involving grossly overloaded vessels. The 95-foot patrol boat *Cape Gull* (WPB-95304) intercepted and brought into Key West the oceangoing tug *Dr. Daniels*. Chartered for seventy thousand dollars, officials at Key West found 449 people crammed onto the tug, with only enough lifesaving equipment for about a third of the people. U.S. Customs seized the tug.

Meanwhile, the cutter *Ingham*, on station near Cuba, received a report from a pleasure craft heading north that the 150-foot *America* expected to take on at least nine hundred passengers for passage to Key West. This intelligence caused Admiral Stabile, commander of U.S. Coast Guard District 7, to send two teletype messages to the Cuban Border Guard asking about the reported nine hundred Cubans being allowed on the *America*. Admiral Stabile pointed out that Cuba had signed the Safety of Life at Sea (SOLAS) in 1960, the international agreement that specifically outlines such items as lifesaving equipment on board a vessel. Stabile went on to state that should a potentially unseaworthy vessel put out to sea, "in the interest of safety of life that you advise Coast Guard of name and country of registry of vessel, time of departure, number of passengers, and life saving and fire fighting equipment on board."[6]

Admiral Stabile's next message to the Cuban Border Guard discussed the condition of the *Dr. Daniels*. After again stating his concerns for the possibility of loss of life in unseaworthy and overloaded vessels and craft, Stabile closed his message: "To avert a tragic maritime disaster, I urge that the principles of safety set forth in the SOLAS convention be observed."[7] The commandant of the U.S. Coast Guard, Adm. John B. Hayes, held a news conference the next day, Wednesday, May 7, and reinforced what Admiral Stabile had said about averting a disaster. Hayes stated that if the Cuban government did not follow the SOLAS agreement they were "courting disaster."[8]

On Thursday, May 8, the captain of the *America* radioed the U.S. Coast Guard that he had been forced to depart Mariel with Cubans on board, but crews from two Cuban patrol boats boarded the vessel four miles outside of the harbor and ordered it to return to port.[9]

By Saturday, May 10, a strategy meeting convened to discuss the future implications of the continued boatlift. Among those present: the Commandant of the U.S. Coast Guard, the U.S. Coast Guard District 7 commander, and other federal agencies. The meeting hammered out a plan of seizing or detaining vessels and craft in violation of the law in two categories. Pleasure craft, usually escorted into Key West, made up the largest group of the first category. If a boarding team found violations, such as lack of enough lifejackets, or firefighting equipment on board, the craft could not leave the harbor until the violations were corrected. Commercial vessels found bringing in Cubans without visas would be detained until the operator could pay "the collateral" for the fine of bringing in undocumented people into the United States.[10] This marks the beginning of a stronger emphasis on law enforcement. Prior to the meeting, only six vessels were detained or seized, but afterward "it was not unusual to have half a dozen or more vessels terminated or detained on a single day."[11]

On the same day of the meeting, the 110-foot red, white, and blue catamaran *America*, halfway between Cuba and Key West, ran into difficulty. The captain of the vessel claimed that the Cubans forced the seven hundred people on board his vessel. The 210-foot cutter *Dauntless* (WMEC-624) arrived on scene to find the *America* "literally . . . sinking under the weight of its passengers."[12] Transferring untrained people from one vessel to another at sea remains an operation fraught with danger even in the best of conditions. With people frightened of going into the sea from a sinking vessel, the risk factor multiplies by many factors. Yet the crew of the *Dauntless* managed to conduct this difficult task without an injury.[13]

Later, Tom O'Toole, captain of the *America*, and Carey Cole, "officially in charge," spoke to the news media. The *Miami Herald* claimed that "not a single relative of the Cuban-Americans who chartered the *America* was on board," much to the disappointment of the eighty Cuban Americans from Miami, New Jersey, and Puerto Rico who paid one thousand dollars apiece for chartering the catamaran and five hundred dollars for each relative. According to O'Toole, Cuban authorities said that "we are in Cuba now, under Cuba[n] regulations. And that we'd take what they gave us or they'd take the boat."[14]

Cole claimed he "furiously" argued with the Cubans about the overloading and that he "had not come down here to pick up these people [forced upon him]. They said if I didn't take them they would seize my boat, name it Fidel, and put me before a firing squad."[15]

The next day, May 13, the *Miami News*, reporting on the new focus on law enforcement, quoted U.S. Customs spokesman James Dingfelder: "You're going to see more seizures in the next few days. We're finally getting our act together and learning how to coordinate with the other agencies involved."[16]

On the same day that Dingfelder spoke, the U.S. Coast Guard continued to handle the many people still trying to transit from Mariel to Key West. The 210-foot cutter *Diligence*, for example, escorted a convoy of twenty-three vessels, with an estimated fifteen hundred Cubans on board. At nearly the same time, because of a previous massive anti-American demonstration that led to violence in front of the U.S. Special Interest Section in Havana, the U.S. Coast Guard sent out a marine broadcast of a Department of State's warning. The broadcast recommended that "non-essential travel to Cuba as in the water surrounding Cuba should be postponed."[17]

On Sunday night, May 11, Lt. David W. Kunkel served as the duty pilot at U.S. Coast Guard Air Station Borinquen, Puerto Rico. During the night he received a telephone call from RCC in District 7, Miami.[18] The RCC officer said, "We'd like you to launch and go to Great Inagua Island and spend the night there." Great Inagua Island is to the northeast of the eastern point of Cuba.

Lieutenant Kunkel replied, "What's the deal?"

"We can't tell you what is going on, but we want you to go there and stand by for instructions." At this time no secure telephones connected District 7 and the air station.

Kunkel thought the order strange, so he called the station's operations officer. The officer said if the "District wants you to go there, you had better go."

Kunkel and his crew, made up of copilot Lt. (jg) Joseph Drazek and crewmen Carmelio Gonzalez and Edward Gonzales, flew a HH-3F helicopter, number 1438, to the island. They arrived at the airport and then telephoned the District. Kunkel received word that the District RCC still would not tell him anything. The RCC officer did tell him to find a hotel room and "plan on getting up early and calling [so he would learn] what to do."

The next morning brought difficulties in finding a telephone at the hotel and finding a taxi to the airport. Eventually, Lieutenant Kunkel succeeded in returning to the airfield. He telephoned RCC and received orders to search Cay Santo Domingo, a small, uninhabited sandy island approximately forty-five miles off Cuba's eastern tip. After performing the normal preflight checks, the 1438, with its crew of four, lifted off for Cay Santo Domingo.

Twenty-nine years later, Kunkel, now a retired rear admiral, recalled that his orders stated he should search the island for survivors. He remembered, however, that no one mentioned the survivors of what. The 1438 held enough fuel for about six hours of flight, from lift off to landing.

As the crew of the helicopter proceeded to the cay, they spotted a U.S. Navy ship. Kunkel entered into a radio conversation with the warship. A voice over the radio said, "Coast Guard, good seeing you out here searching. Don't worry we will be looking out for you." Kunkel then began to wonder "what is going on here? What am I missing?" Again, there was no secure communications available.

Lieutenant Kunkel began searching his assigned area at three hundred feet altitude when he received a radio call from the warship. "Coast Guard 1438: be advised we have two bogies [unidentified and possible enemy aircraft] near your position. Don't worry, we'll watch you."

Kunkel remembered thinking, "Now I am really wondering: what's to watch out here?" Lieutenant Kunkel then asked what was happening. Back came the response, "Obviously, you haven't heard." The naval communicator then spelled out, in a roundabout way, "what's to watch out here."

Earlier, on Sunday, May 11, the Royal Bahamian Defense Force patrol boat *Flamingo* seized a Cuban fishing vessel in Bahamian waters. The *Flamingo* took the vessel under tow and made for Ragged Island, the nearest

Bahamian populated island, some four hundred miles east of Mariel. Two Cuban MiG-21 jet fighters attacked the patrol boat with gunfire and sank the *Flamingo*, killing four. The Puerto Rican news media had not been running the story, so Kunkel and his crew had no idea they were looking for survivors of an attack by hostile jet fighters.

The unarmed helicopter obviously could not outrun the jets. Lieutenant Kunkel wondered, "What am I going to do?" The Navy ship then transmitted the position of the MiGs, "just like in a movie."

"MiGs are at twelve o'clock high," radioed the Navy. "They are now coming down your right side, making an approach."

Kunkel recalled, "I am at three hundred feet at 100–110 knots and going straight toward the island. I wanted to get close to land. I didn't know if I was going to try to land or just get out of the way. "I was listening and observing. They came in from the back and my entire crew was on the alert."

The two enlisted crewmembers, both of whom were Spanish speakers, excitedly reported: "Mr. Kunkel, they're coming around. I see them now." Then the two burst into Spanish, which Kunkel did not understand, interspersed with curses in English.

"Guys, just tell me where they are," Kunkel said.

Then Kunkel recalled, "Before I knew it, there is a MiG-21 not more than one hundred feet away. The Cuban pilot is trying to stay with me and he couldn't because of [our] low speed, and I knew that. Then Joe flips him the bird. And the guy gives it back. The other guy just sort of flew by us."

The navy ship radioed: "Looks like they're leaving. Uh, no, they're at twelve o'clock high and coming back."

Twenty-nine years later, Kunkel recalled, "now the Gonzalezs' are really getting excited. I start getting lower and slower so [the MiGs] can't stay with me. I ask the crewmembers where are they? They reply in Spanish."

The Navy ship radioed: "They are at your 180" (to the rear of the aircraft).

Suddenly, "this manic [Cuban pilot] passes *beneath* me and puts on the afterburner and shoots up into sky, just to give me a 'thump,' to give me a thrill, [and it] shakes my helicopter. The other guy just speeds by."

In the Navy ship's report, they claimed one of the U.S. Coast Guard pilots said the MiGs "almost blew me out of the sky."

The Navy ship called Kunkel: "You all right? Why don't you come over here and visit me?"

The two MiG-21s finally departed.

Kunkel recalled, "I was a bold Lieutenant [then] and kind of brash. I told one of the crewmen to get on the radio and call the District." Kunkel demanded to speak to the District Commander to complain about not being told completely about the mission. The District Commander did not come on the radio, but the Chief of Operations for the District did. He told Kunkel the District RCC could not transmit the information over unsecured radios or telephones. The operations officer ordered Kunkel to hover over the Navy vessel. "I did not hover, as that would waste too much fuel, so I circled the ship until released by the District and the ship."

Kunkel flew to Great Inagua Island, refueled, and departed for Borinquen. Amazingly, on the long return flight they spotted a vessel with fourteen people from the Dominican Republic in trouble. Kunkel and his crew hoisted the people to safety. Later, the news media reported on the story of the MiG-21 encounter, and the crew then received a great deal of attention.

About two days later Kunkel again had duty and received a call about the increasing tempo of Mariel. The District wanted a helicopter from Puerto Rico to make the journey to Key West and join in the effort. On the journey he landed at South Caicos, approximately two hundred miles northeast of the eastern tip of Cuba, which had a small U.S. Coast Guard LORAN (long range navigation) station on it.

In the middle of the night, Kunkel heard a knock on the door. A voice said, "Is there Coast Guard in there?" After receiving an affirmative, the voice said, "Is this Lieutenant Kunkel?"

"Yes," said Kunkel.

"I am a Petty Officer from the South Caicos LORAN Station. The District wants to talk to you on the radio." Kunkel and his copilot, Lt. Benjamin Thomasson, then got into a jeep. The petty officer drove them to the isolated station.

The radio brought orders to launch and do a medical evacuation at a given position. Kunkel looked at the position and then replied to RCC: "Do you know who you are talking to?" Back came the reply, "We know exactly who we are talking to."

Kunkel: "You are sending me to a place where less than a week ago I was buzzed by two MiGs. Have you cleared this?"

"We did."

"You said that a week ago."

It turned out that a woman on a cruise ship needed medical care. The District wanted Kunkel and his crew to depart at first light.

Kunkel recalled that he and Ben, his copilot, spent a restless night wondering about the mission. The next morning "even the crewmembers were saying maybe we shouldn't do this mission." Kunkel and his crew, however, decided to undertake the mission and successfully brought the woman off the cruise ship and landed her at a hospital in Nassau, Bahamas.

This ended the MiG-21 incident for Kunkel. He and his crew received congratulations from the District Commander. Rep. Don Ritter, of Pennsylvania, Kunkel's home district, wrote a letter of praise to Kunkel's mother.

The Cuban government later said they thought the *Flamingo* was a pirate ship attacking the Cuban fishing vessels. Later they apologized for their pilots buzzing the U.S. Coast Guard helicopter. The Cuban government also agreed to pay $10 million in reparations for the sinking of the *Flamingo* and the deaths of the four crewmembers.

Four days after the "open heart and open arms" speech, on Wednesday, May 14, President Carter reversed himself and completely changed policy. Although stating that he took this action "to welcome the Cuban refugees in a legal and orderly process," the changed policy in effect meant that the United States now ended the boatlift as practiced up until this date.

Known as the "five-point plan," Carter tried to bring an orderly sealift or airlift within the immigration laws of the United States. It also featured prior screening of Cubans in the U.S. Special Interest Section in Havana. He offered priority screenings to Cubans who had relatives in the United States; former political prisoners; those who had sought refuge in the Peruvian embassy; and those who sought refuge in the U.S. Special Interests Section. The plan clearly spelled out the various federal organizations' legal duties and the legal steps needed to carry out the law. The U.S. Coast Guard, for example, would communicate with vessels en route to and from Cuba, and within the harbors of the United States and Mariel, that they should return to the United States without taking on board Cubans. The service would also continue to check for violations of boating safety laws. If Cuban Americans followed this directive, they had "nothing to fear from the law."[19] The plan also called for a family registration office in Miami "to receive the names of those Cuban relatives of U.S. permanent residents who will be eligible for immigration." Carter also warned Castro about forcing boat owners to take hardened criminals and mental patients. Carter wanted it known that the United States welcomed "Cubans, seeking freedom, in accordance with our laws, and we will pursue every avenue to establish an orderly and regular flow."[20]

To carry out President Carter's plan, the U.S. Coast Guard suggested fifteen boarding teams formed to meet the incoming vessels. Each team consisted of a U.S. Coast Guard marine investigation officer, a U.S. Coast Guard boating safety detachment member, a U.S. Customs officer, and an INS officer. The U.S. Coast Guard marine investigation officer and customs officer duties included interviewing the master and crew of the vessel. The U.S. Coast Guard boating safety detachment member duty consisted of checking for safety equipment, and the INS officer removed the Cubans. The team also had the duty of recommending the type of legal action against the vessel or boat to the U.S. attorneys.[21]

The U.S. Coast Guard began an Urgent Marine Broadcast in English and Spanish:

> All United States citizens in Cuban ports and en route Cuba are advised to return to the United States at this time. The U.S. government will arrange alternative transportation for Cuban citizens desiring to emigrate through an organized sea lift that will ensure safe and orderly transportation. Vessels not under charter or hire by the U.S. government are subject to heavy fines and possible seizure if they transport Cuban citizens in violation of U.S. immigration laws. All U.S. boats in Mariel and those en route Cuba are advised to return to the United States without delay.[22]

The day after Carter's announcement of the five-point plan, estimates of from 564 to more than a thousand vessels still remained in Cuba. U.S. Coast Guard aviation and surface units received reports via radio from several boat and vessel owners in Mariel. Some boat owners reported that the Cuban government did not allow them to leave without taking people with them, that they had been turned back by gunboats when they attempted to leave without passengers. Other reports said Cuban officials allowed some craft or vessels to depart. The master of the fishing vessel *Mr. Gardner* radioed the cutter *Dallas* that "he wanted to leave Mariel without refugees, but that the passengers who chartered the vessel threatened the lives of the crew."[23] President Carter's shift to making the boatlift illegal increased the need for additional help in stemming the tide. Additional U.S. Coast Guard and U.S. Navy surface and aviation units received orders to work in the Straits of Florida.

Despite a reduction of vessels and boats within Mariel, by May 17 an estimated 341 remained in the harbor, with continued high numbers of passengers in northbound craft. For example, of the sighted 91 vessels bound for Key West, only 4 had no passengers on board.

On Saturday, May 17, Cdr. Alan F. Miller, commanding officer of the 210-foot cutter *Courageous* (WMEC-622), witnessed the dangers facing those trying to cross the Straits of Florida. Commander Miller received a radio report of an injured passenger on board a northbound boat. He ordered flight quarters and then launched an HH-52A helicopter. The aircrew's orders: fly from the cutter on a bearing received from the boat with the injured passenger. Unable to locate the boat, the aircrew flew over the northbound craft in the area and then started back to the *Courageous*.

The pilot suddenly radioed, "Just a minute. I want to take a look at something in the water over here. I'll get right back to you."

A few minutes passed.

"There are people in the water here," the pilot radioed, "there's a partially submerged boat, I'm going down to assist."

Another anxious few minutes passed as the pilot brought his helicopter closer to the surface of the sea.

"I need assistance. There are many people in the water. I'm going to hoist as many as I can." The pilot and his crew rescued eleven people.

Meanwhile, Commander Miller ordered a change in the course to the location, about two to three miles from the cutter, and ordered the engines full ahead. Miller also radioed a request for another nearby 210-foot cutter, the *Vigorous* (WMEC-627), to assist.

Upon arrival on scene, Commander Miller later recalled, "It was a terrible sight. The bow of the *Olo Yumi* could still be seen; there were people and debris everywhere. There was screaming, shouting, crying—pandemonium."

Commander Miller immediately issued a myriad of emergency orders: he directed the cutter's small boats launched; he put swimmer's nets over the side and the cutter's swimmers to help those capable of swimming to the cutter; he radioed Coast Guard Group Key West to provide aircraft; and he informed the cutter *Dallas* and the USS *Saipan* of the situation. In the laconic manner of a seaman, he later reported, "From there, it was just a matter of picking up survivors and bodies, then searching for those still missing." Of the fifty-two people on board the *Olo Yumi*, the rescue effort saved thirty-eight people. Ten bodies were recovered; four remained missing.

Later investigation pieced together what had taken place on this terrible day in the straits. The 35- to 40-foot *Olo Yumi* had lost one of its two engines and then developed steering problems. This caused the craft to work into the trough of four- to five-foot seas. The rocking of the boat caused the fifty-two passengers to move aft to see what was happening. This overloaded the stern area and pushed the transom (the stern area of the boat) under water. The flooding immediately caused panic among the passengers, who began to push, shove, and trample each other as the *Olo Yumi* capsized. Commander Miller believed the four missing people became trapped inside the boat when it sank. "Many of the people we picked up had lacerations to their arms and legs to indicate the shoving, pushing, the panic that ensued." One fifteen-year-old girl who survived lost both parents, both sisters, and a grandparent. Commander Miller recalled that the case of the *Olo Yumi* "was the most tragic thing that we saw."[24]

Despite this tragedy and the loss of unknown others trying to make the transit to Key West, the boats and vessels continued their north and south treks, along with all the dangers of overloading unseaworthy craft.

The day after the *Olo Yumi* incident, the master of the fishing vessel *Atlantis* claimed that Cuban authorities forced him at gunpoint to take on board 354 people, although he had only 80 lifejackets on his vessel. Later the cutter *Dallas* received a distress call from the *Atlantis*. The cutter arrived and, finding the *Atlantis* in disrepair, maneuvered close to the fishing vessel. This provided a lee in the six-foot seas. Seeing the cutter nearby calmed nervous passengers; the cutter escorted the *Atlantis* to Key West.[25]

For the rest of May the work never slackened. After finally arriving in Key West after their long flight from Borinquen, Puerto Rico, Lieutenant Kunkel thought he had landed in the middle "of a Wild West town, with military everywhere." He and his crew soon found themselves caught up in the hectic pace. For example, Kunkel recalled that on the night of Monday, May 19, two days after the tragic *Olo Yumi* incident, they launched to help Cubans on a boat aground on a reef with more than forty people on board. "It became a race between three helicopters," Kunkel recalled, "one HH-3F from [Air Station Mobile, Alabama,] one HH-52A," and his aircraft. "The HH-52A hoisted seven people, the other HH-3F, nineteen. I told Ben Thomasson that we can do better than that. We picked up twenty-one."[26]

Those on patrol boats also continued their hard work through the rest of May. The 82-foot patrol boat *Point Huron* (WPB-82357), for example, received a mayday call on May 18. Upon arrival at the scene, the patrol boat crew found a 35-foot pleasure craft. Boarding the boat, the U.S. Coast Guard crew found three people dead and twenty-seven others suffering from carbon monoxide poisoning. The operator of the boat and his crew, who were above deck, remained unaffected.[27]

Work at sea is inherently dangerous. The duties of those working with undocumented migrants proved no different. While working on Mariel on May 28, 1980, the U.S. Navy ocean minesweeper USS *Leader* (MSO-428), lost a crew member overboard. An immediate search, which lasted for six hours, miraculously found and recovered the sailor "without injury."[28]

Near the end of May, the U.S. Coast Guard estimated that 90 percent of the northbound boats were either overloaded or carrying the maximum number of passengers. The service also estimated the known deaths of twenty-four people since the boatlift began in April. Juan M. Clark, critical of almost all aspects of the federal government's role in the Mariel Boatlift writes that "one aspect of the government's performance which should be highly praised and which Cubans have not forgotten, but receives little, if any, press coverage. This is the humanitarian aid rendered by the U.S. Coast Guard and the Navy. These two entities contributed significantly to the saving of hundreds of lives."[29]

Near the end of May, the U.S. Coast Guard began broadcasting in English and Spanish that vessels departing Mariel were being tracked "to insure a safe transit and arrival at Key West processing center." If a vessel failed to arrive at Key West, it would be considered "evidence of intent to violate U.S. law." Then matters shifted to seizing the craft and prosecuting the owners.[30]

Yet another item joined the stack of "what next?" in the straits. On Saturday, May 24, at 10:13 p.m., the cutter *Acushnet* (WMEC-167) patrolled alone north of Mariel Bay. Three Cuban gunboats approached the cutter and began circling it, seemingly intent on forcing the *Acushnet* into Cuban waters. According to Petty Officer (PO) Robert Dyche, U.S. Coast Guard, "They were . . . often within 60 feet of us, severely limiting maneuverability; we could not break free without hitting at least one of them." The gunboats switched on their searchlights and attempted to light up the bridge of the cutter, thereby destroying the night vision of those on the bridge.

The commanding officer of the cutter, Cdr. G. C. Nelson, contacted the commander of U.S. Coast Guard District 7 and requested assistance from U.S. Navy aviation. The Navy scrambled a pair of Navy A-6 attack aircraft. Meanwhile, the Cuban gunboats continued their efforts to herd the cutter into Cuban waters.

Petty Officer Dyche later recalled that as those on the decks of the *Acushnet* watched the Cuban gunboats, the bridge announced "that a change in the status quo was about to take place, but no word was passed as to what that meant. We found out less than a minute later; the two A-6s had come up astern with no lights at all, skimming about 100' above the water. When they were just astern they 'lit up'; green cockpit lights (an eerie effect in an A-6) and [their] landing lights. One pass and the gunboats decided they had had enough fun, and backed off; two left the area immediately." Another cutter joined the *Acushnet* and both ships stopped their engines. The third Cuban gunboat then departed.[31]

The U.S. Coast Guard sent a message to the Cuban Border Guard asking the intentions of the gunboat. The return message from Cuba stated: "The Cuban Patrol craft No. 308 was in the area on a patrol."[32]

Another problem arose before the close of May: the possible use of foreign-flagged vessels to transport the Cubans trying to reach Florida. On May 29, the U.S. Coast Guard learned of a large ship, the *Red Diamond*, of unknown registry, loading passengers at Mariel. At almost the same time, another 276-foot Panamanian ship, *Rio Indio*, was en route to Mariel to pick up passengers. Panama authorized the U.S. Coast Guard to stop and board the ship, if on the high seas, for SOLAS violations. Panama also authorized the boarding team to advise the master that if he took passengers on at Mariel for transportation to Key West, he violated Panamanian law and stood to lose his master's certificate.

The cutter *Courageous* located the *Rio Indio* on the high seas and placed a boarding team on the ship. Claiming a destination of Mobile, Alabama, the master then changed his mind and said that Cuban Americans in his crew forced him to sail for Mariel. In a message to his higher command, the commanding officer of the *Courageous*, Commander Miller, stated that he believed that force remained the only way to prevent the ship from entering Mariel. Admiral Stabile, however, overruled this recommendation.

Upon receiving Admiral Stabile's order, Commander Miller then had his boarding party return to the cutter. He ordered his cutter to follow the Panamanian ship along the Cuban coastline until it entered the Mariel harbor. However, on June 1, shortly before the vessel entered the harbor, Panama authorized the United States to reboard the *Rio Indio* to inform the master that Panama prohibited the transportation of Cubans from Mariel to the United States. Commander Miller contacted the ship and directed the master to proceed to twelve nautical miles outside of Cuba for reboarding.[33]

The U.S. Coast Guard people most intimately connected with enforcing President Carter's five-point plan must have wondered what June would bring. The answer came soon enough.

Meanwhile, back in Cuba, Mirta Ojito recalled that the "police came on May 7." An official said, "There is a boat waiting for you at the port of Mariel. Are you ready and willing to abandon the country at this time?" Thus began Mirta's voyage to the United States during Mariel.[34] Mirta's family gathered the possessions they could carry. She took a photograph of Varadero Beach, "a chocolate-colored lipstick, and two pens, a gift from her uncle." Her mother took a small image of Our Lady of Charity and a "jeweled pin in the shape of a perfume bottle" bought for her by her father on their honeymoon.[35]

Mirta, along with her father, mother, and younger sister, made their way in a police car to a recreational club, the first assembly point. They joined large groups of people sitting on the grass waiting for information. A loudspeaker called out names, and eventually the family learned the name of Oswaldo's chartered vessel: *Valley Chief*. "From then on, *Valley Chief* was our new identity." No one in the government called them by their family name.[36]

Another family of four made up the people in Mirta's group, plus a man whose brother came to get him, an old woman and her son, and a couple with a baby. All warily eyed one another, but after hours together, the groups grew closer.

During the long hours of the day, Mirta eventually talked her mother into leaving the area to make a telephone call to her friends. The street outside of the recreation club swarmed with those protesting the people leaving Cuba. A group spotted Mirta and her mother and chased them. Both managed to make it back to the club. Mirta recalled, "I'd learned a lesson: I had become the enemy."[37]

At eight o'clock the next morning, the Ojito family heard *Valley Chief* called over the loudspeaker. They made their way to an office. There the family together underwent a series of questions and were then ordered to board a bus with no windows. The windows had been removed so people along the streets could throw tomatoes and eggs at those inside.

They arrived at Mosquito and found long lines of people. Eventually, the family appeared individually before officers; one officer took Mirta's pens and passed her to a cubicle with a woman officer who conducted a thorough search to see if she had hidden anything in her underwear. Unbeknownst to the family, her sister had hidden a plastic bag in her underwear that contained a picture of their grandfather and a letter from a friend. The officer let her keep the material. Her father had his remaining pesos and their identification papers taken from him.

When the family finished this process, they came out a back door that led them to what looked like "a tropical concentration camp." They remained there until ten o'clock the next morning when they heard the name of their boat over the loudspeaker. Throughout the entire process, Mirta observed families tearfully separated, others removed from the lines and never seen again.[38]

The family boarded yet another bus for the two-and-a-half-mile trip to the Mariel harbor. Eventually, they were allowed off the bus and, after tearful embraces with Uncle Oswaldo, boarded the *Valley Chief*. Oswaldo told the family that he had spent sixteen days in Mariel's harbor waiting for the family.

Later in the afternoon the Cuban authorities brought approximately two hundred men to the boat. Oswaldo explained that the Cubans told the captain of the *Valley Chief* the people came from the Peruvian embassy. These men seemed something else. They had shaved heads and dressed in either prison or hospital clothes. One of the men asked Mirta's father for a nail clipper. The man explained that he "wanted to slice [his] veins open." This and his vacant look made Mirta's family move as far away from the men as possible.[39]

The next day, when the *Valley Chief* tried to get under way, the number of people on the boat prevented it from moving. The engine did not work and the captain said he had no parts. Someone would have to either go to Miami for parts or pay a very large sum to get a mechanic from another boat to fix the engine.[40]

Oswaldo managed to find a disabled U.S. veteran of the Vietnam War, Mike Howell, and his fishing vessel *Mañana*. The Cubans had already placed on board the *Mañana* the people Howell had contracted to take out. Anxious to leave, he agreed with a Cuban army officer to take the *Valley Chief* in tow into international waters where the U.S. Coast Guard would pick them up. Howell transferred the women, children, and elderly to his vessel, leaving the men, including Mirta's father and uncle, on the *Valley Chief*.[41]

Earlier, a *New York Times* reporter, Edward Schumacher, watched the overloaded *Valley Chief* and another vessel, the *America*, with families and prisoners or hospital patients on board. Schumacher interviewed some of the men on the *Valley Chief* and filed the first proof of another class of people being sent out of Cuba during Mariel.[42]

Howell towed the *Valley Chief* out into international waters and then dropped the tow. "I could tell [my mother] was scared," recalled Mirta. "She was forty years old and alone with her daughters for the first time in her life. She did not know how to swim, she'd never been in a boat, and she'd rarely ever been away from my father."[43]

The *Mañana*, with a badly seasick Mirta aboard, entered Key West on Mother's Day, Sunday, May 11, thus ending her passage from Cuba. Her father and uncle rejoined them later in Key West. "I had entered the world of the exile," Mirta later wrote, "a zone where one must always walk alone, at one's own pace, and only after burying a part of one's soul."[44]

In June another U.S. Coast Guard unit entered into the federal mix. The U.S. Coast Guard Auxiliary, a volunteer force of private citizens, began patrolling the reef line from the northern end of the Keys to Key West. Operation Key Ring used thirteen sites, and members of the Auxiliary used their boats of from 18- to 36-feet and came from as far away as Atlanta, Georgia, and Charleston, South Carolina. The patrolling lasted until June 15.[45]

The day after Operation Key Ring began, the *Red Diamond* sailed from Mariel. By this time Panama had claimed the ship and had canceled the registry of the ship as well as that of the *Rio Indio*.

The cutter *Acushnet* intercepted the *Rio Indio* immediately after it reached twelve nautical miles outside of Mariel. Crewmen from the cutter found 731 passengers, including 35 infants, crammed into the grossly overloaded ship. Petty Officer Dyche later recalled that no one could "comprehend" just how many people the ship held. Dyche reported that even at the start of the voyage that the captain of the *Rio Indio* had already reported taking on water. "[The] master informed us that many of his passengers were either very old or very young, and that a number of them were in need of medical attention."[46] Commander Nelson, commanding officer of the cutter, ordered his hospital corpsman, HM1 Christopher Parks, USCG, to board the *Red Diamond* and report on the condition of the passengers. Petty Officer Parks reported that some of the passengers "were mothers with very young children, some only days old . . . [and] that some of the [people] had been aboard for at least three days prior to departure from Mariel." Parks also reported that many of the passengers were suffering from lack of food, and "dehydration was already a major problem."

Commander Nelson felt it best if the *Acushnet* escorted the *Red Diamond* back to Key West. Nearing Key West, Petty Officer Parks reported a young mother and her child suffering from dehydration beyond his abilities to help them. He recommended immediate helicopter evacuation.

Meanwhile, U.S. Coast Guard Public Affairs Chief Petty Officer (CPO) Louis Parris, in the *Acushnet*, had provided the news media with running accounts of the plight of the passengers on board the *Red Diamond*. The helicopter evacuation of the mother and child brought even more media attention. As the cutter and ship approached the Key West sea buoy, boats loaded with camera crews and reporters approached the *Acushnet*.

Petty Officer Dyche said that all the publicity "had its own down-side." The on-scene commander, the commanding officer of the cutter *Dallas*, ordered Commander Nelson to transfer the escort of the *Red Diamond* to the *Dallas*. In a large understatement, Dyche remembered that this order "was met with, shall we say, less than enthusiasm; we had given a lot of time and attention to this particular group of refugees, supplying them with all of the food and water we could spare, as well as a lot of hygiene and toiletry items that came out of the crews' own pockets. It would not be wrong to say that we had developed a bond with, and a liking for, these people, and we wanted to take them ourselves, finishing what we started." Adding even more to the disappointment, as soon as the *Acushnet* passed control over to the *Dallas*, the *Acushnet* immediately set out to sea again. "We were not even allowed to follow *Dallas* in to see our charges safely landed," said Dyche.[47]

On Tuesday, June 3, President Carter approved a six-week involuntary call up of a limited number of U.S. Coast Guard reservists. He limited the total number of reservists on duty at any one time to three hundred, with a total of no more than nine hundred. By the end of the month, six hundred reservists received their orders to report for duty.[48]

On the same day, the U.S. Coast Guard officer commanding the cutters near Cuba reported that more than half of the vessels departing Mariel needed assistance. Better news focused on the fact that Cuban officials refused to put Cuban passengers on a Panamanian vessel and the now stateless *Rio Indio*. This indicated that Cuba honored Panama's request not to load passengers on board their vessels at Mariel. This did not mean that overloaded vessels and craft did not continue to depart from Mariel. The 38-foot Bahamian *Veronica Express*, for example, departed with 222 people on board while towing the cabin cruiser *Once More* with 69 people on board.[49]

As the middle of June approached, the flood of Cubans trying to leave Cuba from Mariel slowed. On June 9 the commander of U.S. Coast Guard District 7 released the naval resources assigned to the Mariel Boatlift, with the exception of naval aviation overflights of the area.

On Thursday evening, June 12, the U.S. registered *God's Mercy* arrived in Key West. The ex-minesweeper, purchased in Boston by a New Orleans church group, sailed to New Orleans and there received its new name. The 110-footer carried 422 Cubans. The *God's Mercy* was seized and the owners and crew arrested for bringing in undocumented migrants. They were released on their own recognizance.

In the words of a U.S. Coast Guard publication on the Mariel Boatlift, after the middle of the month the flood slowed to a trickle. "Cuba now released a few boats carrying 50 to 100 people. This occurred three or four days in a week."[50]

The "trickle" continues. At times over the next twenty-eight years, the numbers rose, but the number of Cubans in one narrow span of time never equaled Mariel. The official U.S. Coast Guard total for those saved stands at 125,000. In reality, there is no way an accurate accounting can be given of just how many Cubans willingly took their chances to cross the Straits of Florida. Nor can there ever be an accounting of those who died making the effort. Nevertheless, one of the few authors on the political machinations taking place during the Mariel Boatlift, Dr. Mario Antonio Rivera, writes that by the end of August 1980 the "influx had reached 121,511, almost 1.3 percent of Cuba's population."[51]

Rivera has pointed out that decision making at the highest levels of the federal government, in charitable terms, proved indecisive. The most visible example of this is President Carter's "open heart, open arms" speech, followed a short four days later with a policy that seemed not so liberal. Some have pointed out that Carter focused more on the Iranian hostage situation and the upcoming presidential election to put the time in for the needed decision making for this major event. Yet, as Rivera has pointed out, White House staffers have stated that at times Carter "was personally involved, though episodically, in deciding relatively mundane problems."[52]

Rivera has succinctly outlined the major reasons the Carter administration failed to stop the Mariel Boatlift. The administration did not recognize the signals of "pent-up" pressures in Cuba following the ending of the "freedom flights." The administration, even though claiming to have intelligence of a mass exodus, remained sluggish to react. The White House felt it could persuade the Cuban government to accept the Refugee Act as the basis for resuming Cuban immigration, while the State Department refused to consider other quick strategies. After the Peruvian embassy incident, the Carter administration had no alternatives to solve the crisis other than to persuade the Cuban government to accept the American proposals. Rivera, in a nice bit of understatement, notes that the Carter administration's "persuasive powers were evidently not the equal of the Johnson Administration's."[53]

Another factor also had much to do with the Mariel Boatlift. The Carter administration seemed to throw one federal agency after another at the problem, or to establish groups to handle the problem. Yet there seemed no clear lines of cooperation or reporting between agencies, groups, or the White House. Such an arrangement can only lead to a bureaucratic nightmare with little chance for cooperation and accomplishment. What seems clear is that Fidel Castro, who stood to lose a great deal from the Mariel Boatlift, instead gained a great deal.

Mirta Ojito taught herself English and, six years after entering the United States, graduated college with honors. "I never seriously considered a career other than journalism," Mirta later wrote. As Miami correspondent for the *New York Times*, she shared the 2000 Pulitzer Prize. Mirta also has taught journalism at New York University, Columbia, and the University of Miami.[54]

Juan M. Clark, of the Miami Dade Community College in 1981, wrote, "As with the Camarioca exodus in 1965, there is a consensus regarding one aspect of the government's performance which should be highly praised and which Cubans have not forgotten, but receives little, if any, press coverage. This is the humanitarian aid rendered by the U.S. Coast Guard and the Navy. These two entities contributed significantly to the saving of hundreds of lives. . . . Their sailors showed, through their concern, that the American people cared for the welfare of the refugees."[55] A close examination of the Mariel Boatlift does show that from the beginning the U.S. Coast Guard carried out its mission competently and humanely. This does not mean it recognized the impending boatlift, nor does it mean it did not stretch its resources to the maximum, or that it did not make mistakes. Lt. Cdr. Rob Parker, USCG, while a student at the U.S. Naval War College in 1993, noted in a paper on whether the service applied any lessons learned from Mariel to the work during Operation Able Manner (chapter 9): "We [the U.S. Coast Guard] don't seem to look at the operational level for lessons learned, especially if the operation is more than one year old." Furthermore, the service "must also plan for future contingencies rather than simply learn our lessons on 'how to do *this* better next time" (Parker's emphasis).[56] Anyone studying the service's role in dealing with undocumented migrants from Camarioca to the present day quickly realizes that the service is best at reacting quickly to new situations rather than in strategic studies. This quick reaction is due to a culture that relies on people in the service's operational units—cutters, aircraft, and small boat stations—operating with very little resources. Its greatest source, however, depends upon the lowest person in the unit to the commanding officer, using their intelligence and initiative with little or no guidance from higher commands.

5 Dying to Get Here

Haiti

> Racontez nôtre histoire.
> [Tell our story.]
>
> Haitian to photojournalist
> Patrick Chauvel

Haiti lies approximately 750 miles southeast of Florida. It encompasses the western end of the large island of Hispaniola and shares the island with its eastern neighbor, the Dominican Republic. Immediately to the west of Haiti is Cuba, and slightly to the southwest is Jamaica. The land is very mountainous. In 1804 African slaves brought to the island by the French took control of the country in the only successful slave revolt in the western hemisphere. Since that time, Haiti has become almost a stereotype of a third world country. Its history is marked with "turmoil, violence, political corruption, and brutal rule."[1] The United Nations (UN) development program human development index (HDI) in 2005, for example, ranked Haiti 146 out of 177 nations. Among many items, the index put life expectancy in Haiti at 59.5 years, compared to the highest rated country, Iceland, at 81.5 years. In Haiti, the indicator for the population living below US$1 a day showed 53.9, while in Iceland the indicator showed 0. Added to these impersonal statistics is the fact that the country has suffered extreme environmental damage.[2]

"With the possible exception of Cuba, no other Latin American country has had a more tortured historical connection with the United States."[3] President Woodrow Wilson dispatched troops to Haiti in 1915, ostensibly to restore order and democracy but more likely to protect the approaches to the Panama Canal. Not until 1934 under the presidency of Franklin D. Roosevelt as a part of his Good Neighbor Policy toward Latin America did U.S. Marines depart the country. The long occupancy failed to accomplish a stable democracy or economic growth. Soon after the Marines left, the country reverted to "brutal dictatorship."[4]

Most Americans know very little about Haiti, but many have at least heard of two of the most infamous dictators: François "Papa Doc" Duvalier and his son, Jean-Claude "Baby Doc" Duvalier. Elected in 1957, François Duvalier had the National Assembly vote him "President for Life" seven years later. Corruption and terror hallmarked the senior Duvalier's reign. He established the Tonton Macoutes, a rural militia who made their living through crime and extortion. Jean-Claude succeeded to the presidency upon his father's death in 1971. No real changes took place in Haiti, and by the mid-1980s the population felt helpless. Facing pressures from within, and from the United States, Jean-Claude left his country.[5]

The coming to power of François Duvalier in the 1950s marked the beginning of a larger migration from Haiti to the United States. For a nine-year period beginning in 1951, at least 4,442 Haitians, mostly from the middle class, legally immigrated to the United States, settling largely in New York City. Over the next ten years at least 34,499 Haitians legally migrated, again to New York City. Many of these people came from the urban working class.[6]

As the conditions in Haiti worsened, the number of Haitians entering the United States rose. In the 1970s, for example, 56,335 migrated legally, largely to the New York City area and usually by regular commercial air service.

The 1970s marked the first attempt by poor undocumented Haitians to enter Florida via the sea. At least 7,837 arrived during this period. This influx brought "influential economic and political leaders in south Florida" calling for federal action to stop the Haitians entering via the maritime route. The Florida groups said that "the boat people were a disruptive force, destroying the community and draining public resources."[7] Washington heeded this argument by placing most of the boat Haitians in Florida camps and then returning them to Port au Prince—Haiti's capital—as soon as possible. Hoover Institute Senior Fellow Thomas H. Henriksen points out that, in general, "Haiti slipped in and out of Washington's political consciousness until early in the 1990s."[8]

The 1980s began one of those periods when Haiti occupied "the political consciousness" of Washington, but only for a few months. Little known to most Americans, except to Floridians, at the same time as the U.S. Coast Guard faced the wave of 125,000 undocumented Cuban immigrants during the Mariel Boatlift, at least 25,000 Haitians jammed into small sailing craft called *yolas* and also fought to enter the Sunshine State.

As with the Cubans, the U.S. asylum policy was "blatantly affected by U.S. foreign policy interests; petitioners fleeing repressive regimes friendly to the United States tended to be denied, while those seeking shelter from left-wing governments usually had a greater chance of receiving asylum."[9] Unfortunately for Haitians, their government has generally supported the United States. What took place during the Mariel Boatlift is illustrative of what those trying to escape Haiti would face in the coming years and, as of 2009, still face.

While decision makers wrestled with what to do with the Haitian influx during the Mariel Boatlift, U.S. Coast Guard personnel who had to work with what took place at sea grappled with their own problems. More than twenty-five years after Mariel, Wayne Marshall, a retired U.S. Coast Guard senior chief petty officer, related one incident.

> I was stationed on the West Coast and received temporary orders to proceed to Florida for duty to help with what was taking place [during Mariel]. Along with other crewmen, I was assigned to a 41-foot boat operating out of Islamorada[, Florida]. One day, we came upon a boat full of Haitians who were in very bad condition. We gave them what help we could, and then started the tow into the harbor of Islamorada. As we entered the harbor, we heard some noise that we could not identify. We cut our power to see what was happening. What we heard was the Haitians singing "God Bless America." They had been practicing it since they left Haiti. This certainly made us feel good.
>
> Still feeling good, we tied up the Haitian's boat at the dock. Then INS

came on board the boat and started to treat the Haitians badly. They then herded them off to someplace. This did not make us feel too good.[10]

Some time after this incident, the Carter administration came up with a new status for the Cubans and Haitians during the Mariel Boatlift period: "Cuban-Haitian Entrant." The status permitted most of both groups to remain in the United States. Soon after the official ending of Mariel in September 1980 and the election of a new U.S. president, another policy came into effect, but *only* for the Haitians.[11]

In 1981 the governments of the United States and Haiti agreed to allow U.S. Coast Guard cutters to work close to their shores to stop *yolas* loaded with undocumented migrants before they ventured too far off shore. Furthermore, the U.S. Coast Guard received orders to stop suspected vessels on the high seas and remove any undocumented Haitians for return to Haiti. Haiti also agreed not to punish those returned by the U.S. Coast Guard. "Sometimes a hearing to establish potential eligibility for political asylum . . . [was] accorded these Haitians [intercepted at sea] and sometimes not."[12] This agreement and procedure is, as of this writing, still in effect, despite the many changes in the Haitian government.

Most news accounts and editorials derided the policy of returning the Haitians, who had suffered so much in their own country, and sympathized with their attempt to flee to a better life. Despite the often negative publicity, it has never been enough to change the policy. Furthermore, there have always been those who agree with the procedure.

From 1981 onward, the U.S. Coast Guard usually stressed that they rescued Haitians from the sea, not that they followed policies dictated to them, nor that their main mission by 1981—labeled Haitian Migrant Interdiction Operation—was to intercept and return Haitians. While some may point out this smacked of a bureaucratic word game to hide a policy the U.S. Coast Guard had to enforce, one can make a very good argument that many Haitians in fact would have perished at sea if not for the work of the crews of the U.S. Coast Guard. In most cases, the work accomplished by the U.S. Coast Guard crews went unnoticed. Vincent C. Thomas Jr., a contributing editor for *Sea Power* magazine, is the exception to this generalization. Thomas sailed on board the 378-foot cutter *Hamilton* (WHEC-715) in 1984. He commented on the "youth of the *Hamilton*'s crew and the confidence of these young people in their ability to perform." He derided the "ineffective way in which the Coast Guard communicates to the media and general public the accomplishments of its people. Heroics at sea by Coast Guard personnel are an everyday occurrence; those accomplishments should be communicated routinely to higher authority as a matter of practice, so that the information is at least available for release to the public. That simply is not happening now; as a result, a horrendous vacuum of newsworthy information exists."[13] Thomas's remarks came about because of one incident he observed during his short stay on the cutter.

On the afternoon of June 6, 1984, a U.S. Coast Guard helicopter operating out of the U.S. Naval Base at Guantánamo spotted an overloaded Haitian sailboat in the Windward Passage between Haiti and Cuba. The *Hamilton*, on patrol in the area, responded. The cutter's helicopter located the *yola*. By 5:00 p.m. the *Hamilton*'s commanding officer, Capt. Albert C. Buechler, with seventeen years at sea in both the Merchant Marine and U.S. Coast Guard, had his cutter hove to nearby. He ordered two 25-foot boats lowered and sent to board the Haitian sailboat. Both of the boats had twenty-one-year-old coxswains. (A coxswain is the person who drives the boat and is in charge of the craft while under way.) Each boat had a boarding party. The two boats plowed through eight-foot seas, facing thirty knots of wind (34.6 miles per hour). Captain Buechler, a cautious mariner, prepared a large raft and a fast 17-foot inflatable boat, "just in case."

In one of the boats rode Chief Warrant Officer [CWO] Boatswain Michael Scanlon, who had conducted "literally thousands" of boardings on law enforcement patrols in the North Atlantic. Later, he related that in all his boardings he "had never seen a life lost, nor had he himself suffered serious injury." Also preparing to board the Haitian vessel were two INS agents, Harold Boyce and Haitian-born Jacques Crevecouer, a Haitian interpreter who had just become a naturalized U.S. citizen.

The transfer of people from one ship to another can be accomplished in at least two ways. One method is for a ship to put some of their crew in the ship's small boat, lower it, motor over to the other vessel, and take aboard the passengers. The receiving vessel can either have the people climb a rope ladder, called a Jacob's ladder by sailors, or an accommodation ladder, which looks like a stairway up the side of a ship. The latter method takes some time to rig. Both a Jacob's ladder and an accommodation ladder can be difficult, if not dangerous, in any type of seaway. The second, and safest, method is to hoist the boat with passengers on board the receiving ship using the receiving ship's own davits—the devices containing the gear used to raise and lower small boats from a ship. This way the passengers can step from the boat directly onto the deck of the ship.

On this June evening in the Windward Passage, Captain Buechler opted for the safest method. This meant transferring about six Haitians at a time from their vessel to the cutter's small boats. The small boats with the Haitian six passengers would be hoisted on board the *Hamilton*, who then debarked on the cutter's deck. The small boat would again be lowered and return for more Haitians. While one boat unloaded on the cutter, the other small boat received the next six Haitians.

Everything began as planned. Boatswain Scanlon, INS agent Boyce, and interpreter Crevecouer scrambled on board the Haitian vessel. Crevecouer asked the passengers in the sailboat's hold to remain where they were while six of the passengers transferred to the small boat. After loading the Haitians, the coxswain pulled away to the cutter while the next boat pulled alongside the sailboat. Six more Haitians began moving into the boat. The *yola* rolled heavily to starboard. Those still in the hold panicked and rushed topside, throwing their combined weight to the starboard side. The vessel righted itself briefly before rolling again deeply to starboard and capsizing.

Only Scanlon, Boyce, and Crevecouer wore lifejackets. None of the Haitians could swim. The three men found themselves grabbed by many Haitians trying to keep afloat. Amidst screams and cries for help, Scanlon and Boyce held on to many of the desperate people. One woman Boyce held gave up and died in his arms. Five people grabbed Crevecouer and dragged him under. His body was never found.

The seas quickly dispersed the people struggling in the water. The crew of the *Hamilton*'s second boat grabbed at anyone they could reach; the other boat tied onto the standby life raft and towed it to the area. The first boat then went back to the cutter. In an amazingly short time, the boat was hoisted on board the cutter, off-loaded, put back into the water, and sped for the area of the sailboat capsizing.

In the second boat, Chief Gunner's Mate (GMC) Samuel Spears went into the water to help the Haitians. Within twenty minutes after the capsizing, the crew managed to save sixty-three people. While the boat crews toiled, other crew members worked on the deck of the cutter, applying CPR and artificial respiration. Two Haitian women were in critical condition; crewmen worked for a half hour trying to revive them but could only save one.

At midnight a U.S. Coast Guard helicopter transferred three Haitians who desperately needed more medical help—including one woman about to give birth—to the naval hospital at Guantánamo. The search for any possible survivors continued throughout the night. On board the *Hamilton*, crew members volunteered clothing for the survivors.

During the first two years of the 1990s, with one exception in 1991, the U.S. Coast Guard's orders concerning Haitians remained basically the same: intercept *yolas* and other Haitian craft at sea and return most undocumented Haitians to their country.

During the exception of 1991, the administration of President George H. W. Bush faced a crisis in Haiti that again pushed upward the numbers of Haitian trying to leave their beleaguered country. In February of that year, Jean-Bertrand Aristide, a former Catholic priest, became the first popularly elected president in "Haiti's troubled dictatorial history."[14] Aristide's largest supporters were among the poor. Aristide's radical politics, dictatorial behavior, and the brutal acts against his political enemies—which included the infamous "necklacing," placing burning tires around his enemy's necks—caused his overthrow by a military coup d'état within eight months of his taking office. President Bush declared the coup a threat to American security, granted asylum to Aristide, and continued to turn back Haitians trying to flee their country. He also froze Haitian state assets in the United States in an effort to have the military leaders restore democracy. None of these efforts succeeded.[15] The numbers of Haitians trying to escape by sea continued to grow after Aristide assumed the presidency.

On April 28, 1991, for example, the U.S. Coast Guard intercepted a 45-foot sailing vessel with 215 Haitians on board. The service's patrol boats came upon the scene and took the people off. The 270-foot cutter *Northland* (WMEC-904) received orders to bring the boat people on board and return them to Haiti. The next day, with the Haitians on board, the cutter intercepted another sailboat with twenty-three people. Eventually, the 270-foot cutter had 467 undocumented migrants on board, 455 Haitians and 12 Cubans. Upon questioning the first Haitian passengers, the commanding officer of the cutter learned that at least 10 people "had been thrown overboard alive" without lifejackets. This news did not come as a shock. Another cutter had previously reported one group had stated at least 100 people had been thrown over the side to drown. The commanding officer of the *Northland* ordered a search pattern but found no bodies.[16]

When all 467 passengers had settled on board the cutter, crew members volunteered to act as security teams to ensure order among the boat people and to distribute food and clothing. The commanding officer felt fortunate that two crewmen "spoke fluent French." Crew members quickly volunteered to give clothing to the Haitians because "several men and women arrived virtually naked."

The cutter transported 447 Haitians back to their island while 8 had provided a reason for further investigation into their status. In his final message, the commanding officer noted that the operation to repatriate the Haitians had been a "demanding task." The remaining passengers were turned over to the INS for processing as refugees. Near the end of the message, the commanding officer commented: "No-one aboard [*Northland*] escaped emotional stress during the execution of this task. To help crewmen cope with the events of the last few days, an open forum was conducted to all members allowing a free expression of views and opinions. Command oversight ensured an explanation of migrant versus political asylum and the Coast Guard's role therein." In other words, some in the crew questioned the policy of returning the Haitians.

The reports of political violence in Haiti made the number of fleeing undocumented migrants grow. It also made decision makers in the United States realize that quickly returning Haitians to such chaos would not play well in the United States and the national media. The numbers made it impossible to hold the undocumented migrants on the decks of cutters for any length of time. The answer seemed, once again, the naval base at Guantánamo, Cuba. A tent camp sprung up. Extensive INS hearings were held, and a higher percentage of Haitians were allowed to enter the United States. By the end of February 1992, 32.6 percent of the Haitians at Guantánamo received permission to apply for asylum. By May of 1992, however, with the number of Haitian undocumented migrants continuing to rise, the government again changed course. The United States closed the camp in Cuba and began escorting all Haitians back to Haiti without a review. Richard Boucher, of the U.S. State Department, said, "It was increasingly clear that the camp was acting as a magnet and causing more Haitians to get on boats in the hopes of getting there."[17]

During the 1991–92 crises, the U.S. Coast Guard had fifteen cutters assigned to Haitian operations, out of thirty-three available for the eastern seaboard of the United States. The numbers and length of operations caused friction among some in different U.S. government organizations. The Department of Defense was unhappy about the number of Haitians at Guantánamo, feeling that it might make the Cuban government flood the camp with a Mariel-like operation. Some in the leadership of the State Department criticized the INS for allowing so many applications for asylum. Both INS and State Department found fault with the U.S. Coast Guard for the number of cutters sent to near Haiti's shore, claiming that "they might actually encourage emigration."[18]

Seventeen years later, Capt. Michael Inman, USCG, recalled what happened at Guantánamo when he was a senior lieutenant serving in the 378-foot cutter *Dallas*. "There was a stand-off between DoD [Department of Defense] and the other involved government agencies, including INS, who wanted to get the Haitians ashore. DoD did not want us to land the Haitians. It was the first time I had ever seen brinkmanship in play. It got so we had six to seven [cutters] with three to five hundred Haitians on each cutter just waiting. We were almost at the point of putting them ashore and telling DoD you have them."[19]

The large number of Haitians waiting led to one of the major difficulties mentioned by all veterans of the U.S. Coast Guard's duty in undocumented migrant operations: becoming too attached to the people they have intercepted. This is doubly true for those dealing with Haitians. Most Haitians come from terrible poverty and are forced to return to the conditions they tried to flee. Captain Inman illustrated what could happen when crews became too attached to the people they were trying to help, and then the decision finally came to repatriate the Haitians back to their country and the poverty that awaited them.

Captain Inman explained that the cutter *Dallas* had a very diverse crew, including many African Americans. Homeported in New York City, the crew of the *Dallas* brought some of that city's attitudes with them. When the orders came to return the undocumented migrants back to Haiti, Captain Inman said,

> The crew was very upset. A junior officer came [to me], in tears, asking did they have to take them back. Her feelings mirrored many in the crew.
>
> I took out my ID card and held it up to her and said, "Until I am given an unlawful order, I serve at the pleasure of the President. We have been given an order and we will carry it out."
>
> Did it make the junior officer feel better? No, but I wanted to show her that we obey lawful orders and that we were operating as an instrument of national policy and security. It is the reason we do what we do.[20]

All this took place during a U.S. presidential election year. Candidate William Jefferson Clinton saw in Bush's actions a good target. He noted that if elected he would seek to "buttress democratic forces in Haiti, Peru, Cuba, and throughout the Western Hemisphere." Clinton continually pointed out that Bush played "racial politics" by repatriating Haitians. Clinton said, "I wouldn't be shipping those poor black people back."[21] All of this rhetoric, of course, made many believe the policy would change if Bush were defeated. However, statistics of intercepted undocumented migrants show that the actions of the Bush administration caused the flow to slacken.

The stream of Haitian migrants never actually stopped. While most of the world seemed to care little for what took place in the Windward Passage, there are a few who wanted to tell the Haitians' story. In 1992, for example, Patrick Chauvel, a French photojournalist, wanted "to photograph men and women willing to plunge into the sea in overcrowded, leaky sailboats on the slim hope they would make it to America—and the even slimmer hope they would be allowed to stay."[22]

Chauvel paid out hundreds of U.S. dollars to what can charitably be described as unusual characters. He asked one so-called captain how he intended to avoid the U.S. Coast Guard. "I will create a storm which will encircle my boat and they won't see me." And he explained his method of accomplishing this: "prayers, God and a few slaughtered chickens."

The captain led Chauvel to a house where twenty others waited. All clutched small parcels of American clothing. The Haitians planned that when the boat reached the shores of the United States, all would leap ashore, change into their American clothing, and hitch a ride.

At three o'clock in the morning, Chauvel awoke to loud banging and the shouts of, "Police! Police!" Four men with rifles ran into the room, slapping people around. Despite the offer of more money, the journalist, along with the others, found himself in jail. It took four days and two hundred dollars to gain his release.

Showing the same determination as the boat people, Chauvel again located his captain and eventually ended up on a deserted island called Rat Island, or Arras. There he remained, waiting for the boat. Seeking relief from the oppressive heat, Chauvel took to swimming. No one else joined him because few Haitians can swim. Two mothers with babies, five months and eight months old, were among those waiting for three days on the island. Chauvel awakened each morning to find the creatures the island was named for crawling over him.

When the captain finally returned to the island with a boat, Chauvel was horrified: it measured only twenty to twenty-three feet in length, and had no deck. He could not believe people would attempt a six-hundred-mile voyage in "that deckless ruin."

Chauvel talked to the captain, pointing out it would be suicide to make the voyage. The captain roared with laughter, pointing out that with his juju they would "be in Miami in four to five days."

"What's this juju?"

"I've sacrificed a chicken and paid a priest. Now we will be invisible because of two storms that will follow us, giving us a good wind, and the Coast Guard won't see us."

Later, Chauvel admitted feeling "petrified." As the captain examined his boat, he reached over the side and brought up a human skull. The captain claimed such a find was a good omen. "I look at the skull," wrote Chauvel, "covered in a sort of green moss. It's sinister. As he says, an omen."

Night brought lashing rain. The passengers used the ragged sail in a vain attempt to keep dry, but it leaked. For the remainder of the night, everyone held up the leaky canvas while the captain slept undisturbed.

At five o'clock in the morning, the captain assembled his twenty-five passengers. He told them to board quietly so they would not alert other people of their departure. But word circulated about the attempt and others crowded in.

The boarding dissolved into chaos. Chauvel snapped a photograph of a Haitian in the water trying to board and crewman swinging a machete at him. Three times the boat rolled, each time perilously close to capsizing. At last, with forty-four people on board, the boat departed. Chauvel glanced at the boat's freeboard, estimating it at only twenty inches. In other words, less than two feet now separated the passengers from the sea for the next six hundred miles.

Under way, everyone succumbed to seasickness, with the babies vomiting constantly. The boat sailed toward La Tortue, along the north coast of Haiti. After eight hours, everyone on board remained "totally silent. The only sign of life . . . : a fellow who alternates between reading his Bible and emptying his stomach."

Late in the afternoon, Chauvel noticed the captain was very agitated. A large sailboat then hove into view, ten men lining its deck, with two brandishing machetes. Chauvel's captain handed out his own five machetes. One of the boat people said, "Pirates. They want our money, our cigarettes, our food and our women." The Haitians in Chauvel's boat quickly covered him. They understood that to the pirates a white man meant he had money and this meant a sure effort on the part of the pirates to board the craft. The pirates, however, decided not to board the overloaded boat and sailed away. As the sun set, everyone again lapsed "into a miserable stupor." The babies remained in terrible shape.

Night brought rain and coldness. The boat people had no shelter. Daylight brought the sound of shouting: Two people apparently had fallen asleep and slipped overboard. Everyone realized the hopelessness of searching for them. The day continued with people cooking some food over charcoal in a tub filled with sand. The food caused more vomiting.

Later in the day, the boat people sighted a fishing craft. With Chauvel's captain acting as an interpreter, the journalist managed—for a price—to get his film to the fishing craft with a promise to mail it to *Newsweek*. Later Chauvel found, much to his surprise, the film had reached the magazine in time for the deadline.

The third day of the voyage brought the unwanted sight of building cumulus storm clouds. The captain turned his craft and tried to make land,

and rain pelted the sea and the boat people. Chauvel had the only two lifejackets. He gave both to the mothers. People bailed water, but the boat listed dangerously. As the sea turned white from breaking waves, the Haitians prayed, sounding like "a long moan."

At 11:00 p.m., the craft struck a reef. Seawater flooded the boat. People screamed. The mast snapped, carrying people with it over the side. Knowing Chauvel could swim, the Haitians grabbed at him. A mother handed her screaming five-month-old child to the journalist. Chauvel, carrying the baby, struck out for the beach and somehow managed to reach shore.

Fishermen gathered on the beach. Chauvel handed them the baby and dashed back to the water to help others. Someone yelled: "The army is coming!" Everyone scattered. Chauvel followed a man who knew the area. They ran through a rice paddy. The two found a house with people willing to hide them—for a price. The next morning the army captured Chauvel and he again found himself back in jail. He spent three days in confinement but received no beatings. His boat mates did not fare as well. Chauvel wrote that "a very friendly commandant" set him free without demanding money. Upon his release, the journalist could account for only fourteen of the forty-four passengers in the boat. The mother of the five-month-old baby managed to find her child. The people in the village informed Chauvel that no bodies washed up on the beach, reminding him, "there are many sharks in the water."

Chauvel later admitted that by that time he thought like a boat person, and he again tried to find another boat. He felt he must try to make it to Miami.

After locating another captain, Chauvel arrived at the bay of Acui in darkness. He boarded a sailboat about twenty-five to thirty feet in length with about one hundred people on board.

Chauvel awoke in the morning to the sound of whistling. Heeding a very old sailor's superstition, the passengers were trying to whistle up the wind.

The seasick boat people lay on the open deck and some below decks. Three passengers managed to signal a fishing boat and leave the sailboat. It took the craft six hours to travel three miles.

Another boat approached, and two more people leapt aboard the overloaded craft. Chauvel recognized one man from the wrecked boat. The man disappeared below deck and Chauvel followed him, where he beheld a horrible sight. The heat of the hold, plus the packed human bodies, fogged his camera lens. A river of seawater and vomit sloshed around the hold. Chauvel used his flash to photograph in the dark hold. The light reminded him of "stories of the slave ships that carried their ancestors to Haiti. Five hundred years later, they are still slaves to poverty and injustice, and they remain [as] slaves in their attempt to escape to freedom." As Chauvel retreated from the ghastly scene, a strong hand grabbed him and a voice said in French, "Racontez nôtre histoire. Merci." (Tell our story. Thank you.)

As he left the compartment for the relative comfort of the crowded deck, he heard singing from those below decks. The singing spread throughout the ship.

Another night began. Those on deck had to go below to allow those in the hellish compartment to come out for air, but no one wanted to go below. The captain and one sailor beat on those chosen with pieces of rope, but even that did not work.

The captain and his crew prepared to pass out food as the boat people sang a hymn to God. The same containers people vomited into now provided for the distribution of food.

The sailboat had no keel. Instead, humans provided the ballast, keeping the craft from capsizing. By the next afternoon, the boat finally sailed away from land and into the open ocean.

Later the same afternoon, a U.S. Coast Guard Falcon jet flew over the craft, making several passes. Shortly thereafter, a U.S. Coast Guard cutter with a deckload of earlier survivors from another Haitian craft hove into sight. When the U.S. Coast Guard crew found Chauvel on board, they informed him he had been reported missing. Because the cutter was overloaded, the cutter crew said another cutter was estimated to arrive in eight hours. The Haitians began questioning the journalist about life in the United States.

Eventually, two Zodiac boats from the next cutter approached the sailboat. An amplified voice echoed across the sea: "I don't suppose you'd go back to Haiti willingly?"

"No! No! No!"

"I must intercept you."

The U.S. Coast Guard crew told Chauvel they had no jurisdiction over him and he could continue on with the sailboat if he wished. He quickly declined, which brought laughter from the U.S. Coast Guard crew. Recognizing that too many people on deck might cause a capsize, the cutter crew passed instructions that created an orderly transition from the sailboat to safety.

The next day Chauvel and the boat people transferred to a larger ship going to the U.S. Naval Base at Guantánamo, Cuba, for processing. The Haitians were searched. Chauvel learned from the commanding officer of the unnamed cutter that they had found "weapons and drugs in the past." The Marines and U.S. Coast Guardsmen tried to calm the Haitians "by joking with them, but raising their arms in front of uniforms is a trauma they know all [too] well." Later in the day, many U.S. Coast Guard crew members came to sit and talk with the Haitians.

When Chauvel departed he remembered the sight of the Haitians with their arms in the air being searched. "Their eyes seem to say: 'So. This is freedom?'"

Despite Chauvel's feelings for the boat people, he realized that even though everyone on board the boat wanted to reach Miami, "if the [U.S.] Coast Guard had allowed us to continue, there would have been trouble." He admitted: "The [U.S.] Coast Guard is saving these people's lives by intercepting them before tragedy."

As 1992 ended, the sights and information that U.S. Coast Guard crews saw and heard can make even the burliest sailor feel helpless. A master chief petty officer said the most difficult thing to grasp concerned the children of the boat people: "I once reached over and picked up a Haitian child whose arms were like matchsticks, the first sign of starvation."[23] Hearing stories of Haitians callously thrown over the side to drown does nothing to improve one's outlook on the human condition. What happens is best described in 1984 in *Sea Power* by Vincent Thomas when he accompanied the cutter *Hamilton*. The young U.S. Coast Guard people, Thomas wrote, "aged and matured, when face to face for the first time with death on the high seas."[24]

Chauvel's observations help to understand what the Haitians endured during their attempts to reach the United States. To better understand what U.S. Coast Guard crews faced when trying to intercept undocumented Haitians, Rear Adm. Arthur E. Brooks, commander of Coast Guard District 17 (Alaska), discussed his work during Haitian operations as a younger officer on one cutter.[25]

Brooks' first encounter came as a lieutenant commander and executive officer of the 210-foot medium-endurance cutter *Confidence* (WMEC-619) homeported at Cape Canaveral, Florida, from 1988 to 1990. Then–Lieutenant Commander Brooks had no experience in migrant operations and a green crew.

Admiral Brooks recalled that after they realized they were dealing with "real people and in great danger," then the first problem dealing with bringing Haitians on board focused on the fact that a 210-foot U.S. Coast Guard cutter "was not built to take passengers, or had facilities for passengers and [we] were going to take potentially hundreds of people" on board. Furthermore, the passengers normally "didn't ask to have a ride." Brooks felt, however, that the crew should do everything they possibly could "to make their stay as comfortable and safe as we could possibly make, given that neither party was completely prepared for the experience."

On the cutter *Confidence* at this time, the crew set up processing stations on the fantail (the back of the cutter). They brought "people on board from terrible overloaded boats." Next, the crewmembers tried to identify the Haitians, "do medical screens" and check for weapons. "The Haitians always arrived with a bag," recalled Admiral Brooks. The bag contained some food and "one good set of clothes to wear in Miami." Brooks treated the bags differently than on some other cutters. Instead of just placing the bags in one pile, the crew on *Confidence*, after checking their contents, let the Haitians hold onto their own bags. This provided a calming effect for the migrants.

The crew of *Confidence* had to constantly think of crowd control. "You are going to be outnumbered four to one, six to one and you can't let them inside the ship," Admiral Brooks pointed out. The cutter's crew prepared fire hoses to spray water for possible use in crowd control. They also started security patrols of U.S. Coast Guard crew members near the Haitians. Some crew members received the duty of "a response team that would go into the group and pull out the leaders [that were agitating the migrants] and segregate them and then everyone would deflate." If the agitators calmed down, they were then allowed into the larger group. The Haitians responded favorably to all of the processing procedures if the "whole process was structured and professional."

The crew of the *Confidence* quickly learned that Haitians could not eat rich American food. If not fed a diet of beans and rice, they became very sick.

Interestingly, keeping an accurate count of the undocumented migrants on cutters during operations proved to be one of the most onerous functions of the mission, especially during the early years. As the migrants were brought aboard, they were counted. Then they were counted at meal times and at night to make sure no one had fallen or been pushed overboard. Another count came when they left the cutter at either Guantánamo or Haiti. "Counting at night and in the rain is one of the hardest things," said Admiral Brooks. "A lot of people back in Washington, D.C., used to get really excited: 'What do you mean you screwed up the count?' As long as I brought back more that I picked up when I went into Port au Prince, I was okay. Short, we were going to have to search the ship really hard." Then the service started issuing plastic wrist bracelets, much like those used in hospitals. While not perfect, it did help the crews.

After the migrants went through the processing stations, then the crew of the *Confidence* now faced the difficulty of trying to make a large number of people comfortable with limited supplies and room. For example, how do you provide showers for four hundred extra people when it is difficult to make enough fresh water for your own crew? Crewmembers on the *Confidence* rigged a saltwater type of shower. "It did not work well," recalled Admiral Brooks, "but it was an attempt to provide humane treatment and make them comfortable." Brooks stated that he appointed the engineering officer as "'Mr. Marriott,' he was the hotelkeeper. The engineers, because of their . . . [expertise], were the best people for setting up toilets, showers, chow lines, and other lines."

Another two major problems to overcome centered on where to put the migrants. The first problem: where to keep the Haitians while on board the cutter. They had to sit on a hard deck, with nonskid paint applied to it. (Nonskid paint has gritty material within it to keep sailors from slipping on wet decks.) This meant that people with very little clothing had to sit on an abrasive surface. The crew handed out blue mats for the migrants to sit on.

The second problem centered on the hot Caribbean sun and weather. To provide relief, the crew of the *Confidence* obtained a large green parachute and rigged stanchions (poles) around the deck, which made a tent. "It was ugly," said Brooks, "but it worked."

The stanchion-rigged tent provided a "memorable night." More than twenty years later Admiral Brooks recalled:

> We were hauling a load of [Haitians] from GITMO back to Port au Prince. We had 250 on board and transiting over night and had a line of thunderstorms [pass over. The storm] knocked down the tent and it fell onto the Haitians. That was bad enough, but when we piped all hands on deck to clear the tent from the Haitians, we had forty to fifty [crew members] come in the night with knives to cut the tent free. When the Haitians saw the white men coming up in the night with knives, they got excited. We had some drama, shall we say, for a moment until the Haitians realized the [U.S. Coast Guardsmen] were coming up to cut the tent off of them and not kill them.

In the tight quarters of a cutter, crews learned the cultural differences between the Haitians and themselves. The *Confidence* crew found that Haitian "males always treated women very badly; children did not exist at all. In their society, the men came through the [food] line first; they did not care if the women and children ate at all." The crew, on the other hand, felt the order should be "children and then the women eat first, then the men."

"I would not tolerate anyone abusing a migrant," Admiral Brooks said emphatically. "These were our guests. They were unwilling guests, they didn't want to be there, we didn't want them there, but they were there. I was committed to making them as comfortable, as safe as I could until immigration gave us a decision [as to their disposition]." If they caused problems, however, then security would tighten "and it would not get to be fun anymore."

Admiral Brooks went on to point out that, at least on his cutters, no one did abuse a migrant; in fact, the "crews always sympathized with the migrants. The hardest thing for the commands of the ships was to keep the crews professional, keeping [them] detached." Admiral Brooks pointed out that people in the U.S. Coast Guard tended toward being "do-gooders. We came in to do search and rescue and to save people. You just saved a whole bunch of people." The average person in the service embraced the saving of the Haitians. Most crew members wanted "to play with the babies, wanted to give them presents, wanted to communicate and relate on a personal level; that is the kind of people we are. And so, it was difficult to keep it professional." In fact, Admiral Brooks said that the security group on the cutter sometimes had to keep the crew from the migrants, or they would lose detachment.

Interestingly, at this time the cutters working migrant operations had no uniform policy on how to process the migrants. All the procedure was "done individually by the ships, [but] we got ideas from each other." Admiral Brooks recalled that his philosophy for the humane treatment of the migrants came from now-retired Capt. Randy Beardsworth.

Admiral Brooks remembered another unusual night on the *Confidence*.

> Off the north coast of Haiti [all the migrants were] quiet through the night. [Suddenly,] we started getting these red sparkles in the sky. Then the whole sky was sparkling red. The Haitians *knew* that was [their] Voodoo gods coming to save them. The Haitians went nuts. Everybody came up. Everybody started dancing, chanting. That was one of the most exciting times I had. Later we found out it was a very rare intrusion of the northern lights into the Caribbean. But, if you had just been picked up by the Americans and the sky lights up like that, you just know that someone is coming to help you out. We got them calmed down after a while, but it was one of those dramatic nights to remember.

Almost anyone who works or has worked migrant operations mentions that the mission is very hard. The U.S. Coast Guard crews worked with very little time off. "Besides watches," as Admiral Brooks pointed out, "you are doing security, processing, feeding, this and that. [The] physical fatigue was real. The more important part was emotional fatigue. You are looking at the poorest people in [a large part of the world.] People at the very ends of their means and you feel this overwhelming sympathy, but you have to be professional and stay detached. The crews became very, very tired" for as long as the migrants remained on board.

Admiral Brooks said,

> One of the things I had very little toleration for was people on the beach who did not understand the explosive potential of a [medium-endurance cutter] with four hundred people [who] did not want to be there and [on

> a cutter] not designed to carry four hundred prisoners or detainees. [There were] no facilities and the control mechanisms [were very limited]. You [were at] great risk organizationally and personally when you had large numbers of migrants on board and if you did not understand that risk you missed the point. I always approached these things with a sense of urgency, because if you got the migrants off in a day or two, it wasn't bad, but if you held them for three or four days, or a week, it got worse and worse and more and more explosive, [as] the migrants tolerance [level went down] because of sitting on a nonskid deck in the Caribbean in the sun. The fun factor is very low. The potential for a problem was always there it and grew over time. As the crews got more and more tired, tempers flared, so it could be a very tough environment.

Admiral Brooks pointed out that because of all the factors he mentioned, "You can't do migrant operations without having your heart broken. It's easy to empathize with any one of these people. Even the worst ringleader of the Haitians [on board a cutter] is a person with inherit human dignity. In a different situation, they might have been a friend. Reacting to that on a human level was always very hard. They merited our respect and they merited our care."

Admiral Brooks related,

> My concern when I brought my first load of Haitians into Port au Prince [for repatriation was] that everyone [in the Haitian government] would show up on the dock and treat them badly. It was worse than that. What happened is nobody showed up and nobody *cared*. The Red Cross showed up. But no one from the government showed up. I realized that the [migrant's] government cared nothing for them. In many ways, it would [have been] better if they were persecuted and abused, at least then they would have had some value, but the reality was that their government did not care for them at all. I thought that was the saddest thing: their government did not care at all.

6 To the Golden Mountain

> Farmers put down their tools,
> students discarded their books,
> workers quit their jobs, and
> everybody was talking about
> nothing but going to America.
>
> Chinese journalist

Many Cuban and Haitian undocumented migrants suffered greatly while trying to enter the United States via the sea. Migrants from the People's Republic of China faced all the dangers of Cubans and Haitians, multiplied by very long voyages. A quick glance at any map of the world shows the enormous distances involved. From the Chinese southeastern coastal city of Fuzhou to San Francisco, for example, it is 6,492 miles (10,447 kilometers). History shows, however, that some Chinese have willingly made the long journey, both legally and illegally, since at least the nineteenth century. In Mandarin Chinese, America is *Meiguo*, the "beautiful country."

The movement of Chinese entering into the United States falls broadly into three periods. The first began in the nineteenth century when many came legally into America to work on the railroads. A few writers, however, believe that the Chinese actually landed in North America before Columbus. In any case, early reports reaching the Middle Kingdom spoke of a new seemingly empty land and dubbed it the "Golden Mountain."[1] Eventually, the number of Chinese entering the United States made many fear a "yellow peril," which led to the Chinese Exclusion Act of 1882. The act remained in effect until 1943. Of course, the act only caused Chinese to enter America illegally. One estimate puts the annual number of Chinese smuggled into the country during the last years of the nineteenth century at twenty thousand.[2] A small but steady stream of undocumented Chinese migrants entered the United States until World War II, which ended the first period of Chinese immigration. After Mao Zedong's communist takeover in 1949, the stream effectively dried up and remained so until shortly after his death in 1976, which ended the second period. The final period began with a slow move toward economic reforms after Mao's death, coupled with internal political instability, as evidenced in actions against protestors in Beijing's Tiananmen Square in 1989.

Prior to 1993, most Americans—if they thought anything about Chinese undocumented migration to the United States—presumed such clandestine operations took place on the West Coast. In the predawn hours of June 6, 1993, however, the ship the *Golden Venture* grounded within a few miles of the Statue of Liberty in New York City's harbor. As events unfolded, law enforcement and rescue responders discovered 286 Chinese undocumented migrants on board the ship trying to jump into the frigid Atlantic. Ten died in their attempt to reach *Meiguo*. (See chapter 7 for a detailed look at this case.) The incident led to a "media circus."[3] A large portion of the population of the United States suddenly learned of events that started in the early 1980s.

Because so little is known about Chinese undocumented migrants, it is necessary to examine the location of where the smuggled Chinese lived prior to their long voyage during the third period, why they chose to make the dangerous journey, how Chinese human smugglers work, and other aspects of this trade in human trafficking.

Prior to the 1980s, most of the Chinese reaching America came from Guangdong Province in southern China. These migrants settled in Chinatowns throughout the United States. Beginning in the 1980s, however, most of the Chinese came from one region, the southeastern coastal province of Fujian (also known as Fukien). Fujian, described as "a 125,000 kilometer (77,671 miles) band of mountains dotted with a few patches of flat land, as 'bandit country' and a hotbed of 'rebellious ideas.'" The province "had nearly 30 million inhabitants in 1990, and increased from just over 12 million in 1950."[4] The population density is the fourteenth largest in China. Eighty percent of the land is mountainous, thus allowing little in the way of farming. Until relatively recent times, the mountains also made it one of the most isolated provinces from China's capital, Beijing. Because of the lack of arable land, most people lived in poverty. For years the residents of the province migrated throughout South Asia.

Fujian's location made maritime ventures, both legal and illegal, a necessity. "Alan Mansin Lau . . . planted the first seeds of Fuzhou's [a city in Fujian Province] New York-based community by jumping ship in the United States . . . following World War II."[5] The province, neighboring the Straits of Taiwan, played an important part in the increase in human trafficking from China in the 1980s.

In 1978 Premier Deng Xiaoping began economic reforms. One year later the government established four special economic zones, including one city in Fujian, Xiamen. The intent of the zones was to attract foreign investment and stimulate the economy. Fujian's closeness to Taiwan immediately pumped a large amount of capital into the region. In 1992, for example, the province "received six billion dollars in foreign investments, whereas other Chinese provinces received on average only half that amount." Before 1979 the annual per capita income in rural Fujian households stood at "134 yuan [US$17.10], compared with 133 [yuan] for China as a whole." What is interesting is that from 1978 to 1992 the province's "rural household per capita income increased by 229 percent versus 179 percent for rural households of China as a whole." Furthermore, this placed Fujian's rural households in eighth place out of thirty provinces in 1992, as compared with its former place of twelfth in 1978. These statistics graphically illustrate that the people of China Fujian Province could no longer be considered poor.[6]

The obvious question then is, why did the Fujianese risk the long illegal voyage to the United States? There are two theories of international migration that suggest the answer to this question. One states that very poor people cannot migrate because they are too busy simply trying to survive and have no real means of finding ways to travel to wherever the transportation is located. Conversely, people who are well off do not need to take the risk of illegal migration. Those who are in between these two extremes are most likely to take a risk. Another theory states that "relative deprivation" caused those in Fujian to take the risk. Relative deprivation means that people make judgments based not only on their personal level of possessions and income but, more importantly, on their relative level of welfare in reference to others in the community.[7]

The "burgeoning prosperity . . . [of Fujian and the] omnipresent construction of four- and five-story mansions rising from the rice fields at the edge of nearly every village" set into motion a movement of people within China.[8] Many left the land to work in the urban areas that prospered. Not all areas reaped the benefits equally, however. Those that prospered had no economic reason to leave China. Those that were displaced from the land might prosper more than those that remained, but some did not do as well as others. Both those that remained on the land and those that did not fare as well in the cities are the in-betweens. They are the ones who looked at their relative position in the community and decided illegal migration worth the risk.

Other factors, such as China's edict on the one-child family, caused some to leave. The corruption of officials drove some to take the risk. Political persecution, especially after the Tiananmen Square incident, caused others to flee their native land. Those Chinese who successfully migrated to America, both legally and illegally, and who returned with apparent wealth for visits influenced others.

In the 1980s there grew an obsession among the Fujians to migrate to the United States. A Chinese journalist who visited the province wrote, "Everybody went crazy. The area was in a frenzy. Farmers put down their tools, students discarded their books, workers quit their jobs, and everybody was talking about nothing but going to America. . . . If people found out someone had just successfully arrived in the United States, his or her home will be crowded with people, both acquaintances and strangers, to come to collect information about going to America."[9] One scholar found villages "devoid of most men and many women between the age of 18 and 45, while others are virtual ghost towns, populated only by old people caring for very young children whose parents are working in the United States."[10]

In the period from 1980 to 1993, few people in the West knew anything about those who trafficked in Chinese people. Were they members of Chinese triads, tongs (both of which are secret societies), or street gangs? Moreover, how were the smugglers organized and how did they develop their routes?

Ko-lin Chin, of Rutgers University, interviewed Chinese smuggled into the United States. His interviewees divided the smugglers into two groups: "little snakeheads" and "big snakeheads." The little snakeheads are people living within China and big snakeheads are Chinese living outside of China. The little snakeheads are the recruiters and "work as middlemen between big snakeheads and customers; they are mainly responsible for finding and screening customers and collecting down payments." Big snakeheads are the arrangers and "investors . . . [that] generally invest money in a smuggling operation and oversee the entire operation but usually are not known by those being smuggled."[11]

One Chinese police officer told Chin that no "typical" big snakehead exists. Some are well educated while others have no education. Others are considered "good" because they try to help those who wish to leave the country. Some are essentially "con men," who promise to help undocumented migrants into the United States but cheat them out of their money. The most they have in common is the ability to fund the operations. Some undocumented migrants looked upon the big snakeheads as wealthy and respected businessmen.[12]

Little snakeheads, also called *lakejia* (recruiters), received the most complaints from the undocumented migrant interviewees. The lakejia work on a fee basis for every passenger they recruit. According to many Chinese, the little snakeheads are the ones most apt to mislead those they try to recruit. In a parody of a shady used car salesman, the lakejia promises anything to get his passenger. One woman said her "little snakehead told [her] that it was going to be a safe trip. You can say he glamorized everything about the trip . . . when he tried to persuade me to leave China."[13] The reality proved far different. Despite the chance for deception, most undocumented migrants contacted the little snakeheads. Prior to the 1990s, most Chinese found their lakejia through friends and relatives from within China. About 12 percent found them through connections from abroad. In 1988, the number of foreign snakeheads rose to 30 percent, and by the 1990s snakeheads shifted their emphasis from recruiters in foreign lands to within China.[14]

It is interesting to note that the views of the snakeheads changed over the years. By 2000, due to more studies on the subject, a somewhat different picture emerged (see chapter 8).

For the period from 1980 to 1992, no one knew how many Chinese smuggling groups existed. Estimates ranged from seven or eight to as many as twenty or twenty-five.[15] Some law enforcement authorities in the United States believed that Chinese smugglers also brought in drugs, some forcing those who could not make their down payments to carry the illegal substances. Chin, however, believed only a few were involved in this trade in 1999.[16]

The attraction for any criminal activity is money. In moving Chinese the vast distances to the United States, little snakeheads charged between US$500 to $1,000 per person. Some undocumented Chinese paid a down payment for the voyage of US$3,000. Most snakeheads received a guarantee from a family, either in China or in the United States. The undocumented migrant then signed a contract. One clause stated that the smugglers could hold a person hostage if the person could not raise the rest of the fee upon arrival in the United States. Chin's interviewees paid an average of US$27,745 total fees, with a maximum of $35,000. "The average smuggling fee [by sea] in 1988 was $22,956 and increased about $2,000 each year after that, with the exception of 1992 and 1993. By 1993, the average smuggling fee was $29,688."[17]

It is unclear exactly when the modern emphasis on smuggling Chinese into the United States by sea began, but it was likely in the 1980s. By the early 1990s the U.S. Coast Guard noticed a steady increase in human smuggling vessels. In almost all cases, the vessels were Taiwanese. Previously, some of these ships worked as drift-net fishing craft. Beginning in the 1980s, largely at the urging of U.S. environmentalists to stop drift-net fishing, the method eventually received international condemnation. Deprived of one form of living, some Taiwanese fishermen turned to human trafficking. This is not unusual. Within the United States, some commercial fishermen turned to illegal smuggling of drugs and people, using their boats when fishing declined. With Taiwan so close to Fujian, it seems obvious that many smuggling vessels came from Taiwanese ports. One researcher felt that the "Taiwanese [were] in total control of the global transportation networks . . . by sea." Others believe the Taiwanese played "an active role in the trade, but they [were] clearly not the only ones."[18]

Once the snakeheads selected a vessel for smuggling, they applied pressure to quickly recruit enough passengers for the voyage and meet a departure date. These are the recruiters most apt to employ the used-car-salesman tactics. A thirty-two-year-old male said his snakehead told him he would travel "on a huge ship and that it would take only about two weeks. . . . My family was [told the ship was] outfitted with a movie theater, a nightclub, and a swimming pool. Once I boarded the ship, I was scared. First of all, there was no theater or nightclub on the ship. Secondly, the ocean seemed endless."[19]

On the scheduled day of a smuggling ship's departure, little snakeheads guided passengers to a specified location. Normally, each snakehead handled groups of ten to twenty people. Some of the passengers traveled by bus, and others reported they made their way in military trucks, indicating government corruption. At the final staging area before embarking on the mother ship, the snakeheads collected the down payments.

Small boats, many of them overloaded, transported the migrants to the mother ship, usually in the dark. The length of time in the small boats varied from a few minutes to two hours. On the longer trips to the mother ship, many became seasick. "Because most of us were seasick, the snakeheads were almost throwing us onto the mother ship." On one ship, there "were 203 passengers, including twenty-three women." Boarding a ship from a smaller craft at sea can be a risky operation. Bad weather and darkness greatly increases the danger, even for old salts. Add to this witch's brew people who have never been to sea and the chances for tragedy increases greatly. "When we were transferred from the small boats onto the mother ship," said one undocumented migrant, "a passenger was hit in the head by a heavy object. He died on the spot." Another undocumented migrant described a twenty-three-year-old man who slipped while climbing on board the mother ship, and "a wave dragged him away and we all watched him drown."[20] In many cases, the dangers of just boarding the mother ship proved a portent of what lie ahead.

Some undocumented migrants had no problems during their long sea voyage to the United States. Most, however, had "nightmarish" journeys. Many Chinese found themselves crammed into areas with too many people, poor sanitation facilities, the chance of sexual abuse, and a lack of adequate food and water. On one voyage of fifty-nine days, one group ate only twice a day and did not have enough fresh water to bathe. Many described the slowness of the voyage, compounded by breakdowns on the journey. One undocumented migrant said it "was like we floated to the United

States from China." One U.S. law enforcement official in San Francisco said of a vessel, "I wouldn't even ride on it from one side of the Bay to the other. It's rotting. You can grab a handful of the wall [bulkhead], and it crumbles in your hand."[21]

Snakeheads hired people called *ma zhais* (enforcers) to keep order among the undocumented migrants. One migrant recalled, "The whole trip was like a nightmare. The *ma zhais* did not treat the passengers as human beings. They assaulted those they disliked and raped the women passengers as well."[22]

If the undocumented migrants survived the long ocean voyage in the mother ship, they then had to survive the transfer to small boats. Some said they waited for almost a month in international waters before a small boat came to take them off the ship. Many lost their lives in this operation. One woman said she felt as if she had "to jump to the ground from the top of a tall building." Another undocumented Chinese recalled that more than two hundred passengers got onto a small boat "almost simultaneously." The craft almost sank. Then the undocumented migrants had to endure another two days on the crowded boat before making shore. Once ashore, many of the Chinese were placed in trucks and sent to their final destination. One undocumented migrant said he came ashore in California and he and 160 others were packed into the trailer of a semi and driven to New York City, arriving there a week later. Yet another, who landed on the East Coast, said after transferring to a smaller boat, all 134 people sailed for another three days and then arrived in Boston. A series of cars arrived in shifts and loaded six to twelve of the passengers at a time. The Chinese rode for about an hour to a private house. After arriving at the house, the next leg of their journey had them herded into a container truck and driven for eight hours to New York City.[23]

The two important changes in the smuggling of Chinese into the United States by sea from the 1980s to 1993 focus on where the migrants originally lived and their final destination in the United States. Most of the migrants from this period came from Fujian, and most arrived in New York City. New York City now has a very large population of Fujianese. Some Chinese scholars remark that strolling through portions of Gotham's Chinatown is like walking a street in the city of Fuzhou, the capital and largest city of Fujian Province. Part of the reason for the desire to reach New York is tied to another reason for Chinese migration. Family is one of the strongest linchpins of Chinese culture. Fujianese began settling into New York City shortly after World War II. The strong migration from Fujian is based largely on people wanting to reunite with other family members, or at least to be near people from their own area.

In Chin's study, the reason given by his respondents for coming to the United States that is easiest to understand is to make money. However, the Chinese may have given this response because they knew most people in the United States would understand this explanation. Nevertheless, the drive for better wages must be considered. For example, one successful undocumented migrant said, "When the income differential between China and United States is 1:2 rather than 1:15 or 1:20, that is when Fuzhounese will stop going and even start to come back . . . Look at it this way—in terms of income potential for the average worker, one year in the United States equals 15 Chinese years."[24]

Once within the United States, the undocumented migrants usually work in restaurants and garment sweatshops. Even the earning of money is not straightforward. Most must first work off the money loaned to them in accordance with their contracts with the big snakeheads. They become indentured servants. Those who have difficulties paying are sometimes forced into crime. (The fate of some of the Chinese who reached the United States during this period is covered in chapter 7.)

Chin wrote that many of the undocumented migrants who came by sea "broke into tears when asked what it was like to spend months on board a smuggling ship."[25] Most said they would never undertake another trip, even if someone paid them a great deal of money. Yet this type of smuggling continued almost unnoticed by most Americans until the early morning hours of June 6, 1993, when the *Golden Venture* ran aground near New York City.

The U.S. Coast Guard and one of its predecessors, the U.S. Revenue Cutter Service, has dealt with intercepting undocumented migrants since at least 1794. They have specifically dealt with the Chinese since the Chinese Exclusion Act of 1882. In the age before large container ships, some Chinese put themselves in "barrels and [marked the barrels] as some import to the country." These undocumented migrants, "imprisoned in such narrow, cramped quarters, suffered the most frightful tortures from which some never recovered." Many were "smothered by the cargo or otherwise died from the hardships."[26] Most of the U.S. Coast Guard's early work concerning undocumented Chinese came as a tack-on mission. An example of this happened in 1919 involving the 205-foot cutter *Manning* operating out of Norfolk, Virginia. The cutter had orders to search for the *Sunbeam*, a schooner that had lost its sails off the Carolina coast. After two days of searching, a radio message reported that the steamer *Chicomico* had the disabled craft in tow. The *Manning* rendezvoused with the steamer to relieve it of the tow. The commanding officer of the cutter learned that *Sunbeam* claimed to be out of Cuba with a cargo of molasses bound for New York. However, the skipper of the *Chicomico* reported seeing a crew of seven but also spotted at least eighteen Chinese. "Looks sort o' funny, eh, what?" said the skipper.

The cutter took over the tow and headed for port. By midnight, the two vessels wallowed through rising seas, forcing the commanding officer of the cutter to cut his speed. In the deep blackness of a stormy night, the lookout shouted that he spotted a bright flash from astern. The towline remained taut, so the commanding officer ruled out a parted line. He reduced speed thinking the previous speed might have been the reason for the signal. With the gradual light of dawn, the cutter's crew noticed a slack towline. Full light brought the terrible sight of the sinking schooner. Despite desperate actions, only two undocumented Chinese migrants and five Cubans survived.[27] No reports mention what caused the bright flash.

Prior to World War II, those who attempted to bring undocumented Chinese migrants into the United States used "dozens of ways" to land their human cargo. Some came hidden on board Chinese ships. When the ship tied up in an American port, the undocumented migrants passed themselves off as crew members, sometimes with fake identification, and simply walked ashore. Others slipped over the side of an anchored ship, swam for shore, and then ran to hidden locations.[28] Many of those who plied the human trafficking trade in Chinese during this era preferred the Cuba to the United States route.[29]

Cuttermen who worked in the service's long and frustrating war of trying to stop the illegal entry of alcoholic beverages into the United States during Prohibition also encountered human smuggling. The trade in undocumented migrants proved an additional bonus for smugglers. Ernest Hemingway's 1937 novel *To Have and Have Not*, for example, has Henry

Morgan running both liquor and Chinese from Havana to Florida. Even though the smuggling route from Cuba to Key West represented the shortest leg of the distances involved from China, it also represented one of great danger for the Chinese. Unlike Hemingway's protagonist, Henry Morgan, many of those running Chinese into the United States from Cuba "were often nothing more than murderers of the worse type." This type of smuggler placed chains on the Chinese brought on board the boat. If a U.S. Coast Guard cutter hove into view, "the Chinese were thrown overboard . . . to drown without a chance to save themselves!"[30] Eventually, some Chinese in the human trafficking trade in Cuba secretly armed the undocumented migrants. Some "bloody battles took place on the high seas." Off the coast of New Jersey in the 1920s, for example, a steamer notified the U.S. Coast Guard of a two-masted schooner adrift and flying a signal of distress. A cutter sped to the location. The boarding party found twenty-one Chinese, none of whom spoke English. No logbook or papers remained on board. The passengers had no food or water. The boarding party found seven of the Chinese with knife or bullet wounds. Officers pieced together a rough idea of the drama that took place on the schooner. Most of the undocumented passengers had made their home in Canton. They had paid two hundred dollars each for the Cuba to United States route. At least thirty-one Chinese and a crew of five had slipped out of an unidentified small inlet in Cuba. At some point in time, the Chinese felt their lives were in danger, or they became desperate from a lack of food and water. In any case, the undocumented migrants attacked and killed the crew, dumping their bodies into the sea. At least ten Chinese died in the struggle. The Chinese never admitted to anything, although at least four Chinese bodies showing gunshot wounds were found days later floating in the sea. The twenty-one survivors' reward: deportation to China.[31]

Human trafficking and rum-running also took place on the West Coast during Prohibition. Warrant Officer (WO) L. A. Lonsdale, for example, commanded the 85-foot patrol boat *Arcata* in the Puget Sound region of Washington State in June 1924. Lonsdale received intelligence that rumrunners planned a delivery in Seattle for festivities on the Fourth of July. In the darkness, the U.S. Coast Guard warrant officer placed his patrol boat in a hidden location near Whidbey Island. Soon the patrol boat crew recognized the sound of a high-powered boat approaching. Lonsdale ordered the *Arcata* under way. In pursuit, the cutter's searchlight lit up the speeding boat. Lonsdale ordered a shot across the boat's bows. The speedboat made a sharp course change and opened fire on the *Arcata*. The cutter's gun crew returned fire. Flames shot out of the rumrunner's boat. Flames and an explosion erupted from the forward deck of the rumrunner's boat.

Warrant Officer Lonsdale maneuvered the *Arcata* alongside the flaming speedboat. Crewmen from the cutter pulled four men from the inferno, along with two badly burned Chinese undocumented migrants.[32]

As mentioned earlier, a steady stream of Chinese undocumented migrants continued entering the United States until World War II and then for a few years after the end of the war. Mao Zedong's communist takeover of China in 1949 dried up this stream.

Reading the U.S. Coast Guard's statistics on the human trafficking of Chinese, the numbers show only 28 Chinese undocumented migrants apprehended from 1982 to 1990 (see the appendix). This does not mean that only 28 Chinese tried to enter the country illegally, only that 28 did not succeed in their attempt. The year 1991 marks a watershed. From 1991 to 1993, the service stopped 2,830 undocumented Chinese migrants. By anyone's calculation, this is a significant increase, even though these are only the ones intercepted. In short, in a relatively short amount of time, the U.S. Coast Guard faced a tsunami of smuggled human cargo on board vessels. By 1993 an internal Department of Justice report on the smuggling of Chinese declared it an "immigration emergency."[33]

The service's tactics in combating this "immigration emergency" essentially continued the same methods used since the nineteenth century, updated with modern technology. The U.S. Coast Guard intercepted some of the Chinese while working other missions, notably cutters on drug interdiction patrols. Information on the sailing of some human smuggling ships came from intelligence gathered from many sources, a method used during the Prohibition era. Once the U.S. Coast Guard received information of a potential smuggling ship, then tracking by radar and aircraft helped in the interception of the human cargo. Even with modern technology, however, the oceans remain a large area in which to hide, with the Pacific the largest of them all.

One of the U.S. Coast Guard's largest problems in combating human trafficking by sea is that traditionally the Coast Guard has always suffered from low funding. In the past, its small fleet of cutters has been technologically outdated without much firepower or speed. Moreover, the service operates with few people spread among a myriad of missions. For example, in 1993, the year of the largest number of Chinese captured, the service operated in the entire Pacific only ten high-endurance cutters capable of sea-keeping for any length of time. Two of the ten cutters had home ports in Hawaii. In 1992 the service had 37,827 active duty people. The next year's active force numbered 39,136. In short, the service operated at a huge disadvantage in dealing with the human trafficking of Chinese.[34]

Between August 31, 1991, and December 22, 1992, the service recorded eleven incidents of intercepting smuggling ships with approximately 1,800 undocumented Chinese migrants on board. During this short span, the cases seemed to follow one upon another. On August 31, 1991, for example, the service intercepted the *I-Mao Number 306*, a Taiwanese fishing trawler with 131 undocumented migrants on board. Then there was a short respite until February 17, 1992, when the service intercepted the *Yu Fong Number 303*, a Taiwanese fishing vessel near Honolulu that had 93 undocumented Chinese migrants, followed the next day by *Fa Shiann Jee*, stopped near Honolulu. This Taiwanese trawler revealed 51 undocumented Chinese on board.[35]

During February 1992 the U.S. Coast Guard conducted Operation Jade in California. A Chinese gang that employed some Vietnamese attempted to smuggle in 125 Chinese undocumented migrants through Long Beach, California, aboard the Taiwanese fishing vessel *Jinn Yin No. 1.* On February 1, one group of the gang traveled northward to the Marina Village Yacht Harbor at Alameda, California. A member of the gang using the name Steven Chang purchased the wooden-hulled 57-foot Chris Craft yacht *Liberated Lady* to transport the undocumented migrants from the ship to shore. He paid seventy thousand dollars in cash.

The new owners worked around the clock to refit and provision the yacht. They installed the latest in electronic navigational equipment. The U.S. Coast Guard soon received information about the yacht. Years later Special Agent Gene Chacon of the Coast Guard Investigative Service related that the service works to build a "community outreach" of those in the maritime world to report on anything different in their world.[36] Besides the relatively large amount of cash used to purchase the craft, what probably raised the interest of the person making the tip centered on the provisions stowed aboard the *Liberated Lady*. The new owners brought "huge cartons of Dramamine and case after case of soft drinks."[37]

The U.S. Coast Guard put a watch on the yacht. By February 8, the *Liberated Lady* had left the San Francisco Bay area and proceeded south to Newport Harbor, to the southeast of Long Beach, near Los Angeles. From around February 10 for the next six days, members of the gang obtained equipment to hold extra fuel for the yacht. During this period law enforcement agents observed members of the gang passing large sums of money. On February 16, the *Liberated Lady* departed southward to an area sixty-five miles southwest of San Diego.[38]

Four days later, on February 20 and again on 21, the Vietnamese unloaded their human cargo at the Long Beach Downtown Marina. Forty Chinese undocumented migrants came ashore. The Vietnamese brought them to two separate motels in the Long Beach area.

Interestingly, a U.S. Army captain in military intelligence assigned to assist the U.S. Coast Guard drove into work early in the morning. Her duties: to head a post seizure analysis team to obtain information for future operations. Within three blocks of the intelligence officer's building in down town Long Beach, she stopped at a red light. As the officer waited for the light to change, she watched a group of Asian men and women "all dressed identically in track suits" and "very obviously new to the country. They walked in a mesmerized state, looking up at the buildings and lights with mouths agape." After the light changed and the Asian people cleared the cross walk, the captain continued on her way. During the short drive, the thought crossed her mind that the Asians might be an international sports team, but she discarded this idea because they appeared "too gaunt." At just about this time, "it all began to click." The captain quickly went to the U.S. Coast Guard's operations center and reported what she saw. This confirmed that the undocumented Chinese now had been landed by the *Liberated Lady*.[39]

Meanwhile, the Vietnamese, once they had the Chinese in their motel rooms, fed them and shortly thereafter began loading them into vans for further transportation, which took place on February 20 and 21.

Having refueled the *Liberated Lady*, the human smugglers again proceeded out of the Long Beach harbor in the darkness of predawn on a course to intercept the *Jinn Yin No. 1* and off-load another group of Chinese undocumented migrants.

At least 8 nautical miles (9.2 miles) astern of the *Liberated Lady*, the 110-foot U.S. Coast Guard patrol boat *Tybee* (WPB-1330) shadowed the yacht. Then, 11 nautical miles (12.7 miles) behind the *Tybee*, the 210-foot cutter *Venturous* (WMEC-625) also followed the yacht, tracking it on their radars. The *Venturous* carried a helicopter on board. The larger cutter had the senior officer, Cdr. Terry Newell, of the at sea operation on board.

At 5:30 a.m., the *Tybee* reported that they had a large stationary target 34 nautical miles (39.1 miles) ahead of them and directly in the path of the *Liberated Lady*. At first light, Commander Newell ordered the *Venturous'* helicopter launched. Lt. (jg) Michael F. White, of the *Venturous*, flew as an observer. The U.S. Coast Guard aircrew and Lieutenant White observed the *Jinn Yin No. 1* and other craft moving rapidly away from the fishing vessel. Using gyrostablilized binoculars, Lieutenant White identified the rapidly moving *Liberated Lady* heading toward the northeast. The aircrew radioed the *Tybee* to coordinate with the 82-foot patrol boat *Point Evans* (WPB-82354), commanded by Lt. Jeff Farrar, to follow the yacht. Once the 82-footer took over, the *Tybee* then resumed its shadowing of the yacht. The helicopter returned to the cutter.

The *Point Evans* and boats from U.S. Coast Guard Station Long Beach/Los Angeles stopped the *Liberated Lady* in U.S. waters and sent a boarding party to the yacht. The boarding party later said they "were stunned by what they found."[40]

In a cabin designed for twelve people, they found eighty-five Chinese "crammed into cupboards, stuffed under the sink and doubled over on top of each other in the bathroom." Some of the boarding party said, "It was like looking down into the hull of a slave ship."[41]

Meanwhile, back on the *Venturous*, and at least forty miles behind the trawler, the cutter received orders to stop and board the *Jinn Yin No. 1*; Commander Newell ordered his cutter to close on the fishing vessel. As they drew nearer, the cutter sent flashing light signals to stop and hoisted the international flag signal SQ-3, which means, "Stop or heave to, I am going to board you." All of this was to no avail: the pursued vessel continued to steam onward. Commander Newell then ordered searchlights to illuminate the vessel and transmitted radio messages to the ship. The *Jinn Yin*

No. 1 continued to ignore the orders. The cutter's helicopter launched again and flew around the fishing vessel to get its attention.

Lieutenant White then took a boarding party made up of Chief Boatswain's Mate (BMC) Salvatore J. Galazzo, Electronic Technician Third Class (ET3) Joe R. Shanahan Jr., Seaman (SN) Joseph A. Jones, and Electrician's Mate Third Class (EM3) Todd Wilmot in the *Venturous*' rigid hulled inflatable boat (RHIB) to see if they could stop the fishing vessel and then board it.

The RHIB pulled to the starboard side of the vessel. Lieutenant White, facing the vessel, "used exaggerated motions to stop after a crewmember stuck his head out of pilothouse window." Again, the *Jinn Yin No. 1* failed to heave to. Lieutenant White then had the RHIB maneuver to within thirty yards of the ship and he "again used [his] hands to signal the vessel to stop." This time the ship began to slow.

This is the official account of the means to stop the vessel. Years later, White, now a captain, related what probably stopped the vessel: he had ET3 Shanahan stand up with a rifle at port arms (held diagonally across his chest) and facing the bow of RHIB. Due to the bouncing of the RHIB, the boarding team members had to hold the crewman upright. Lieutenant White then pointed at Shanahan and then at the pilothouse. They understood these gestures.

Lieutenant White and his boarding team quickly scrambled aboard the vessel. Other boarding parties soon came aboard, including one from the *Tybee*. The teams soon found overwhelming evidence of an attempt to smuggle undocumented Chinese by the *Jinn Yin No. 1*. For example, in the hold of the ship there were many mattresses and blankets and a clear attempt at using the compartment for a living area. The *Jinn Yin No. 1* was seized and its crew placed under arrest.

During the intense period from 1992 to 1993, not all cases happened in the Pacific or on the West Coast of the United States. In April 1992 the 110-foot Taiwanese trawler *Chin Wing* arrived off the coast of Fujian Province. A speedboat transported 151 undocumented migrants out to the trawler, which soon departed. The trawler arrived at Port Louis, Mauritius, in the Indian Ocean, on May 22 for refueling and provisions and departed on May 28. The *Chin Wing* arrived at Port Elizabeth, South Africa, on July 9 and took on board spare parts. On August 16, the vessel arrived at Jacmel, Haiti, about seventy-five miles southwest of Port au Prince.[42]

Two days later, the *New York Times* carried the continuing odyssey of the *Chin Wing*. A boatload of Chinese either swam or took a small boat ashore. Haitian officials quickly rounded up the undocumented migrants. The Haitians had the Chinese put back on board and released the trawler on September 1.[43] Six days later, on September 7, the *Chin Wing* once again surfaced. The radio watch stander at the U.S. Coast Guard Station at Morehead, North Carolina, received a radio message in strongly accented English reporting a vessel broken down near Wrightsville Beach, North Carolina.[44]

A cutter received orders to tow the *Chin Wing* into the U.S. Coast Guard Station at Fort Macon, North Carolina, near Morehead. All of the Chinese undocumented migrants were removed from the trawler and spent the night in a National Guard armory and fed "meals from a local Oriental restaurant." Eventually, the Chinese found themselves on the way to a federal immigration center near Brownsville, Texas, where they appeared before a judge. The captain and crew of the *Chin Wing* faced charges of conspiracy to smuggle undocumented migrants into the United States. On March 9, 1993, the owners of the trawler found themselves convicted of the charges in New York.[45]

An incident beginning in January 1993 in the far reaches of the Pacific Ocean probably made law enforcement people wonder about the coming year. On January 27, 1993, a radio operator at the U.S. Coast Guard's Communication Center in Guam received the call that makes the adrenaline kick in for anyone who works in search and rescue: "Mayday!" the international radio call for desperate distress. As the Guam radio operator listened closely, the radio officer on the Panamanian-registered freighter *East Wood* reported that "the vessel had been taken over by hijackers and that there were 400 people in the vessel's two main cargo holds."[46]

Upon receiving the Mayday call, the U.S. Coast Guard began seeking other ships in the area by radio, requesting that they come to the aid of the *East Wood*. In Honolulu, the 378-foot cutter *Rush* was notified that it should prepare to get under way to the scene. Within twelve hours, Capt. Alan Doty managed to recall his crew, brief them, get underway, and receive on board a helicopter. Meanwhile, another ship, the motor vessel *Venanna*, intercepted another radio call from the *East Wood* and passed on the information to the U.S. Coast Guard. The startling message: ten people "were going to be thrown overboard" from the *East Wood*. The U.S. Coast Guard requested by radio that the captain of the merchant vessel *Patriot* divert from its course and rendezvous with the *East Wood*. A long-range U.S. Coast Guard aircraft received orders to proceed to the position and search for people in the water.

While the *Rush* sailed toward the position of the *East Wood*, a C-130 aircraft from U.S. Coast Guard Air Station Barber's Point, Hawaii, located the ship dead in the water some 1,500 miles southwest of Hawaii. The aircraft crew dropped a portable radio to the ship.

In the interim, through an interpreter on the *Patriot*, the U.S. Coast Guard learned via radio that "eight people from the *East Wood* jumped over the side after a fight with some of the Chinese on board, and that the [ship had] picked up six of the eight people."[47]

Captain Doty and his cutter arrived on scene on February 4. Doty quickly ordered a boarding team to go aboard the freighter. Their radioed report to the cutter found little to support violence on board or a hijacking. But "there appeared to be evidence of mutinous behavior aboard the ship." Most importantly, they found an amazing 527 undocumented Chinese migrants.[48]

The boarding party reported to Captain Doty that the master of the freighter said his crew "feared for their lives at the hands of bad men among the Chinese, who allegedly hijacked the ship near Hong Kong." Doty soon began receiving conflicting verbal accounts and paperwork concerning the *East Wood*. For example, a man identified as a passenger appeared on one manifest and yet on another he appeared as the chief steward. The master and the mysterious man "had a violent argument over the master's claim that the chief steward was the hijack leader." Furthermore, the names of the ship's radio operator and second engineer appeared on the crew list but were missing during the boarding.[49] The boarding party learned that the second engineer allegedly sabotaged the freighter's engines.[50]

Reports back to the cutter told of appalling conditions on board the *East Wood*. "Food has either been cooked over open fires in the compartments or lowered by buckets from the main deck," Captain Doty later recalled.

Surprisingly, the Chinese undocumented migrants, for all their hardships, remained in "good health." A U.S. Coast Guard C-130 aircraft "dropped five loads of food and water containers" for the migrants.[51]

Eventually, Captain Doty received orders to escort the *East Wood* to the Marshall Islands. Doty kept an armed guard on board the ship on the transit to the islands. At Kwajalein, the Chinese received food, water, clean coveralls, showers, and tents and cots. Eventually, 527 Chinese were repatriated and the Indonesian crew sent back to Indonesia.[52]

In April 1993 James Hayes, the assistant director for investigations of the INS, said, "The way these boats have been coming in, I wouldn't be surprised if I saw one land in Topeka, Kansas. They seem to have the ability to show up anywhere." Although said with tongue firmly in cheek, Hayes expressed his frustration over the increasing waves of ships dropping off illegal Chinese migrants. Of course, Hayes had no way of knowing what the next two months had in store for him. If he could have been clairvoyant, perhaps Hayes might not have been so quick to make such a flippant remark.[53]

Less than a month after Hayes uttered his comment, shortly after midnight on Monday, May 24, 1993, one of the more "nervy" smuggling attempts took place in San Francisco. The 250-foot Honduran-registered freighter *Pai Sheng* sailed inbound beneath the Golden Gate Bridge. The vessel continued under the bridge and as far east as the city's Aquatic Park, about two-and-a-half miles from the bridge. The *Pai Sheng* then came about sharply and headed toward the old nineteenth century Fort Point area near the south end of the bridge. Ironically, it moored at a former U.S. Coast Guard pier. Amazingly, 250 undocumented Chinese migrants streamed out of the *Pai Sheng*. The ship then cast off lines and set sail for the Pacific Ocean.[54]

"It was beautifully executed," said David Ilchert, district director of the INS. "They zip into the harbor, do a circle, then they're gone." Ilchert felt the whole operation took fifty minutes from the time the ship entered the bay.

A tollbooth collector on the Golden Gate Bridge called the police to report that a freighter had come alongside an unused pier. The location, within the Golden Gate National Recreation Area, came under the enforcement of the U.S. National Park Service Police. The Park Police arrived near the dock but could see nothing. The officers reported their findings and started away from the area.

Meanwhile, at 1:30 a.m., military police at the large U.S. Army installation of the Presidio stopped a pickup with a camper shell. The MPs found seven Chinese jammed into the camper portion. Remembering earlier radio traffic on a suspicious freighter, they "put two and two together" and detained everyone in the truck and eventually turned them over to INS. Officers from many organizations started converging on the Fort Point area. The first to arrive saw a large group of people who started to run. Throughout the dark of the early morning hours and into daylight, police tracked and captured groups, all of which offered no resistance. Some were found on the Golden Gate Bridge, others wandered throughout the Marina District residential area, and some were found on a public golf course. At least 183 of the fleeing undocumented migrants did not escape, but dozens of others eluded capture. "They'll just blend into the community," said Ilchert.

In spite of boldness and speed, the smugglers did not realize they had been tracked by radar. Located on Yerba Buena Island within San Francisco Bay and approximately 5.5 miles from the Golden Gate Bridge, the U.S. Coast Guard maintained a vessel tracking system (VTS). Radar operators of the VTS tracked ships entering and leaving the bay, much like air controllers track aircraft. The system had been in operation since 1972. The VTS knew about the *Pai Sheng*'s approach and began tracking it twenty miles out from the Golden Gate Bridge. At the time, foreign ships had to announce their names and country and relay their intentions to VTS when in U.S. waters. If it did not, the U.S. Coast Guard could board the vessel. PO Garry Openshaw, USCG, later said, "We were aware of [the ship] for quite some time. We were trying to determine who it was and what it was doing." When reporters asked him what if the ship had terrorists on board, Petty Officer Openshaw replied, "We haven't been attacked by sea since World War II. It is not something that happens very often. We are not going to comment on the what-ifs."[55]

When the *Pai Sheng* headed back out to sea, VTS continued to track the freighter. The U.S. Coast Guard 82-foot patrol boat *Point Brower* (WPB-82372), stationed at Yerba Buena Island, got under way to overtake the *Pai Sheng*. At near first light, a U.S. Coast Guard helicopter located the vessel. The *Pai Sheng*'s master refused to obey radio calls to return to San Francisco. Soon a U.S. Coast Guard 110-foot patrol boat, *Long Island* (WPB-1342), from Monterey, joined the action. This finally convinced the master of the *Pai Sheng* to return to San Francisco, where the U.S. Coast Guard boarded it and took off the crew, plus seven Burmese and four Taiwanese, in handcuffs. The living conditions in the hold proved horrible. One member of an intelligence team remembered when she entered the hold of the ship. "We discovered the location of the bathroom/kitchen. Within seconds of entering this area, everything became very dark, we were in the middle of a swarm of small flies and could barely breathe. I never climbed a three story ladder so quickly to get out of there!"[56] The entire ship had to be fumigated. The Chinese undocumented migrants ended up in detention centers in the Bay Region at Bakersfield or in Alameda County.

Law enforcement officials must have felt they had seen everything. They had not. Less than one month after the *Pai Sheng* case, another ship, the *Golden Venture*, literally came ashore, becoming one of the most important cases concerning the smuggling of Chinese into the United States in the twentieth century.

PART II

1993–2008

7 The *Golden Venture*

> I just started pulling people out of the water.
>
> Seaman Apprentice (SA) Charley Wells

In the predawn hours of Sunday, June 6, 1993, two U.S. National Park Service police officers drove their patrol car near a stretch of beach on the Rockaway Peninsula in Gateway National Park. This portion of the park is located in Queens, one of the boroughs of New York City. The quiet early morning routine abruptly changed.

Two Asian men suddenly appeared out of the darkness waving their arms. The startled officers stopped and cautiously opened their patrol car's door. Immediately, they heard the sound of screams coming from the beach. The full moon gave enough light to see some type of vessel in the surf. As the incredulous officers peered through the lunar light, they saw people leaping from high up on the deck of a ship. Squinting, the Park Service officers recognized people flailing in the water, trying to reach the beach. The officers quickly called the nearest U.S. Coast Guard unit, Station Rockaway, which had rescue boats.

"Initially the call came in as a 50-foot boat in distress," said Petty Officer Second Class (PO2) Tim Clancey, of Station Rockaway. "A few minutes later . . . park police units reported that it was a larger vessel with approximately 100 people in the water."[1] Clancey sent SA Charley Wells to the area to verify the report. Wells later said, "There were people in the water, on the beach, and there were people jumping into the water from the [ship.]" Wells, without hesitation, rushed about twenty yards into the fifty-four degree surf to help. "I just started pulling people out of the water," Wells later said. This quick action saved ten people.[2]

After Clancey received Wells's report, he passed the information up his chain of command. Soon U.S. Coast Guard units, New York City police and fire department, and other emergency responders sped to the scene. Meanwhile, Station Rockaway launched a 41-foot boat.

PO2 Daniel Anderson, in charge of Station Rockaway's 41-footer, received a radio report "of a lot of people in the water." As he approached the stern of the grounded vessel, he realized such an approach "was totally unsafe" because the "surf was kicking pretty good."[3] He backed off, awaiting other units.

CPO Brian Hatfield, in a 21-foot rigid hulled craft, from Shark River, New Jersey, arrived just before daybreak. He remembered the incredible amount of rescue units in the area, from helicopters, small boats, and larger vessels. "As we got closer," recalled Hatfield, "I could see people hanging off the side of the ship on ladders and ropes." Hatfield's crewman, PO2 Jeffrey A. Norton, said, "It was a very challenging operation because of the surf conditions. We would be able to get five or six people and then would have to move out because of the waves. It was hard staying alongside the ship. . . . We almost got caught a couple of times in the surf."[4] Hatfield and Norton rescued twenty-seven people. One New York City police officer said, "It looked almost like the movie about the invasion of Normandy," so many people were trying to scramble off the ship.[5] "Just as you thought you had a grip on it, there were more people coming out of the ocean," said Robert Leonard, an emergency medical technician at the scene.[6]

Rescuers on the beach found many of the survivors emaciated and clad only in their underwear. People leaping into the water from the ship immediately felt the shock of the numbing water. Some went into cardiac arrest. One U.S. Coast Guard petty officer on the beach applying CPR later said, "I could feel the gristle of their bodies, the cartilage. They walked up out of the water, collapsed on the beach, and died."[7] One petty officer said, "Never in my 14 years of working in the Coast Guard have I seen a rescue operation this big."[8]

PO Chris O'Neil, one of the few U.S. Coast Guard people to board the ship, later said, "The first thing that greeted me [in the cargo hold] was a pile of human feces. . . . Everywhere were articles of these people's lives. Slippers, purses, money, a remote control from a VCR, sweaters, pants, anything, everything that you can imagine. . . . The wood was saturated with human perspiration. It was [an] overpowering aroma. The sanitation conditions were much to be desired. It was clear that the living space was being used as a bathroom."[9]

Two days later, the U.S. Coast Guard's final situation report on the incident identified the vessel as a coastal freighter measuring 230-feet and named the *Golden Venture*. The ship remained moored at a military terminal in Bayonne, New Jersey. A previous message indicated a human cargo of close to three hundred undocumented Chinese. Most of the passengers were men, but there were some women and children. At least seven Chinese died in the surf. The largest city in the United States had just had an unwelcome wake up to the smuggling of Chinese into their midst. And they had a story that flooded the nation's largest media market.

Very few scholars have studied the smuggling of Chinese into the United States. Of the few that do, all have pointed out that the *Golden Venture* marks the awakening of interest in human trafficking from China.[10] Arguably, if this incident had happened in Seattle, Washington, the case would probably have had a few days run but then would have been relegated to obscurity, except among those who work to stop human trafficking. The incident, because of its location and amount of media attention, can be used as a textbook case of how those who trafficked in Chinese undocumented migrants by the sea route worked prior to 1994.

A decade after the *Golden Venture* slammed into the beach in the borough of Queens, thirty-two-year-old Michael Chen talked to Patrick Radden Keefe about his experiences in trying to reach the United States illegally. Chen, who owns a restaurant in Columbus, Ohio, grew up outside of the city of Fuzhou. His father farmed during the day and fished at night to make ends meet. Some of his uncles had made their way illegally into the United States. At the age of sixteen, his parents managed to borrow five thousand dollars to pay a little snakehead the down payment to transport Chen to the United States. The total, payable upon arrival in America, amounted to thirty thousand dollars.[11]

In 1991 this snakehead told Chen that he had Thai officials on his payroll. All Chen had to do was take a bus or a motorcycle to Thailand. There, "maybe one week or two weeks, they will arrange [your transportation] by plane to the U.S.A." Chen, along with others from his village, set off for Kunming near the China-Myanmar [Burma] border. After a time, they were smuggled over the border "among bags of rice." Once within Myanmar, the Chinese now had to provision themselves for a difficult and dangerous journey across steep mountains in the region of the infamous Golden Triangle, noted for the large amount of poppies grown for making heroin. Chen dodged drug smugglers at night. He also recalled seeing the bodies of Chinese lying along this dangerous route.

He reached Bangkok early in 1992. The U.S. crackdown on smuggling by air caused a long delay in Thailand, which eventually led to Chen's arrest. At one point he found himself in prison and needed to ask his parents to obtain a loan to bail him out. In all, he remained in Thailand for more than a year.

While Chen made his agonizingly slow passage through China and Myanmar and into Thailand, Hollywood-like events happening in far-off New York City transpired. A violent Chinese gang known as the Fuk Ching began moving into the human trafficking trade. The gang members first worked as enforcers for the big snakeheads, forcing the newly smuggled Chinese to quickly raise the remainder of the money to pay off the big snakeheads. If they could not, the hapless Chinese faced violent acts to make those in China come up with the rest of the money. The Fuk Ching realized great profits from this activity. The gang leadership realized that sentencing for human trafficking generally remained low. If you pled guilty, a person usually received a six-month sentence.

A "charismatic young murderer," Guo Liang Qi, also known as Ah Kay, rose to the leadership of the Fuk Ching. In March 1986 Ah Kay received a conviction of attempted larceny, a prison sentence, and then deportation to China. He soon made his way back to the United States. Although he had committed multiple murders, he received political asylum in the United States in 1991.

Ah Kay knew of the profits to be made from transporting large numbers of Chinese by sea. He arranged for a "mother ship," to arrive off the East Coast of the United States and rendezvous with fishing vessels with Vietnamese captains and gang members as crew. In 1992 Ah Kay learned that a New York City big snakehead wanted to speak to him about combining operations.

Cheng Chui Ping, a middle-aged woman, came to the United States in 1981, whether legally or illegally is unclear. Born in 1949 in Shengmei, a farming village in Fujian Province, she married a fisherman. In the 1970s, they left for Hong Kong, where she opened a convenience store and earned the reputation of being a "clever businesswoman." Soon after settling into New York City, she opened a shop. She also entered into human trafficking.

Eventually, Cheng Chui Ping, the small heavyset woman "with cropped black hair, wide-set dark eyes," became known as "Sister Ping." Sister Ping maintained "a hang-dog expression" and a "gruff demeanor and [wore] simple clothes," radiating the appearance of a peasant. Behind this façade, Sister Ping had, by 1992, become known as the "mother of all snakeheads." Her reach extended to China, Hong Kong, Thailand, Belize, Kenya, South Africa, Guatemala, Mexico, and Canada. Sister Ping helped create the China-to-Chinatown, New York, pipeline in the early 1980s, becoming a Chinatown institution. Very few Chinese spoke harshly about her. She helped preserve her image by refunding money to those undocumented migrants who were captured as she attempted to smuggle them into the county and by paying for burial costs if a migrant died en route. The FBI estimated that in two decades Sister Ping made at least $40 million in human trafficking.

In the summer of 1992 Ah Kay and Sister Ping entered a trial partnership. Sister Ping's portion of the partnership entailed bringing the people in close to the United States. Ah Kay supplied his expertise in unloading the Chinese undocumented migrants at sea and then settling them in New York City. The trial effort, off the coast of Massachusetts, proved successful and both partners decided to collaborate once again.

Meanwhile, another big snakehead competitor, Weng Yu Hui, whom Sister Ping had earlier smuggled into the United States, joined her to charter a cruise ship, the *Naid II*. Their plan was to smuggle at least three hundred Chinese from Bangkok to the United States. The master of the ship, while making a port call in Mombassa, Kenya, quit when he felt he would not receive enough money for hauling the human cargo. Twenty of the people were Sister Ping's customers. Weng Yu Hui met with Ah Kay and another snakehead in a Chinatown restaurant to find a way to get this human cargo to New York City. Eventually the three snakeheads purchased a Panama-registered ship, the *Tong Sern*. Along with a new name, the *Golden Venture*, the vessel came with a crew and Kin Sin Lee, a Chinese, the on board enforcer.

Like most ship owners, the snakeheads realized that sailing empty from Singapore to Mombassa made no profit. In February they decided to order the *Golden Venture* to stop at Thailand and pick up ninety Chinese waiting there, among them Michael Chen. When Chen saw the ship, he thought, "This is the boat?" It seemed too small to make an ocean passage. Nevertheless, Chen and others clambered on board and the *Golden Venture* sailed to another port area in Thailand, where it loaded even more passengers. Once loaded, the ship sailed through the Strait of Malacca and across the Indian Ocean to Mombassa.

At Mombassa, all but two of Sister Ping's customers refused to board such a small ship. They had good reason to hesitate. Chen and close to three hundred Chinese found themselves crammed into a twenty-by-forty-foot hold. Those in the cramped space sweltered in the heat, with the air rank with cigarette smoke, sweat, and the odors coming from the single toilet.

As the months wore on, the food supplies diminished. Eventually, the passengers received only small portions of rice, peanuts, or dried vegetables each day.

Ah Kay's original plan called for unloading the passengers at sea, but then he ran into the machinations of gang leadership. Another member, Dan Xin Lin, decided to split from the Fuk Ching and start his own snakehead enterprise along with some of the Fuk Ching members. Ah Kay solved this problem in a typical gang manner: he ordered a Fuk Ching member to kill the upstart. Unsuccessful, Ah Kay left the United States to go into hiding in China, leaving the management of his affairs with two younger brothers. This led Dan Xin Lin to attack and murder the Ah Kay brothers. The police captured the killers as they sped away from the scene of the crime. This left no one to meet the *Golden Venture.*

Meanwhile, the U.S. Coast Guard had received intelligence of a possible human trafficking operation taking place in June in the Northeast. The First Coast Guard District—which encompasses New England—began alerting all of its units by message. Commands learned that "a large blue hulled 'mothership' vessel [would] offload 150–200 illegal PRC aliens in the 'Boston area' [on the] evening of 05 June."[12] The district's intelligence was consistent with previous operations that Ah Kay conducted. That is, he had the mothership unload near Boston and then moved the passengers to New York City.

Sometime while the *Golden Venture* plodded on its journey, the snakeheads of the illegal consortium radioed the ship that there was no longer anyone to pick up the passengers. Here the story becomes murkier. One account has the enforcer, Kin Sin Lee, leading a mutiny and confining the master of the *Golden Venture.* With the help of the crew, he headed into New York's harbor and ran the freighter aground. Another account simply states that the ship's crew ran the vessel aground.

One day after the story of the *Golden Venture* broke, federal finger-pointing began. Reporter Anne E. Murray wrote that ships "filled with illegal human cargo can easily slip into local waters because officials do not police the coastline for illegal aliens—and because two law-enforcement agencies are pointing fingers over who's responsible." Murray quoted Tom Durand of the INS press office: "The Coast Guard is responsible for patrolling the coast. We investigate smuggling operations, but we don't go out on the high seas and look at these boats." Murray then reported that Lt. Cdr. Dave Marks, USCG, said that ships did not have to notify the U.S. Coast Guard unless they intended to enter the busy area north of Verrazano Narrows Bridge. South of the bridge the waters are relatively wide open. "'A large ship could be in that area without telling us what their intentions were,' Marks said." Lt. James Donovan, another U.S. Coast Guard officer, said, "Specific responsibility for aliens does not come under the Coast Guard." Lieutenant Donovan went on to say that the "Coast Guard's missions are search-and-rescue, enforcing fishing regulations and drug interdiction." John Ingham, another INS official, said that INS knew about the smuggling of Chinese by sea "but can't do much to stop it. We don't have the ability to track a ship."[13]

This complicated story does not end with the rescue and capture of the Chinese on the beaches of Queens and with the federal finger-pointing. Two months after the grounding of the *Golden Venture*, Ah Kay slipped into Hong Kong, where police arrested him. In the United States, the FBI raided the Fuk Ching's buildings and rounded up members of the gang. Ah Kay waived extradition to the United States, pled guilty to murder, and volunteered to help the FBI.

Meanwhile, the FBI gathered more information on Sister Ping. Being the shrewd businesswoman that she was, Sister Ping left New York City and arrived in Hong Kong in the fall of 1993. She immediately rid herself of her passport, thus ending her paper trail.

While Ah Kay helped the FBI and Sister Ping fled the United States, the undocumented Chinese of the *Golden Venture* faced treatment not usually afforded their predecessors. About half of the passengers found themselves deported while others wound up in INS detention facilities scattered throughout the United States. Michael Chen, for example, remained in York, Pennsylvania. Previously most Chinese had remained in custody for only a short amount of time. Most of the passengers believed "that it was not difficult for Chinese migrants to obtain asylum in America." But the events surrounding the *Golden Venture* "embarrassed the Clinton Administration—critics charged that America's policy on asylum had become a magnet for illegal Chinese and all but a few passengers had their claims denied." Lawyers claimed their clients were being used to deter both illegal operations in this country and in China.

Almost four years later, the front page of the *New York Times* revealed that many of the *Golden Venture*'s passengers remained in detention facilities. The *Times* felt the Chinese might have already won their asylum, "had they come ashore a year earlier—when George [H. W.] Bush was president." Eleven days after the *Times* story, President Clinton pardoned the final fifty-three *Golden Venture* passengers.[14]

For seven years after the *Golden Venture* grounded near New York City, law enforcement officials knew Sister Ping lived in the village of Shengmei, Fujian. From there she continued in her business of human trafficking. As the sea trade directly to the United States proved more difficult, she sought new routes, such as ships to Central and South America and then to the United States. In April 2000, acting on a tip, authorities in Hong Kong arrested Sister Ping. Within her purse, police discovered a number of passports and proof that Sister Ping had made at least one trip to America three months prior to her arrest. Sister Ping fought extradition for three years until 2003. The FBI tried to obtain her cooperation, but she refused.

Chen Chui Ping's trial began in May 2003 in federal court in New York City. Now a fifty-six-year-old grandmother, Sister Ping sat stoically during the month-long proceedings. David Burns, an assistant U.S. attorney, described Cheng Chui Ping as "one of the most powerful and most successful alien smugglers of our time." Burns relied heavily on the testimony of Ah Kay and other snakeheads. Lawrence Hochheiser, the attorney for Ping, constantly questioned the testimony of Ah Kay and his ilk, implying they only testified to obtain lighter sentences. Burns admitted that Kay and the others were "killers," but Ping had knowingly hired killers.

On Wednesday, June 22, 2005, the jury brought in a verdict of guilty in conspiring to smuggle aliens and take hostages, money laundering, and trafficking in ransom proceeds. The *New York Daily News* headline proclaimed Ping "Evil Incarnate." Close to thirteen years after the *Golden Venture* grounded in Queens and the Chinese passengers leaped into the cold Atlantic Ocean, Cheng Chui Ping received her sentence on March 16, 2006. The judge asked if she had anything to say. Sister Ping launched into a tirade lasting more than an hour. After she sat down, the judge called the oration "self-justification" that defied belief. He then pronounced her sentence: thirty-five years in prison, the maximum allowed.[15]

The aftermath of the trial proved interesting. Ah Kay, whom one of the prosecutors labeled "an incredibly violent man with zero regard for human life," was released shortly after the trial, having satisfied his sentence. Although the New York press seemed satisfied with Sister Ping's verdict and sentence, this opinion did not resonate throughout Chinatown. A Fujianese community leader said that many in the community said that the government put "Robin Hood on trial." One New York City Chinese-language newspaper reported that "villagers in Shengmei had volunteered to do prison time on Sister Ping's behalf; they described her as a living Buddha." President Clinton's pardon, known as a "humanitarian parole," of the last of the *Golden Venture*'s detainees meant that they could apply for work permits but had none of the privileges of asylum or green card status. Without "presidential or congressional grant, this parole creates an indefinite legal limbo; there is no process for graduating to permanent-resident status."

Once freed, the detainees moved throughout the United States. Michael Chen moved to Columbus, Ohio, and opened a restaurant. He worried, however, about sudden deportation. Chen had good reason for his concern. In May 2001 one of the passengers living in Aurora, Colorado, was suddenly deported. Interestingly, Chen felt the same about Sister Ping as did members of the Fujianese community in New York. "She's a very nice lady," he told Keefe. "Even if some of her customers died by accident, it was not her fault." He did remark that Sister Ping was so much better than Ah Kay, whom Chen labeled "a monster."

In line with the twisted path of everything dealing with the *Golden Venture*, another incident illustrates the frustration of law enforcement officials in attempting to stop human trafficking from the sea. On Saturday, May 30, 1998, five years after the *Golden Venture* grounded in Queens, a 30-foot motor boat aptly named the *Oops II* moved through heavy fog along the New Jersey shoreline. It hit bottom. Out spilled twenty-two undocumented Chinese migrants. The impoverished Chinese ran through Bay Head, New Jersey, with a population of thirteen hundred. Bay Head lies approximately fifty miles south of New York City. Police quickly rounded up the Chinese.[16]

Word of the landing spread quickly in the small community. By Monday, June 1, residents referred to the incident as the Chinese invasion. Katie Dempsey said it was "just perfect" because it was "probably the most affluent town on the Jersey Shore." Lorraine Norwicki, of Whiting, New Jersey, away from the coast, said, "Where are all the patrol boats that are supposed to be patrolling? I think it's unfair that they should come here, take our money, and send it back to China, while we're here starving anyway." Kim Morris, owner of a "fashion boutique," in Bay Head, however, said, "It's so sad. They spend their life savings to get here, they survive weeks on a boat—not that I approve of illegal aliens, but it's sad." Tom Fitzgerald said the incident was "pretty crazy—but it's exciting. Nothing much ever happens in this town."[17]

One of the twenty-two undocumented Chinese on board the *Oops II*, Wang Wu Dong, "a skinny man of forty," amazed even law enforcement officials. Wang led a very unlucky life. Incredulous officials learned that when the *Golden Venture* grounded five years earlier, one of the Chinese captured was Wang Wu Dong. He spent three years in jail at York, Pennsylvania, trying to seek asylum on the grounds of persecution for resisting China's one-child policy. Wang finally gave up and went home, "just months before Congress passed a law in 1996 that would have made his asylum claim more likely to succeed."[18]

The *New York Times* quickly picked up Wang's story. "Lawyers, advocates, officials and a fellow *Golden Venture* passenger" commented on Wang's bad luck, but "tipped their hats to his determination to get to America." Beverly Church, a paralegal "who became a mother hen to many of the *Golden Venture* passengers during their three-year detention in York," said, "To me it's unbelievable he went through all that, then turned around to come back again. It tells me how much he'll go through to be free."[19]

Reports indicated that Wang's plea for asylum centered on the one-child issue, that authorities in China had sterilized his wife. The new change in the U.S. law gave Wang's lawyers "hope that his luck has finally changed." Some members of Congress had expressed interest. Rep. Bill Goodling, whose district includes the York prison, said, "That [Wang] would risk being reimprisoned so soon after he went back shows you how unbearable the situation is."[20]

In "a reversal of fortune worthy of a Chinese poem about faith and perseverance," Wang Wu Dong finally succeeded in his quest to enter the United States. The *Times* felt Wang received "the benefit of the doubt," from the federal judge. Wang received a "'withholding' status, a rarely invoked designation that allows illegal immigrants to live and work in the United States indefinitely without ever having an opportunity to become a full-fledged resident." Amy Otten, a spokesperson for the Eastern regional office of the INS, said, "It's legal, but it doesn't give him a whole lot of benefits."[21]

"'I am very happy to be released,' said a laconic . . . Wang, who looked tired and gaunt, with bloodshot eyes." His short-term plans called for living with his sister in Delaware.[22]

Yet another aspect of the *Golden Venture* story involves art and documentary filmmaking. As the Chinese imprisoned in York awaited their fate, the detainees folded paper from discarded magazines, toilet paper, and any other bits of paper, into works of art. The "first piece survived in the Chaplain's office, a simple figure of a bird reminiscent of the Fujianese practice of paper-folding folk art called zhizha or hushi." Eventually, the Museum of Chinese in the Americas gathered a number of these objects for an exhibit.[23]

In 1997 filmmaker Peter Cohn, who stated that he opposed "our nation's exclusionary immigration policies," learned of the *Golden Venture*'s passengers still detained in York. He eventually made a seventy-minute documentary, *Golden Venture*, that focused on four of the ship's passengers.[24]

The United States Marshall Service sold the *Golden Venture*. Juan Lopez, who "inherited the ship as a custodian for a court case involving previous owners," let it sit in the Miami River. He then sold it to Palm County, Florida, for sixty thousand dollars. Plans called for towing the ship about a mile off the coast of Boca Raton, Florida, and sinking it "in about 70 feet of water to create an artificial reef" for fishing.[25]

Jeffrey Lobach, an attorney in York who helped the *Golden Venture* detainees, said he felt that none of the Chinese passengers "would care to preserve the *Golden Venture*. Their 100 days on there were something a lot of them still have nightmares about." Janet Phipps, an environmental analyst for Palm County, said, "A ship that had an ugly past will become something beautiful."[26]

By the time of the *Golden Venture* case, the U.S. government had increased its interdiction efforts against the human smuggling of Chinese via the sea. The National Security Council entered the arena. By the end of 1994 "the U.S. administration was crediting itself for bringing an end to maritime smuggling. The implication was that the [Chinese] smuggling declined because U.S. law enforcement made it too difficult." The coming years proved the fallacy of this presumption.[27]

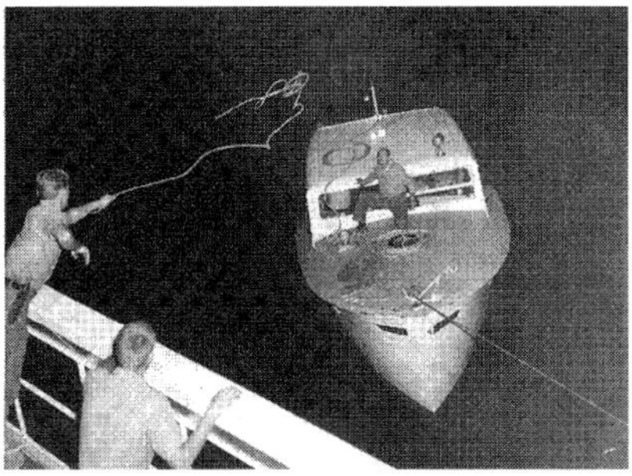

A stranded boat is taken under tow by the U.S. Coast Guard during the Camarioca Boatlift.

The first of the Cuban boatlifts began in 1965 from Camarioca; the small harbor as it appeared in 2008. (Dennis L. Noble)

This scene at Key West during the Mariel Boatlift graphically illustrates the problems facing the U.S. Coast Guard during the operation.

At least 125,000 Cubans departed from Mariel in 1980. Twenty-eight years later the harbor appears relatively sleepy. (Dennis L. Noble)

The wet foot/dry foot policy has made some Cuban migrants turn to violence when intercepted by the U.S. Coast Guard. Cubans in this craft have sharpened sticks to use as spears as the cutter *Matagorda* approaches them.

Balseros attempt the passage from Cuba to Florida during 1994.

A *balsero* who was returned to Cuba under the wet foot/dry foot policy in 1994 drew this diagram of his raft. The raft had three truck inner tubes, a sail, and handmade paddles. Drawn in Havana, Cuba, in 2008; the person did not want to be identified and destroyed the drawing after author photographed it. (Dennis L. Noble)

The U.S. Navy assisted the U.S. Coast Guard during the major undocumented migrant operations. The size of the frigate in the background compared to the U.S. Coast Guard 110-foot patrol boat graphically illustrates just how many migrants could be held on each vessel.

A go-fast boat attempts to out run the U.S. Coast Guard boat from U.S. Coast Guard Station Islamorada, in the Florida Keys. The head of one of the undocumented migrants can be seen just forward to the center consol.

A human smuggler's boat is captured by a U.S. Coast Guard boat from Station Islamorada. Note the fishing poles near the stern of the smuggler's boat.

The U.S. Coast Guard buoy tender *Joseph Appleby* held 103 Cubans during operations in February 2008. Note the awning spread to provide some protection from the sun.

An INS interpreter on board a U.S. Coast Guard cutter pleads with Haitian boat people not to crowd to one side of their overloaded craft.

A U.S. Coast Guard cutter approaches a typically overloaded Haitian sailboat (*yola*). Many more Haitians are probably below decks.

One hundred and thirty-six Haitians jam the flight deck of the U.S. Coast Guard cutter *Harriet Lane* after being intercepted at sea.

How close the *Golden Venture* grounded to the beach in Queens, New York, in 1993 is illustrated in this photograph. Note the tall buildings in the background.

Some of the Chinese undocumented migrant survivors from the *Golden Venture* being taken off the ship by rescuers. One rescuer said it reminded him of a movie of the Normandy landing.

Chinese survivors from the *Golden Venture* wrapped in blankets wait on the cold New York beach for transportation to holding areas.

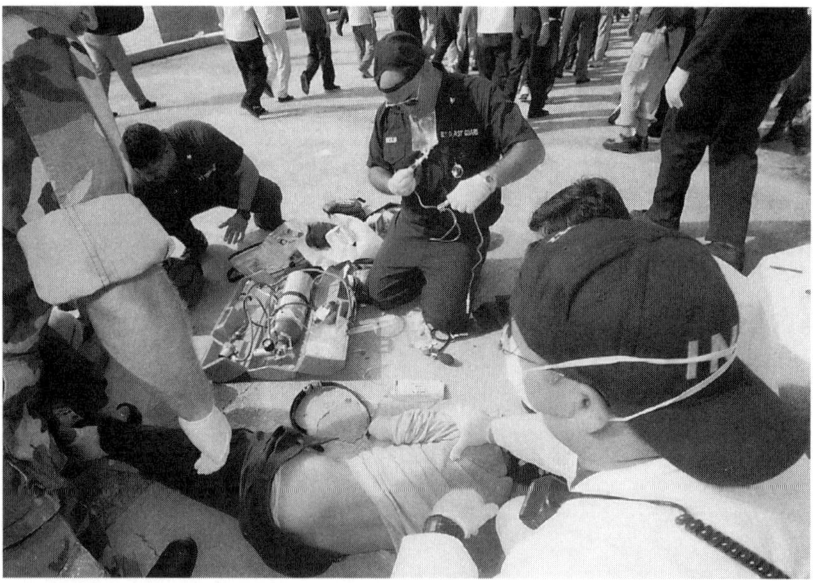

U.S. Coast Guardsmen and an INS agent help stabilize a smuggled passenger from the *Yu Xing* after seventy-five undocumented migrants were brought ashore at Midway Island.

The Caribbean (Tracy Ellen Smith)

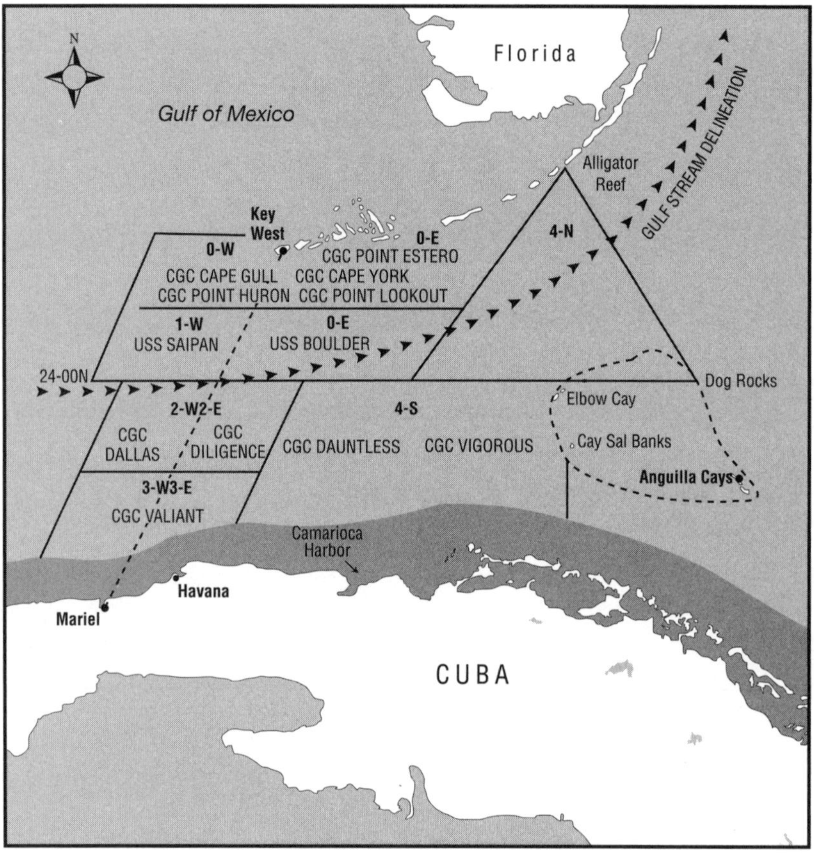

Operational Areas during the Mariel Boatlift (Tracy Ellen Smith)

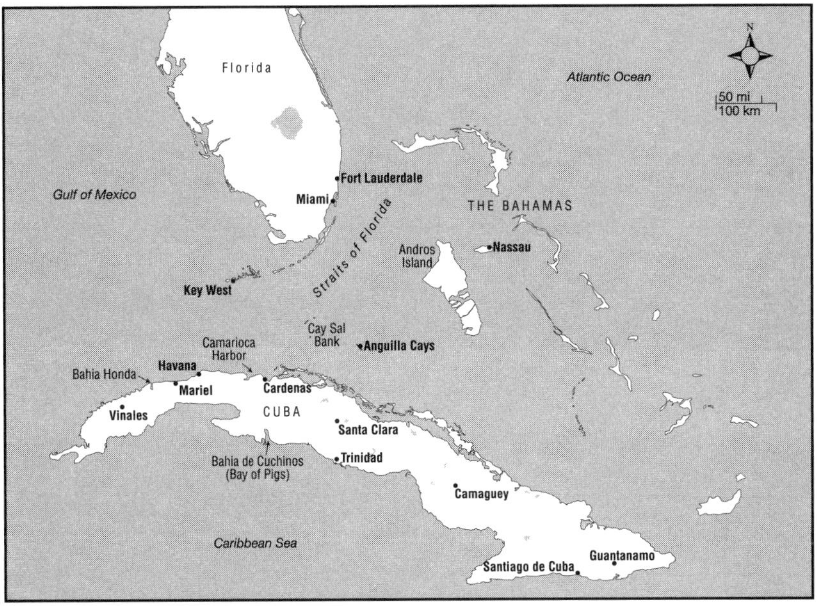

Cuba (Tracy Ellen Smith)

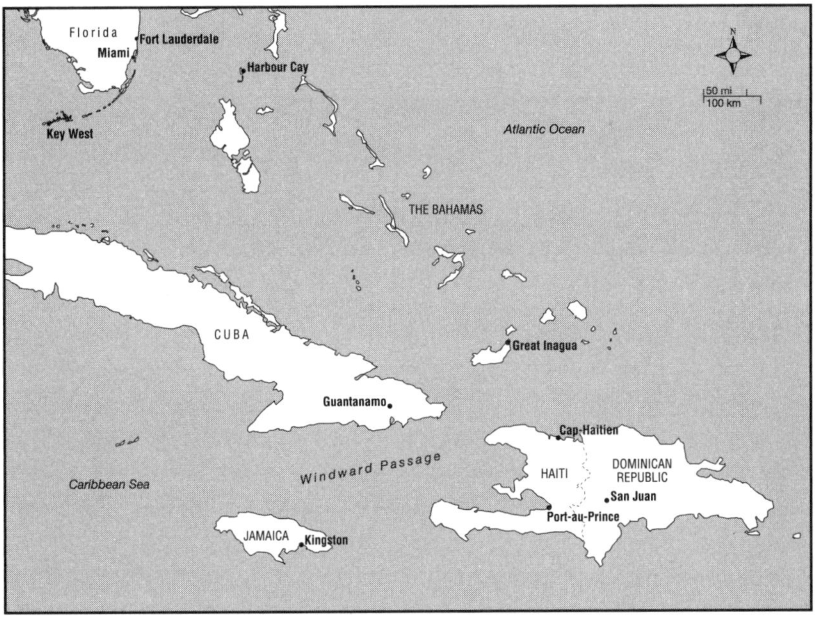

The Bahamas, Cuba, and Haiti (Tracy Ellen Smith)

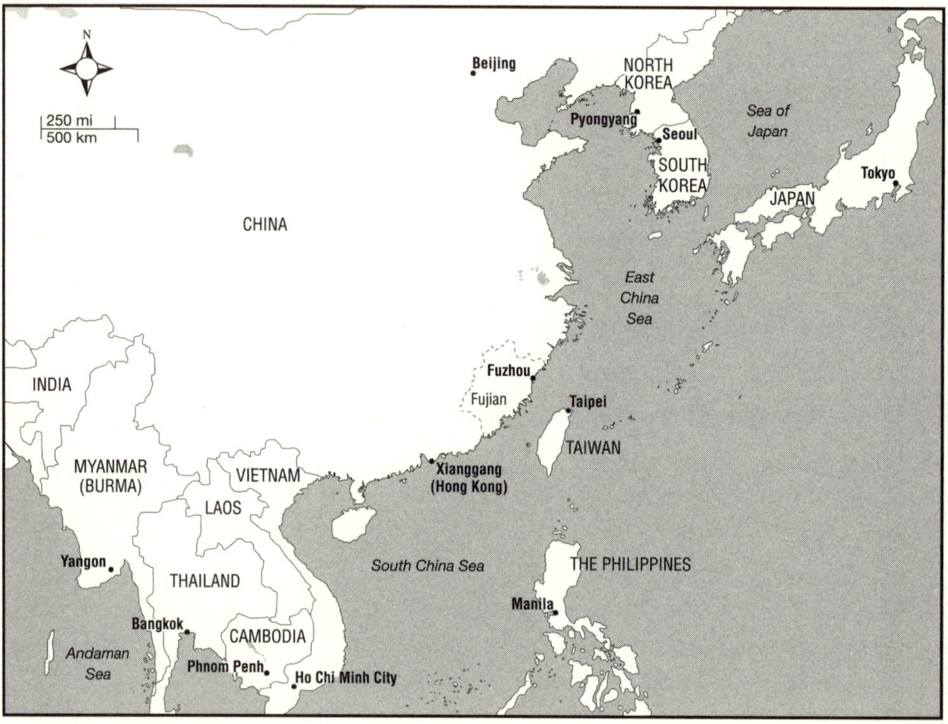

China (Tracy Ellen Smith)

8 Escaping the Dragon

> Lt. (jg) Robert Borowczak lay "awake worrying that his crew might not have captured all of the smugglers and wondering what mayhem might come next."

Prior to the case of the *Golden Venture* incident of 1994, the U.S. Coast Guard faced a flood of undocumented Chinese attempting to enter the United States via the maritime route. The grounding of the ship and the ensuing large amount of publicity marks the slowing to a trickle of the previous flood of human smuggling from the sea. The most significant reason for the lower number of Chinese immigrants was because the Chinese government now allowed more people to obtain visas. The fate of those on board the *Golden Venture* reached Fujian Province, which also contributed to the lower numbers (see the appendix for the number of immigrants). This does not mean that the flow stopped completely—far from it. Beginning after 1994, U.S. Coast Guard crews faced yet another factor in dealing with Chinese undocumented migrants.

By September 1994, nearing the close of Operation Able Manner (see chapter 9), Jan C. Ting, writing in *Asiaweek*, stated that President Clinton's "vacillating treatment of the Haitian boat people have shattered the facade concealing the racially discriminatory immigration policy toward refugees." Ting went on to point out that Chinese received the harshest treatment. Clinton's policy, according to Ting, "leaves Chinese boat people as the only nationality subject to repatriation by the United States without any consideration of asylum claims when intercepted on the high seas."[1]

Ting elaborated. "Of the boat people intercepted by the U.S. Coast Guard or Navy on the high seas, Cubans get brought to the United States for resettlement, Haitians get interviews and safe haven—subject to the latest flip-flop of Clinton administration policy—but Chinese get sent back to China without any hearing or opportunity to state their claims for asylum."[2] Given the date of Ting's article, it is a little off about the Cubans (see chapter 10). Ting is correct, however, in pointing out that Cubans have a strong political foundation in South Florida, and the Haitians have the Black Caucus in the U.S. Congress, but the Chinese have no political voice.

By 1998 the *New York Times* noted the former maritime routes for the human smugglers of Chinese had "become a rarity." Instead, the smugglers had "diversified their routes." Border patrol agents began noticing "a gradual increase" in Chinese showing up along the U.S. southwestern border area, according to INS spokesperson Russell A. Bergeron. Furthermore, human traffickers now demanded higher fees from the undocumented Chinese migrants—in some cases at least US$45,000 instead of the $30,000 at the time of the *Golden Venture* incident.[3]

As if to prove Bergeron's comments, three months later, 174 Chinese, looking "confused, scared," came ashore after spending two and a half months at sea on a rat-infested smuggler's ship. The undocumented migrants planned to land in Mexico and illegally cross over the southwestern border. This group contained 153 men, 21 women, and 35 younger people, the youngest about thirteen years old. Intercepted off the northern Mexican coast, negotiations between the United States and Mexico lasted for three weeks before the State Department ordered the ship escorted into San Diego. The *New York Times* reported that it appeared that only 17 of the 174 undocumented Chinese might "have reason to stay in the United States." Sherman Chow, a specialist on Japan and China at the University of California, San Diego, correctly pointed out that "the capture likely would not deter future attempts." As Chow pointed out, "Their idea is: 'Once I pay off my debts, I will be able to go back a rich person.'"[4]

In the spring of 1999, in the far reaches of the Pacific, there occurred a "Guam Boatlift." At first it defied all the patterns known to INS and the

U.S. Coast Guard. Ships containing undocumented Chinese headed toward Guam, not Hawaii or the mainland of the United States. Most unusual, the captains of the ships had instructions "*not* to avoid interdiction." Moreover, the Chinese had paid the price for a passage to New York City.[5]

The complicated story that was finally unraveled by INS and the U.S. Coast Guard began with a Fujianese presence in the Marshall Islands when Chinese industrialists found a loophole. The Commonwealth of the Northern Marianas Islands (CNMI), although a U.S. territory, administered its own labor laws. Willie Tan of the CNMI island of Saipan felt he could escape the tax laws of both the United States and China by establishing clothing factories on the island. He placed labels in the garments saying "made in the U.S.A." Eventually, however, the U.S. Department of Labor and the CNMI cracked down on the factories. "The relationship between the U.S. and CNMI allowed the CNMI to keep the factories and the Chinese aliens in the islands, since they had become an important part of the economy."

Some of the workers found their way to Guam. They established networks to move undocumented Chinese from the island to New York City. Eventually, the smugglers moved "several dozen" per month.

On January 10, 1999, the U.S. Coast Guard's oceangoing buoy tender *Sassafras* (WAGL-401) and the 110-foot patrol boat *Galveston Island* (WPB-1349) intercepted two vessels containing a total of sixty undocumented Chinese and eighteen crewmembers. They escorted the ships into Guam the next day and were met by the INS and a Chinese lawyer from New York City, who were expecting them.

The INS and the territorial government did not have facilities to hold the Chinese, so the undocumented migrants were flown to the U.S. mainland. By February 9, all were in Seattle, where they were granted a prima facie hearing on U.S. soil. A prima facie hearing "is an initial hearing to determine if an alien might have a case for asylum. The alien who passes the prima facie is allowed to remain and work in the U.S. until their asylum hearing, which is usually a year or more later."[6] By February 27, all of the Chinese had passed their hearing and been bonded out. By March 4 they were in New York City.

By March 21 "the leading edge of the Guam Boatlift arrived when an unnamed wooden vessel was grounded on the Guam coast." Within the first two weeks of April, at last 331 undocumented Chinese had arrived in Guam.

The INS quickly realized their mistake of taking the Chinese to the mainland and started to keep them within the islands. Many were sent to Tinian. The *Sassafras* intercepted the fishing vessel *Teesune* on April 16 and escorted it to Tinian. While en route to the island, the undocumented migrants realized the "legal difference between Guam and Tinian in regards to asylum, the latter being a part of CNMI." The U.S. Coast Guard boarding party, although armed but greatly outnumbered, faced a riot when a boy saw the chart and realized their destination. The boarding party managed to convince the Chinese that the boy was wrong and that they were headed toward Guam.

As the numbers continued to grow, "U.S. policy-making remained confused." Eventually, a decision was reached based upon the Illegal Reform and Immigration Act of 1996, which gave the INS the authority to repatriate the undocumented migrants back to China. By June 11 the undocumented migrants began being repatriated in large groups.

Capt. Bernard Moreland, USCG, in his study of Chinese migration in the Pacific, writes that through the 1990s the U.S. policy centered on "treating the snakehead as a criminal and the migrant as an unwitting victim. Replaceable low-level criminals, usually enforcers, were punished while the migrants themselves were rewarded for their behavior with the prize they most sought, work permits allowing them to stay in the U.S. and make money. While it is satisfying to see thugs in prison and 'hard working immigrants' given a break, this policy predictably encouraged more [undocumented] migrants."

One dangerous new route into the United States mainland for undocumented Chinese began showing up in February 1999. In Long Beach, California, INS officers and U.S. Coast Guard personnel discovered eleven undocumented Chinese migrants hidden in cargo containers on board a huge container ship that had just arrived in the California port.

On April 21 the *Seattle Post-Intelligencer* reported nineteen Chinese, "including three juveniles," in a forty-foot container on board the *Sea-Land Navigator* in the nearby port of Tacoma, Washington. Robert Coleman, deputy district director of the INS in Seattle, explained that the container ship had touched at Hong Kong and Kao-hsiung in Taiwan. The nineteen had spent at least two weeks in the soft-topped container. A soft-topped container has a top made of vinyl or other fabric, thus allowing air to flow into the container so the Chinese could breathe. "This is part of a troubling trend," Coleman said. "This fits an existing pattern of soft-top container smuggling."

Considering that a container ship can carry up to one thousand containers, this seems almost a natural route for human smuggling from Asia. It also highlights just how difficult it is for law enforcement organizations to search such ships.

Coleman said that the nineteen Chinese on the *Sea-Land Navigator* had a "horrible trip," even though they "had food and water, but little else in the way of comforts." A spokesperson for Sea-Land, Inc. said the nineteen were "the first stowaways from Asia [for Sea-Land]."[7]

"In the six months prior to May 2000, fifteen containers [were] seized with a total of 126" undocumented Chinese captured. Furthermore, initial research suggests that "2–3 percent of passengers die" en route.[8]

Human smugglers from Asia chose yet another route after 1994. Smuggled Chinese arrived in British Columbia, then were transported by vans across Canada, and finally crossed the Canadian–U.S. border in eastern Canada. One of the routes led through the Mohawk Nation's reservation on New York State's border with Canada.[9]

Ed Offley and Joel Connelly of the *Seattle Post-Intelligencer* reported the use of high technology and cooperation between the United States and Canada in an effort to track smuggling ships across the North Pacific. The reporters wrote that both nations used spy satellites, patrol aircraft, underwater acoustic sensors, and electronic sensors to track ships suspected of smuggling into Canadian waters. Navy officials from both nations, not too surprisingly, did not wish to go into specifics. "It would give an advantage to people we are trying to intercept," said Canadian navy spokesman Lt. David McKinnon.[10]

Despite stepped up surveillance, the container route continued. In January 2000, both the *New York Times* and the *Washington Post* featured articles on the subject. One case concerned the container ship *Cape May*. As the containers from the *Cape May* came ashore on Monday, January 10, 2000, fifteen "dazed, dehydrated and gravely hungry" Chinese staggered out of a container. They pointed to the interior of the container and investigators found the bodies of three men who had died on the trip from Hong

Kong to Seattle. INS official Coleman said, "I've simply never seen people so disoriented, so distraught." In Washington, D.C., Ken Elwood, deputy executive associate commissioner of field operations with the INS, pointed out that rips in the top of the container indicated that the Chinese men had tried to escape from the container but to no avail. Elwood said, "Psychologically this had to be terrible. Evidently they had tried desperately to tear the top off the container and get out. It's horrific to think what happened to them."[11]

Five days after the *New York Times* story, Rene Sanchez, writing in the *Washington Post*, reported that since Christmas at least fifty Chinese undocumented migrants had entered via containers at Long Beach and other large container ports on the West Coast of the United States and Canada. "This is a huge smuggling operation we're up against," said Michael Fleming of the U.S. Customs Service in Long Beach, California, and Los Angeles. "And it's getting harder to discover. There's no way we could look inside most of the containers that come off these ships every day."

Sanchez noted that this is "an old story with a new twist. For decades U.S. Coast Guard and Customs officials on the West Coast have regularly caught groups of young Chinese nationals trying to get smuggled into the country." Many came on fishing vessels. When the human traffickers realized this route was no longer profitable, the smugglers turned to containers.[12]

While some smugglers opted for containers and others tried to bring their human cargo over the Mexican–U.S. border by land, still others continued with the older means of transportation. In January 2000, although U.S. Coast Guard, Customs, and INS officers recognized the increase in container smuggling, the U.S. Coast Guard faced the case of the Taiwanese freighter *Wing Fung Lung* and yet another "old story with a twist."

On December 9, 1999, the 378-foot U.S. Coast Guard cutter *Munro* (WHEC-724), home ported at Alameda, California, intercepted the *Wing Fung Lung* approximately three hundred miles off the coast of Guatemala. What took place over the next six days and nights helped the service declare that intercepting undocumented migrants now had "become a more dangerous business than running down drug smugglers."[13] (This change to violence is also detailed in relation to Cubans in chapter 10.)

The *Wing Fung Lung* case for the U.S. Coast Guard began when the Taiwanese ship, described as a 200-foot fishing vessel with "rusted hull" and a white superstructure, aroused the interest of an aircrew on a U.S. Coast Guard C-130 aircraft patrol. One of the reasons for the pilot's suspicions: no fishing gear was "visible on deck." Furthermore, when the aircraft flew over the vessel, the hatches were open. But when the aircraft made another pass, the hatches were closed, as if they were hiding something.[14]

Capt. Wayne M. Justice, commanding officer of the *Munro*, received a message of the suspicious freighter. Captain Justice, a twenty-two-year veteran with extensive experience in the Caribbean basin, broke off his drug patrol and headed toward the position of the suspect ship.[15]

As the *Munro* neared the fishing vessel, Captain Justice launched the cutter's helicopter to locate the ship. Once spotted, the cutter approached the *Wing Fung Lung*. Bringing the *Munro* near the Taiwanese ship at night, Captain Justice hailed the *Wing Fung Lung* on the radio in English, Chinese, and Spanish, with no response. Justice opted to follow at one nautical mile astern of the fishing vessel during the night.[16]

The next day, Justice ordered a boat from the cutter with a boarding party, which included PO Andrew Ha, a Chinese-speaking crewman, to approach the ship. The master of the ship refused to allow the U.S. Coast Guard to board his ship. Later, a second boat from the *Munro* came alongside the *Wing Fung Lung* and attempted communications via a megaphone. The master had claimed he did not respond to the radio calls because of radio problems.

The ship's master stated that they carried a cargo of plywood. When asked how the plywood was loaded, he said instead that they carried rice. The officer said he shipped a crew of six. The U.S. Coast Guard crew in the cutter's small boat reported they observed at least nine people. The master of the Taiwanese ship refused an inspection boarding. Captain Justice ordered the small boat back to the cutter. He continued to have the *Munro* follow covertly at a distance of ten to twelve nautical miles hoping that the vessel might return to its normal routine. After the C-130 aircraft passed over the *Wing Fung Lung* the second time the ship's crew had closed the hatches. Justice worried that if there were Chinese undocumented migrants on board, the closing of the hatches might make the migrants suffer. Furthermore, if the master of the Taiwanese ship felt the cutter had departed, he might allow the migrants up on deck and could then be spotted. The master turned the *Wing Fung Lung* in a circle to see if he was being followed.[17]

In the morning, the *Wing Fung Lung* stopped. Flares suddenly shot up from the ship. Captain Justice ordered the cutter's helicopter launched for another look at the ship. Back came the pilot's message of "hundreds of people on . . . deck." The pilot also reported the ship "wallowing in the sea" and at least two hundred panicky people on the ship.[18]

The *Munro* then closed on the *Wing Fung Lung*. Captain Justice ordered Lt. (jg) Robert Borowczak to take a boarding party of twenty-five crew members and board the freighter. The weather cooperated, with winds approximately ten knots, seas at two feet, and swells cresting at a low three feet. The visibility remained good, with the cutter's thermometers registering eighty degrees Fahrenheit.[19]

As the boarding party pulled along side the *Wing Fung Lung*, they reported back to the cutter a number of disturbing events. The U.S. Coast Guard people were, of course, not welcomed aboard. A large crowd seemed to be fighting among themselves; whether it was the fishing vessel's crew and the migrants, the boarding party could not determine. Ten years after the events on the *Wing Fung Lung*, Justice, now a rear admiral, recalled that the boarding party "almost had to fight their way on board." They encountered "mass confusion on the ship." Then eight migrants leaped into the sea. This caused a distraction, to say the least.[20]

Once the U.S. Coast Guard's boarding party scrambled aboard the deck of the *Wing Fung Lung*, Lieutenant Borowczak immediately ordered the engineers under his command to check the ship for seaworthiness. The engineering force reported "a foot of water in the engine room" and evidence of an attempt to scuttle the ship. Other members of the boarding party found the only life raft on the ship "partially inflated."[21]

Later, at a debriefing, Captain Justice said, "After they saw our helicopter, the smugglers apparently concluded we were coming after them and decided to sink the ship right there, leaving more than 200 people to their fates while they escaped."[22] Eventually, the *Munro*'s crew pumped out the freighter and the cutter took the ship under tow.

Meanwhile, Lieutenant Borowczak's boarding crew found that more than two hundred Chinese males had lived "without sanitation facilities or bedding" during the long voyage. "I remember going down into the hold and [the Chinese crew had rigged] salt water [to run] down the hull inside the hold and it was full of feces and just unbelievable," said Admiral Justice.

"There were about twenty women on board, . . . all kept topside in their separate cabins, for some sort of servicing manner."[23]

Admiral Justice recalled that U.S. Coast Guard crew kept the men on the forecastle, with fire hoses laid out to spray them with water in case they became unruly. "We tried to treat the women a little better until they started to get unruly. We had our female crewmembers assigned to take care of the Chinese women. [Eventually,] we had to pepper spray some of the Chinese women. That disturbed some of our crew. Somehow pepper spraying women was different than pepper spraying men."[24]

Borowczak and his boarding party, following standard procedures, began searching for the Chinese enforcers who controlled the migrants. "You spot the ones that are bigger, better fed, better dressed," Lieutenant Borowczak later said. "You find the ones with tattoos and the ones who are shouting orders." The boarding party rounded up about a dozen men fitting these descriptions and separated them from the other Chinese.[25]

Fortunately, Lieutenant Borowczak had Petty Officer Ha, the Chinese-speaking crewman from the *Munro*, in his group to translate for him. Borowczak learned that the migrants had not eaten in two days, nor received water for more than twenty-four hours. The boarding party reported the condition of the migrants, and Captain Justice ordered meals sent over to the ship.

Recalling events from ten years past, Admiral Justice remarked that feeding the migrants eventually led to a mistake on his part. He had one crew on the ship the entire day and needed to rotate them. Admiral Justice noted that he sent them over at feeding time. He also sent the same number of people. "The new people didn't really know what they were doing. The snakeheads saw a moment of weakness and acted."[26]

The enforcers began to yell at the migrants, apparently telling the hungry migrants to hurry or they would not receive the food. "People rushed toward the buckets of rice and jugs of water, and began fighting over the food. Almost simultaneously two fires broke out below decks."[27]

Lieutenant Borowczak said later, "We realized we had to get the enforcers out of there or we were going to have a riot on our hands."[28] Two enforcers attacked a boarding party member, who used pepper spray on the enforcers. Other enforcers refused to move. This caused wrestling matches between the boarding party and some of the suspected enforcers. Other suspects "threw feces at the Americans." The boarding party began hitting the resisters in the legs with their batons, which took the fight out of most of the enforcers. Lieutenant Borowczak and another boarding party member, however, ran into even more difficulty. They cornered the apparent head of the enforcers. Admiral Justice recalled that the head enforcer was "a wiry little guy as tough as nails and full of adrenaline." He swung a heavy length of wire. The man charged. Stinging pepper spray to the face did not slow the man. His momentum caused all three to fall to the deck. The trio struggled for a pistol. A shot rang out. Fortunately, the bullet did not strike anyone. The sound of the shot caused two other members of the boarding party to rush to the scene. They swung their batons at the fighting enforcer, which quickly brought him under control.[29]

That night, as Lieutenant Borowczak spent his first night aboard the "floating nightmare," he laid "awake worrying that his crew might not have captured all of the smugglers and wondering what mayhem might come next."[30] Apparently, Lieutenant Borowczak's boarding crew had either isolated and handcuffed all the enforcers or at least taken the fight out of those unidentified that remained because nothing happened for a few days. The U.S. Coast Guard crew erected tarps as awnings to help the Chinese escape the harsh sun. During this period, one of the migrants suffered a concussion and was medically evacuated.

One afternoon Lieutenant Borowczak came on deck to find the migrants tearing down the awnings. Admiral Justice remembered seeing mattresses being flung into the sea and wondering, "Now what are they doing?"[31] Towing the *Wing Fung Lung* did not allow Justice to maneuver the cutter alongside the other vessel.

Several of the Chinese began putting on all the clothing they owned. Having observed the earlier medical evacuation, the migrants concluded the heat might get them off the ship. Several Chinese fainted from the heat.

Lieutenant Borowczak hit upon an interesting solution. In plain view of the migrants, Borowczak had a medical technician establish an intravenous line into one of the fallen Chinese. Borowczak later wryly observed, "They didn't seem too anxious to get stuck with a big needle and went back to behaving themselves."[32]

Nothing untoward happened for the rest of the trip, and the cutter and its tow arrived off the coast of Guatemala. A total of 249 Chinese found themselves repatriated and 4 suspected smugglers brought to the United States to face "a variety of criminal charges."[33]

Eventually, Hsin-Yung Yeh, Yuan Dian Wang, and Jian Zhou Li of the *Wing Fung Lung* were flown to Washington, D.C., and tried there. Captain Justice and Lieutenant Borowczak received orders to serve as witnesses at their trial. All three smugglers received long sentences; each appealed their sentence but lost their appeal.[34]

In 2002 Sheldon Zhang and Ko-lin Chin wrote that smugglers of Chinese used three main routes to bring in their human cargo to the United States. The first route entails reaching Mexico and then somehow illegally crossing the Mexican–U.S. border. Another method "involves flying into the United States either directly or via several transit points outside China." The final strategy was the maritime route. Zhang and Chin believe the "use of air routes, far less hazardous and torturous than the fishing trawlers, has become the preferred choice of transportation for entering the United States by those with connections and financial resources." The professors point out that it appears the maritime route remains "reserved mostly for the peasantry and villagers from small townships . . . [and] is usually considered unacceptable to many urban dwellers and better-educated would-be 'smugglees.'"[35]

As of 2009 the flow of undocumented Chinese continues. "Few doubt the magnitude of the social and legal ramifications were the influx of illegal immigrants to continue from the world's most populous nation."[36] Stanley Rosen, University of Southern California, remarked that this smuggling "has a long history, and its very sophisticated. There's also a lot of money involved."[37] In the case of the *Golden Venture* (chapter 7), much was made of Sister Ping and her wealth from human smuggling. Zhang and Chin had an informant who stated, "Sister Ping was fortunate because she got in the smuggling business early. . . . She was only successful for a short while in the early 1990s, but her days are long gone. I know people in Fuzhou right now who are far more successful than Sister Ping and have made an enormous amount of money."[38]

9 A War without Bullets

Operation Able Manner

> We got stuck in the middle, where there was no right answer. Taking them [the Haitians] got us in trouble. Trying to take them home got us in trouble. Locking them up *really* got us in trouble.
>
> National Security Council official of the Clinton administration in charge of overseeing the Haitian crisis

The Hoover Institution's Senior Fellow Thomas H. Henriksen noted that presidential candidate Clinton's comments on domestic affairs seemed full of "confidence and enthusiasm" while his "views on foreign policy questions belied a sense of both personal unease and disinterest."[1] The attitude toward undocumented migration from the sea during the Clinton administration presents a constantly changing set of policies for Cubans, as discussed in chapter 11, and especially for Haitians. During this confusing time, the Haitian situation caused the U.S. Coast Guard to face its largest peacetime operation since the end of World War II. One officer who participated in the operation called it a "war without bullets."[2]

As pointed out in chapter 5, President George H. W. Bush in 1991 faced a serious situation in Haiti. Jean-Bertrand Aristide became the first popularly elected president in Haiti's history. His term ended eight months later when overthrown by a military coup d'état. President Bush declared the coup a threat to American security, granted asylum to Aristide, and forcibly repatriated those Haitians trying to leave by the sea. Because the camps at Guantanamo were full, the Haitians received no screening.

During the election campaign, Clinton strongly criticized the president's policies on returning the Haitians. As inauguration day approached, Clinton's criticism of Bush's policies began to waver. On November 12 President-elect Clinton said, "I believe there is a legitimate distinction between political and economic refugees. Sending them back to Haiti under the circumstances which have prevailed for the last year was an error." But two days later he said to the Haitian people, "I have been deeply concerned by reports that many of you are preparing to travel by boat to the United States, and I fear that boat departures in the near future would result in further tragic losses of life. For this reason, the practice of returning those who flee Haiti by boat will continue, for the time being, after I become president." The next day, a statement reported: "I will end the practice . . . when I am fully confident I can do so in a way that does not contribute to a humanitarian tragedy."[3]

In Haiti, Luc Salomon, an unemployed father of four, said, "As far as I am concerned, after the good Lord comes Bill Clinton, and as soon as Bill Clinton is sworn in, you'll see me go."

The *Washington Post* on December 3, 1992, reported that the U.S. Coast Guard had intercepted 640 Haitians, "including a woman who was hemorrhaging and had to be airlifted to a Florida hospital." The *Christian Science Monitor* reported four days later that information coming out of Haiti suggested that Clinton's "promise may have done more to spark the hopes of desperate Haitians that it did to win votes at home on an issue few Americans are familiar with."[4]

On January 15, 1993, The *Washington Post* quoted Sen. Daniel Patrick Moynihan (D-NY) as saying, "This week has been rather the clatter of campaign promises being tossed out the window." On the same day, Clinton indicated he would keep the Bush policy in place but, he continued, "I still believe the policy should be changed. . . . Give us a chance to see if we can make it work. I haven't even taken office yet."[5]

Amid the heated charges and rebuttals over what Clinton said, Adm. J. William Kime, commandant of the U.S. Coast Guard, called a press conference in Miami on Friday, January 15, 1993. He announced that the "U.S. Coast Guard will continue to carry out the policies of the government of the United States to protect the safety of lives at sea. In addition, the traditions of my service mandate that we be always ready to deal with any contingency or potential disaster. To that end, I've directed that the Coast Guard deploy significant resources in an effort to prevent the possibility of major loss of life, should a surge of Haitian migrants occur."[6]

Admiral Kime named the effort Operation Able Manner. The commandant said that, even as he spoke, cutters and aircraft were moving into positions around Haiti. Capt. Fred Wilder received the task of controlling efforts off Haiti as fleet commander in the 378-foot cutter *Gallatin* (WHEC-721); he reported to the U.S. Coast Guard District 7 commander, Rear Adm. William Leahy.

When asked if such an operation might hurt other U.S. Coast Guard missions, Admiral Kime said he felt the service had sufficient resources to handle the new mission. A reporter asked if it might not be better to just let the Haitian vessels reach the United States. "We have safely interdicted and rescued over 40,000 Haitians: men, women and children, without the loss of a single life in the interdiction effort. I think certainly by far this the safest, most prudent thing to do."[7]

"If there is a major or even a moderate exodus, people will die," U.S. Coast Guard Lt. Cdr. James Howe said, "Our primary concern is the safety of these people."[8]

The *Los Angles Times* reported that Admiral Kime stressed the operation was "not a blockade" but a "humanitarian move coordinated with both the Bush and incoming Clinton administration." Other officials also "refused to call the mission a blockade, a term with hostile overtones."[9] However, Rick Swartz, an attorney for the National Coalition for Haitian Refugees in Washington, D.C., pointed out, "Whether it's called an encirclement or a white picket fence, a blockade is a blockade. Blockades are acts of war."[10]

Kelly M. Greenhill notes that Able Manner "meant there would be a substantially larger naval presence in the area under the 'humanitarian' Clinton than the 'racist' Bush, who had tasked only two or three cutters . . . since the September 1991 coup."[11]

The first full day into the operation, the news media began to put forth differing stories of the expected exodus. Haitian officials said that they believed the estimates of at least 250,000 Haitians making the attempt to enter the United States after Clinton became president were "overblown." The numbers reflected "the longstanding anxieties of south Floridians and U.S. policymakers about this Creole-speaking Caribbean nation, more than a real threat of a refugee flood."[12]

The *Seattle Times* reported that Cdr. Larry Mizell, the U.S. Coast Guard's liaison officer in Haiti, stated that he expected "some increase in the number of Haitians headed to the United States after Clinton takes office, but hesitated to compare the exodus with May, when President Bush ordered all boat people to be quickly returned."[13] Commander Mizell thought there would be a surge, but that it would not be long term.

On Tuesday, January 19, the Pentagon reported that it had ordered five U.S. Navy ships to support the U.S. Coast Guard's efforts. By Thursday, January 21, Douglas Farah, a reporter for the *Washington Post*, wrote that Operation Able Manner appeared "to be working, at least temporarily." However, Farah also pointed out that Haitians felt "they thought the halt would only last until the United States tired of the Coast Guard patrols or a political settlement was reached returning ousted Jean-Bertrand Aristide to office." Many of the Haitian boat builders also stated they would not leave if Aristide returned to power.[14]

In March President Clinton further changed his rhetoric. He said that "perhaps he had been too harsh on President Bush."[15] However, he felt that his administration was proceeding in the right direction.

By July President Clinton concluded talks on Governors Island, in New York City's harbor, with Haiti's military leaders and pressed for a United Nations agreement that called for the return of President Aristide and democracy by October 30.

The United States dispatched the USS *Harlan County* (LST-1196) with lightly armed Canadian and U.S. troops to implement the October agreement. The military junta of Haiti staged an armed demonstration against the landing at the dock. The week previously, in Somalia, a clan leader's followers attacked and killed U.S. Army Rangers. Not wishing to have a repeat, the Clinton administration ordered the ship to return to the United States. "The message was clear—the United States could be pushed around and humiliated by weak but determined thugs."[16]

The United States successfully urged the United Nations to reimpose sanctions on Haiti in order to force Gen. Raoul Cédras to step down. The Clinton administration sent naval warships to enforce a blockade of arms and oil. Cédras and the junta refused to step down. As the blockade stretched on, the people of Haiti suffered. "Unemployment reached 70 percent. Imported food disappeared." The sanctions also caused "a thousand deaths a month among children under five years of age."[17] All of this, of course, caused Haitians to again take to the boats.

President Clinton threatened the junta with even stronger sanctions if Cédras did not relinquish power by January 15, 1994. When the date passed and nothing happened, both Aristide and Cédras felt Clinton's threats "amounted to mere bluffs."[18] Another inducement by Clinton to the junta again failed.

Clinton faced mounting criticism from all sides for the constant changes and apparent lack of direction. Randall Johnson, the head of the TransAfrica Forum, for example went on a hunger strike in the spring of 1994 "to protest Clinton's lack of a 'moral compass.'"[19]

Rumors in Washington began to circulate of military action against Haiti. The Clinton administration worried about another Somalia. Administration critics, even in the Democratic Party, continued pressing for an armed solution, "impelling the administration to edge glacially toward military intervention."[20]

Clinton again turned to the United Nations, which imposed a near-total trade embargo on Haiti. The White House gave Cédras two weeks to comply with the Governors Island agreement. The junta, caring little for the Haitian people, refused. Again, the date imposed by Clinton came and nothing happened. Under the increasingly harsh conditions in Haiti, at least five thousand fled each week during the summer.

The Clinton administration now changed its policy once again. Two days after the UN Security Council voted on the sanctions, President Clinton announced that the United States would no longer immediately repatriate Haitians. The United States also stopped commercial air travel between the two countries, cut off travel visas, and froze U.S. assets of Haitians.

By midsummer 1994 very strong rumors continued about military action. There was little support for this by Congress or the American public. Aristide called for the international community to remove the military junta. At the end of July the Clinton administration sought and received authorization for an invasion from the UN's Security Council, with no date fixed for the action.

Trying for a last minute diplomatic solution before a military invasion, President Clinton dispatched former President Jimmy Carter, former chairman of the Joint Chiefs of Staff Colin Powell, and Sen. Samuel A. Nunn Jr., (D-GA) to talk to the junta. After the visit, General Cédras agreed to step down.

The invasion—Operation Restore Democracy—proved a peaceful intervention.[21] Media attention on Haiti diminished after the intervention and Aristide's return to power. In effect, this caused the policy of intercepting Haitians at sea to return to the status quo. That is, the U.S. Coast Guard intercepted Haitians, the INS interviewed the Haitians, and those who had no credible fear of returning were treated as economic migrants and returned to Haiti. This policy continues today. However, this does not mean that the problems of Haiti were solved. Indeed, conditions continue to be appalling. One U.S. Coast Guard officer said in 2006, "Things have changed in Haiti. When I first went to Port au Prince, I saw at least twenty bodies lying in the ditches alongside the road. Recently, I returned and saw only twelve."[22]

While the diplomatic and political machinations took place between Haiti and the United States, Operation Able Manner continued. Eventually, seventeen U.S. Coast Guard cutters, nine U.S. Coast Guard aircraft, and five U.S. Navy ships took part in the mission.[23]

The pressure on the U.S. Coast Guard never slackened. At first the statistics later compiled for Operation Able Manner indicated that the numbers of Haitians intercepted between January and June of 1993 were below 200 for each month, but from July 1993 the numbers reached 240. From that month until the end of the mission, the numbers never dropped below that amount.[24] For example, at 3:15 a.m. on Friday, January 29, 1994, a Miami Beach police officer noticed a small group "of what he believed to be . . . Haitians" walking from the beach. The police officer went to a pier to investigate and found a 15-foot rowboat below the pier. He could also hear shouts for help coming from the sea. In the moonlight he could see a boat in the surf about one hundred yards offshore. The police officer quickly radioed the U.S. Coast Guard.

By 3:20 a.m. U.S. Coast Guard units responded from Station Miami Beach, Air Station Miami, and Station Fort Lauderdale. The boat crews prepared "for the worse." Arriving on scene, the boat crews found a 65-foot wooden freighter. Once they established the safety of everyone on board, the largest U.S. Coast Guard boat on scene, a 41-footer, took the freighter under tow. The boat crew estimated "numerous people" on board. This caused the service to divert the 110-foot cutter *Farallon* (WPB-1301), another 110-foot cutter, *Maui* (WPB-1304), and the 270-foot *Seneca* (WMEC-906) to assist.

Eventually, a boarding team from *Farallon* along with an INS agent and interpreter boarded the freighter. The team found twenty-two men, seventeen women, and seventeen children on board the vessel that had been without food for three days. The vessel was towed to Base Miami Beach, and the Haitians were turned over to the INS.

Less than a week later, a HH-65A *Dolphin* helicopter attached to the cutter *Thetis* (WMEC-910) located fifty-five Haitians on a "dilapidated 30-foot sailboat 25 miles southwest of the northern [coast] of Haiti. *Thetis* and the patrol boats *Nantucket* (WPB-1316) and *Nunivak* (WPB-1306) all worked to bring the Haitians onto the *Thetis*. The crews encountered a mother and her two sons. "The youngest son, a two-month old infant, had a high fever. The mother and the other boy were also sick." Helicopters flew the three to the hospital at Guantánamo.

On Sunday, February 7, four Haitians died in the surf trying to make shore near Fort Pierce, Florida.[25] By June 1994 the numbers of Haitians who were intercepted climbed into the thousands per month. The cause of this large increase can largely be blamed upon the military junta not allowing Aristide's return.

Two days later, the bodies of four Haitians—a man, woman, and two children aged five and seven—drowned in the early morning darkness near the central Florida coastal town of Stuart.[26] Border Patrol assistant chief Herbert Jefferson said, "It's a tragedy, but we've come to expect this. This is how desperate these people are to come here. And it's going to continue." Jefferson went on to say that it appeared two boats containing Haitians dropped off their human cargo. The twenty-four survivors of the boat near Stuart were separated by approximately forty miles. The other boatload of thirty-two came ashore outside the grounds of Mar-a-Lago, a beachfront estate owned by financier Donald Trump. As 1994 progressed the U.S. Coast Guard and the other sea services found Border Patrol official Herbert Jefferson's statement that "it's going to continue" to be prophetic.

10 The Human Factor

> Nothing maritime is easy.
>
> Brig. Gen. Michael J. Williams, USMC

The photographic files of the Historian of the U.S. Coast Guard in Washington, D.C., contain wrenching forgotten images of what crews of cutters and small craft saw on the boats of the Haitians. During Operation Able Manner, one senior petty officer working in the public affairs division at headquarters recalled several petty officers and chief petty officers receiving a call to attend a meeting with the captain in charge of the division. A photograph taken by a service photographer on board a cutter in the Caribbean had arrived, and the captain wanted the views of the division on whether to release it.

> Given the refugee crisis faced by the Coast Guard [and the possibility of a Haitian invasion by the U.S.] anything that could be seen as inflaming American public opinion was to be avoided. The photograph could not have been more inflammatory. It showed two Coast Guardsmen [in the water] attempting to rescue a Haitian man.
>
> The expression on the Haitian's face was a combination of horror, terror and desperation. All we had to look at was a Xerox copy, so you couldn't even tell if the man was still alive. We argued for over an hour whether the image should be released. There was no doubt that it would be controversial, but the captain always leaned on the "release it all" school of public affairs,

> and eventually we all agreed. It was later I heard the issue eventually went all the way to the White House, which refused to allow the release of the photo. It was apparently considered so inflammatory that it could start a war.[1]

Those who worked very closely with the Haitians at sea—the crews of U.S. Coast Guard boats, aircraft, cutters, and Navy ships—soon found themselves again faced with people willing to gamble with their lives for the chance to reach the shores of the United States. The numbers of Haitians steadily increased, reaching a crescendo by the summer. Cutter crews also faced other emotional dangers while working on Operation Able Manner. Capt. Michael D. Inman recalled fifteen years later the case of the Haitian ferry *Neptune.*

On Tuesday, February 16, 1993, the 150-foot *Neptune* departed the town of Jeremie on the overnight 120-mile voyage to Port au Prince. The cargo included "75 oxen, some sheep and goats, and sacks of coffee and charcoal." The estimates of the number of Haitians on board the triple-deck ferry ran from fifteen hundred to two thousand. Caught in a storm, the passengers apparently panicked and the ferry capsized. Madeleine Julien said, "The sea was full of people. I kept bumping into drowned people." Poor communications in Haiti prevented anyone from learning the true extent of the disaster until much later.

Captain Inman, then a lieutenant commander and operations officer serving in the 378-foot cutter *Dallas*, remembered that they received information that a ferry had sunk and there were at least two hundred plus people in the water. After the United States received permission to enter Haitian waters, the U.S. Coast Guard provided many units, including aircraft—a C-130, HU-25, and HH-65—along with the 378-foot cutter, a 210-foot cutter, and a 110-foot patrol boat as part of a task force. The service conducted search-and-rescue operations all day. Retrieving the bodies of the Haitians fell to the smaller U.S. Coast Guard units. "The crews of the 210 and the patrol boat took excruciating care to properly take care and protect the bodies. There were no body bags on board, or in theater. There were maybe five body bags in Guantánamo."

Captain Inman vividly recalled a decade and a half later "standing on the bridge wing of the *Dallas* on a full moon night next to then Capt. Jimmy Hull (now vice admiral, retired), and passing close aboard the 210 and seeing on their flight deck eighty green blankets in a line covering the dead Haitians. It is one of those moments that gets your attention, even takes your breath away, and stays with you for a lifetime."

Later newspaper reports indicated that only 285 people survived the disaster. The *New York Times* labeled the capsizing as "one of the world's worst ferry disasters."[2]

Near sunrise of Thursday, April 21, the crew of the U.S. Coast Guard 82-foot patrol boat *Point Barnes* (WPB-82371) viewed "an amazing sight." Ahead of them a wooden 65-foot freighter packed—packed is probably too mild a word—with hundreds of Haitians. In one photograph, so many Haitians crowd the stern of the freighter that one has difficulty in locating the cabin on the vessel. In a bit of unintended understatement, BM1 James Robertson, executive petty officer of the patrol boat, said, "When the sun came up we could see all the people on deck and we knew we had a big case on our hands."[3]

The final count of the Haitians on board totaled 411; recall that this vessel measured only 65-feet in length. Two other patrol boats, *Point Glass* (WPB-82336) and *Manitou* (WPB-1302), and 41-foot boats from U.S. Coast Guard Stations Miami Beach and Fort Lauderdale quickly arrived on scene. Even with these units nearby, such a transfer of so many people on these small units was still considered unsafe. Next, the cutter *Mohawk* (WHEC-913) received orders to leave Key West and proceed to the scene.

The plan developed by U.S. Coast Guard District 7 headquarters focused on stabilizing the scene with the patrol boats and the 41-footers until *Mohawk* arrived. Helicopters from U.S. Coast Guard Air Station Miami brought out gallon jugs of water and lowered them to the patrol boats to pass on to the Haitians. The 41-foot boats brought medical personnel and interpreters to the position of the freighter.

As the day wore on and the sun beat down upon the freighter, problems developed. One Haitian appeared to have an epileptic seizure and another suffered heat exhaustion. Both were placed on board Station Fort Lauderdale's 41-footer and quickly taken ashore.

The *Mohawk* arrived at approximately 10:00 p.m. It took nearly three hours to bring most of the Haitians safely on board the cutter. During the transfer, three more Haitians needed immediate medical attention, and Station Lake Worth Inlet brought them ashore in its 41-footer. By this time the freighter had drifted to near West Palm Beach.

At noon of April 22 the freighter, with the remaining Haitians on board, came into Base Miami Beach. The incident required more than thirty hours of effort, ending finally when at least one hundred South Florida media watched as the Haitians disembarked and were taken away by the INS.[4]

As the numbers of Haitians increased and the political policies remained hazy at best, the sea services of the Department of Defense also faced problems. What "did emerge clearly from Washington was a general reluctance . . . to maintain refugee camps surrounded by barbed wire on an American base [Guantánamo]."[5] The U.S. Marine Corps put into effect a plan of action that stressed a procedure to keep the migrants moving, either back to Haiti or to the United States, but not to a camp.[6] At about this time, President Clinton had decided to stop the direct return of Haitians without interviews and issued orders to have them screened in "facilities in the region" or in ships lying off shore. On May 24, 1994, Brig. Gen. Michael J. Williams, USMC, became commander, Joint Task Force 160 (JTF 160). General Williams received orders to prepare for missions to put Marines on ships for security during shipboard migrant processing, and to establish a facility for processing migrants at Grand Turk Island and maintaining "a presence at Guantanamo to support such initiative."[7]

General Williams first focused on how to process the migrants away from Guantánamo. The Navy sent the large hospital ship USS *Comfort* (T-AH 20) from the West Coast through the Panama Canal to the Caribbean. After a "tortuously complicated set of negotiations," Jamaica agreed to allow the *Comfort* to anchor in its waters. The operational concept had a processing center on the hospital ship. During the processing, the Haitians had to remain on the ship. None could be released into Jamaica.[8]

The operational concept further had U.S. Coast Guard cutters bringing the Haitians they had intercepted to the *Comfort*. There they would receive medical screenings and interviews by INS agents to determine who would be allowed to enter the United States. If allowed into the United States (screened-in), the migrants next were flown to Guantánamo for further processing. Those to be returned to Haiti (screened-out) would be taken by cutters back to Port au Prince. A company of Marines remained on board the *Comfort* to maintain order. Interestingly, if the cutters proved overloaded, JTF 160 had rented a Ukrainian cruise ship, *Gruziya*, at the cost of thirty thousand dollars a day, to transport the Haitians. The *Gruziya* might have been the perfect fit for the operation, but the contract ran out before it could be tested. Instead, the successor, *Ivan Franko*, proved "to be much less capable of meeting the demands of the operation." A company of Marines remained on the *Ivan Franko* to provide security.[9]

There appeared nothing wrong with the Marines' operational concept, but actual operations soon revealed "flaws" in the plan. The flaws centered on the same problems U.S. Coast Guard officers earlier faced in processing migrants aboard cutters, as described by Admiral Brooks in a previous chapter. The operational presumption held that at least five hundred migrants a day would be processed. This "proved wildly optimistic." One problem, for example, was screening for infectious diseases, such as tuberculosis, with only a limited number of x-ray machines. Furthermore, how do you handle patients with infectious diseases in the *Comfort*? The hospital ship had a self-contained heating, ventilation, and air conditioning system. The migrants had to be taken within the ship to be examined for infectious diseases. Once the migrant was within the ship, the *Comfort*'s system would spread the disease throughout the interior of the ship. Someone eventually "found a portable x-ray machine that worked outdoors."[10]

Recognizable by captains of U.S. Coast Guard cutters, other problems concerning sanitation and fresh water soon appeared on board *Comfort*. Because of the hospital ship's huge size, smaller craft could not pull alongside it. General Williams's comment that "nothing maritime is easy," would be echoed by many in the U.S. Coast Guard.[11] Eventually, again because of its huge size, tent camps sprang up on the hospital ship's deck, especially on the flight deck. To Lt. Col. John R. Allen, commanding officer of the 2nd Battalion, 4th Marines, "it looked like the infamous Civil War prison camp at Andersonville." The Marines' official history of their work in the Caribbean during these years remarked, "But [Allen] and the Haitians made it work."[12]

Reports of Haitians killing other Haitians circulated amongst U.S. Coast Guard crews almost from the beginning of the large numbers of Haitians trying to escape from Haiti by the sea back in the 1980s. Lieutenant Colonel Allen soon came face-to-face with this on *Comfort*.

When a U.S. Coast Guard cutter came alongside *Comfort* with migrants, Allen and Luis A. Moreno, an officer of the U.S. State Department, went on board to brief the Haitians through an interpreter about the routine on *Comfort*.

Lieutenant Colonel Allen usually found the mood of Haitians "buoyant and hopeful and often cheered." On this particular cutter, however, he found the mood "noticeably subdued." Both Allen and Moreno asked their interpreter for an explanation. The interpreter revealed that one of the migrant boats had been overcrowded and "some of the men had decided to throw 'excess' migrants overboard." The interpreter pointed at a woman in the helicopter shelter on the flight deck. She clutched her baby, rocking back and forth. The interpreter said, "She was next."

Lieutenant Colonel Allen asked the interpreter if he knew who had thrown the people overboard. As soon as the interpreter said yes, then Allen ordered the Marine reaction force on the *Comfort* to the cutter. "Dressed in helmets, body armor, and riot gear, the force came streaming onto the cutter." After Lieutenant Colonel Allen briefed the noncommissioned officer in charge of the detail, he "pointed to the first suspect and the marines laid hands on him. The effect was electric. The previously subdued migrants leaped to their feet, pointed to the others the interpreter had named and began cheering when they were led away."[13]

As the numbers of Haitians increased, "it became clear the Jamaican option was not working. There was simply too many Haitians."[14] At just this time, the Clinton administration changed the policy so migrants could select to return to Haiti or go to a safe haven, which was not defined but somewhere outside of Haiti. They could stay there until General Cédras stepped down.

Faced with the increase of migrants and the new political policy, General Williams decided to shut down operations with the *Comfort*. He would have the migrants moved to Guantánamo, instead of Jamaica. The remaining Haitians would be taken to the naval base on board the *Comfort*. The Jamaican government protested that the U.S. government had contracted to keep the hospital ship in their waters and to use their facilities for a specific amount of time.

The State Department moved slowly to remove this deadlock. Meanwhile, the approximately one thousand Haitians on board the *Comfort* felt marooned and grew angrier and angrier as time dragged on. The situation led to some Haitians whipping up the migrants into a riot state. The Marines, however, quickly separated the speechmakers, and this effectively ended the tense situation.[15]

It was not until July 20 that the *Comfort* departed from Jamaica and eventually docked in Guantánamo. Once at the naval base, the Haitians did not want to depart the ship and their Marines to the "unknown soldiers waiting on the pier." After much cajoling and entreaties from Marine officers and Red Cross officials, the Haitians departed. Before leaving, the Haitian leaders presented Lieutenant Colonel Allen with a hand-lettered certificate of appreciation "attesting the Marines had accomplished their work."[16]

At the same time that Marines struggled with their part in Operation Able Manner, the U.S. Coast Guard continued its unglamorous work of intercepting badly overloaded *yolas* and dealing with people near the end of their endurance. From June 24 through June 28, 1994, for example, the service intercepted 1,486 Haitians. Jason Vest, writing in the *Seattle Times*, reported that many of the Haitians arrived on the cutters "hungry and dehydrated."[17] Vest wrote, "Out on the hot, hazy waters of the Windward Passage off Haiti, the Coast Guard faced the first challenge in handling the new movement of people." Near sunset, the cutter came upon a small yola that held twenty people on deck and twenty jammed below decks. As the Haitians came on board the *Hamilton*, "the dazed-looking Haitians slumped against one another. Several had to be helped aboard the ship by crew members, all of whom wore surgical masks and latex gloves." One officer said, "They're too dehydrated to walk." Few had any possessions, and only "a few had shoes." The *Hamilton*'s crew made quick medical examinations.

As they "gulped paper cup after paper cup of water," the Haitians, through interpreters, told of being at sea for three days. They had run out of food and water the previous day.

Cdr. Robert Reininger, the executive officer of the *Hamilton*, said, "It feels as if they have got all these boats and we don't have enough ships. Some of the stuff happening here is just amazing." Commander Reininger's comment proved prophetic. A few days after the article appeared, the cutter's crew faced a difficult case that stretched the crew.[18]

The case began near the end of June 1994 when the Haitian 55-foot sailing vessel *Merci Jesus* departed Haiti with an amazing 468 Haitians crammed into the vessel. That is at least eight people per foot of the *Merci Jesus*. On July 1, the U.S. Coast Guard cutter *Hamilton* received a report from an aircraft of a grossly overloaded sailing vessel. Once the cutter located the *Merci Jesus*, the commanding officer sent over two rafts to make contact with the Haitian vessel. (The "rafts" described by Terry Rey were probably the cutter's rigid hull inflatable boats.) Twelve years later, Rey recalled that "each of the rafts contained a rescue swimmer, a Marine, a captain [an officer], a driver [coxswain], and a Haitian Creole interpreter." Rey served as interpreter on one of the rafts. The crews of the rafts quickly passed over lifejackets to the Haitians.[19]

The transferring of the Haitians began with each raft holding at least ten passengers. "The seas were three to six feet, and there were sharks circling *Merci Jesus*."[20] Ferrying no more than twenty people at a time, of course, consumed a great deal of time. The commanding officer of the *Hamilton* decided to bring the Haitian craft and the cutter closer together.

Rey recalled that by this time the skies cleared and the strong Caribbean sun beat down upon the scene. On board the *Merci Jesus* the passengers were "vibrant with glorious hymns of thanks and praise to the Virgin Mary . . . , and 'Queen of the Seas, Mother of Haiti.'" The "chanting voices of hundreds of sun burnt and exhausted but prayerfully hopeful black people in blazing orange life jackets rose toward the scorching Caribbean sun" moved Rey. Then he noted a "tall U.S. Marine" standing next to him "in tears."[21]

Once alongside the *Merci Jesus*, the crew of the *Hamilton* rigged two rope ladders (Jacob's ladders) for the Haitians to scramble up onto the cutter's deck. The process suddenly came to halt when someone spotted a body lying face down in the water near the sailing vessel.

The crew of the *Hamilton* lowered a stretcher and brought up the body, a boy. Two U.S. Coast Guardsmen "miraculously" revived sixteen-year-old Frantz Lubin. Upon reviving, Lubin asked for "his lost rubber sandals, his lone worldly possessions." Lubin's mother and father had been killed in the village of Au Boigne the week before.[22]

Professor Rey noted that the cutter *Hamilton* "developed a kind of mythology among some would-be Haitian *botpipel* [boat people]." An ABC television reporter noted that *Hamilton* was believed to be the "first cutter to intercept a Haitian sailboat." The Haitians did not have words for Coast Guard, so they spoke of when the *Hamilton* shows up.[23]

On July 3, Jason Vest, writing for the *Washington Post*, observed, "Of all the key players in the Haitian crisis, perhaps none have a tougher role than the Coast Guard crews who patrol the Windward Passage. While the U.S. Navy enforces the trade embargo against Haiti . . . , the Coasties, as they call themselves, have the more vexing job of loading and intercepting Haitian refugee boats."[24]

As if the case of the *Merci Jesus* did not prove Commander Reininger's comment about amazing things happening during Operation Able Manner, reporter Vest detailed what took place on the 210-foot cutter *Dependable*. Late on a hot evening, the cutter crew came upon another small, overloaded wooden sailboat. Following normal procedures, the commanding officer ordered the cutters RHIBs to approach the Haitian boat.

The *Dependable*'s boat crew drew near to the sailboat. They heard a man talking in "loud, almost threatening tones, desperation saturating his voice." He held a baby near the gunwale of the sailboat.

"This guy was holding an infant over the side, threatening to throw it overboard if we were going to send them back to Haiti," said Lt. David Ford. "Then the master of the ship said, 'If we're going to die, we'd rather die at sea than back there.' We managed to calm them down and get them all off safely, but the whole thing was really troubling."

Very few writers accompanied U.S. Coast Guard crews during Operation Able Manner. Vest was one of the few who recognized that "the difficulty goes beyond the mere physical task. There is the human factor."

CPO James "Doc" Amster, the cutter *Hamilton*'s medical corpsman, said, "When you see a 45-foot boat with between 50 to 200 people who've been at sea for days, in this heat and with minimal food and water, it becomes pretty clear to you that these are very desperate folks. It's obvious that things are horrible in Haiti. But I try not to think about that. I concentrate on making sure they're in better shape when they leave this cutter than when they came on."

Normally, the *Hamilton*'s home port was San Pedro, California, but it had been deployed to the Caribbean in the service's efforts during the operation. Weapons technician Alyar Rissanen had worked Haitian operations for two years before transferring to the cutter. He felt he had seen the end of migrant operations.

Commenting on his first experiences with Haitians, Rissanen said, "It made me think. I was a spoiled kid, and then I saw these people; it made me realize just how good we have it in America. I think that's why they keep coming—because they have hopes and dreams, kind of the same way my ancestors came to the U.S., looking for a shot at something better."

Rissanen, and many other U.S. Coast Guard crews, felt "troubled." He believed that taking the Haitians off the overloaded, leaky boats was a humanitarian act, but he had "reservations" about what happened when the cutter crews turned the Haitians over to the immigration people. "Sometimes I worry about what's going to happen to them. I've been to Port au Prince, and I'm afraid to get off the ship. I'm sure they're more afraid than me, for good reason."

Despite being "troubled," the crews continued to do their mission. As mentioned earlier, most of the times the number of Haitians observed on the deck of a yola proved only a small percentage of those on the craft. "One rule of thumb is, multiply the initial head count by the boat's length and you'll get the actual number of Haitians," said Lt. Tex Coffey. "It's not uncommon for over 200 people to be wedged on a 40- or 50-foot boat."

By the time Operation Able Manner reached full swing, the procedures for handling Haitians on larger cutters had evolved. The cutters approached to within five hundred yards of a migrant boat. Then the cutters sent small boats to pass out lifejackets to the Haitians. Once the Haitians were in lifejackets, then the boats brought back small numbers of Haitians to the cutter.

ET John King's duties for migrant operations on the *Hamilton* centered on inspecting the Haitians small amount of possessions—their bundles. "I feel bad about doing it," said King. "I don't like people going through my stuff, but we have to do this for safety."

King pointed that some carried clothing in their bundles, but "many just carry bundles of food." Any knives he found went over the side. The most common item in the bundles was cans of condensed milk. "A lot of them have Bibles, which they keep, but we throw other trinkets, like voodoo powder, overboard," King said.

King went on to relate that previously one Haitian performed a voodoo dance and placed a curse on the ship. The electronics technician said no one felt any ill will against the Haitians for this, but since the increased boat activity, some "are wondering if his mojo was really working."

The sight of Haitian children gave most U.S. Coast Guard people pause.

"I'm hardened to a point, but when I see a baby being passed from a raft up to the ship, I'm not going to get emotionally involved, but I feel real sad," said Quartermaster First Class (QM1) Kathy Hoyt, a fourteen-year U.S. Coast Guard veteran. "And when [the Haitians] see us, they'll change into their best clothes. There's something sad about that too."

Hoyt said she did not like to look into the Haitian's eyes. "Most of the time, they're absolutely blank. Given what they've gone through, I guess this isn't surprising. As much as I keep it at arms length, those looks can get to me."[25]

By Saturday, July 9, the headline of the Portsmouth, Virginia, newspaper, the *Virginian-Pilot*, reported that the number of Haitians intercepted stood at 9,687, and, according to the paper, it was "the busiest time in two centuries of Coast Guard history."[26] The article went on to explain that the sea services had intercepted 20,698 Haitians so far during 1994, with 12,345 early in the month of July. The record for a single day came on July 4, when 3,247 were rescued.

The commandant of the U.S. Coast Guard, Adm. Robert Kramek, praised his crews. "The men and women of Operation Able Manner have had little rest, no time for port calls or holiday routine. But, without complaint, they continue, as their predecessors have done for nearly 204 years."

Admiral Kramek pointed out the actions of the *Hamilton*. He also mentioned that the cutter *Harriet Lane* (WMEC-903) intercepted a 34-foot sailboat with an amazing number of Haitians on board—134, including 28 children. The craft had only two inches of freeboard. On the same day, another sailboat sank alongside the cutter *Escape* (WMEC-6), putting twenty-eight into the sea. "All, including an infant, were saved."[27]

By October of 1994, with Aristide restored to the presidency, the numbers of Haitians began to taper off—although Haitians continue to make their desperate voyages up to the present day. Even as the numbers of Haitians began to diminish, the U.S. Coast Guard crews had little time to reflect on what they had accomplished as another large migration flow began from Cuba, beginning yet another mass migration: Operation Able Vigil.

11 Balseros

Operation Able Vigil, Part 1

> When [the rafters] hear that only four of every 10 make the trip, they say that gives them hope. They think a forty percent chance at freedom is better than no chance in Cuba.
>
> Arturo Cobo, director, Transit Center for Cuban Refugees, Key West, Florida

Cubans continued trying to flee their country by sea after Mariel, although nothing approached the hectic months of the boatlift. In fact, the rest of the 1980s remained relatively uneventful. For eight years, beginning in 1982, the U.S. Coast Guard intercepted 493 Cubans. The 1990s, however, brought about a period as stressful as Mariel. During the first year of this decade, the service intercepted 443, nearly equaling the number intercepted during the previous eight years. The U.S. Coast Guard's statistics on the number of Cubans escaping from their country steadily increased, reaching a peak in 1994.[1] That year marked a number of important events: a large influx of undocumented migrants, deemed a "slow Mariel;" a major new policy concerning Cubans; and what is now called the *balsero* (rafter) phenomenon.

On Tuesday, May 7, 1991, the service stated that for the previous week they had recorded thirty cases of intercepting Cubans, totaling 130 people. Three cases during that single week illustrate the mix of duty facing U.S. Coast Guard people during the three-year period from 1990 to 1993.

On Monday, April 1, at 6:45 a.m., the radio watch stander at Station Islamorada received a call from the master of the fishing vessel *Ocean Runner* reporting he had come upon a twenty-foot steel vessel *El Coral*, home ported in Havana. The master of the fishing vessel reported twelve Cubans on board and in good condition. The station dispatched a 41-foot boat to tow the *El Coral* and the ten men and two women on board into their station.

On the same day, at 9:00 p.m., the U.S. Coast Guard received a radio report from the pleasure craft *Mac II* stating they had recovered two Cubans from a raft near Elliott Key, approximately twenty-five miles south of Miami. When the service debriefed the two men, they learned that their raft had been in company with another raft of two men. On the night of Tuesday, April 30, the rafts had become separated, tragically, within sight of land.

U.S. Coast Guard Air Station Miami launched an HH-65 helicopter, number 6520, to begin searching for the missing raft. It searched until low on fuel and then returned to base. Refueled, the next day the helicopter crew spotted and retrieved the body of one of the missing Cubans. The search continued for the missing man but without results. The search was eventually called off.

On Saturday, May 4, Station Islamorada received a radio call from the master of the fishing vessel *Grumpy* reporting they had taken on board two persons from a raft and requested U.S. Coast Guard help. The station dispatched their 41-foot boat to the area and notified U.S. Coast Guard Air Station Miami. The air station again sent helicopter 6520 to the scene and hoisted the twenty-six- and twenty-five-year-old Cuban men and landed at Station Islamorada. Members of the station's crew drove the men to the hospital. INS later took the Cubans into custody. Both men were suffering from saltwater exposure and sunburns. One man had been so thirsty he had drunk seawater. The men told the U.S. Coast Guard they had departed from near Havana and had spent eight days on their raft.[2]

Still, this did not approach Mariel. What is evident, however, is that unlike Mariel, when Cubans usually made the transit across the straits in pleasure craft or chartered fishing vessels, a new means of escaping the island entered the picture. By the 1990s, homemade rafts using inner tubes, packing material, planks, and anything that floated now appeared in the water between Cuba and the United States. Lashed together, the devices used for flotation usually also had crudely fashioned paddles and a sail. In such flimsy "craft," Cubans attempted crossing the dangerous ninety miles across the Florida Strait. The largest usage of this type of craft came in 1994 and became known as the balsero (rafter) phenomenon. "But many [did] not survive the trip," said Arturo Cobo, director of the Transit Center for Cuban Refugees in Key West. Cobo "estimated that only four of every 10 who leave the island survive to make it to the United States. . . . But when [the rafters] hear that only four of every 10 make the trip, they say that gives them hope. They think a 40 percent chance at freedom is better than no chance in Cuba, no chance to eat, no chance to work, no chance to live." Rafters continue today but in far fewer numbers than in 1994.[3]

The number of Cubans trying to escape from Castro's government escalated throughout the first three years of the 1990s, from 443 in 1990 to 2,882 by 1993. In 1993, as shown in chapter 8, Haitians in increasing numbers also tried to enter the United States, which led to Operation Able Manner. As this influx of undocumented Haitian migrants slowly wound down, events in Cuba in 1994 caused another major operation in the Straits of Florida.[4]

By the summer of 1994, some analysis pointed out that the situation in Cuba seemed dangerously close to those that heralded Mariel. First, Fidel Castro's government again faced a deteriorating economy. Its gross domestic product "had declined 35 percent between 1989 and 1993 following the demise of the Soviet Union" and its guaranteed trade, plus Castro had announced "the worst sugar harvest in decades."[5] Second, a series of incidents from May to August took place at embassies in Havana. On May 28, more than one hundred Cubans forcibly entered the Belgian ambassador's residence. Other entries at the German and Chilean embassies happened in July and August.[6] Third, the most probable catalyst focused on hijackings. The incidents involving embassies did not involve violence. Hijacking proved another matter.

On Wednesday, July 13, 1994, Fidencio Ramel Prieto Hernández put a night watchman of a harbor tug "to sleep with thorazine" and helped load about sixty-three people aboard the tug in Havana harbor. Built in 1879, and unsafe for the open sea, the tug had only enough lifesaving equipment for four people. Nevertheless, the hijackers had the vessel put out to sea while being pursued by three other tugs and a Cuban patrol boat. In the pursuit, thirty-two people drowned, including Prieto, when two vessels of the Cuban Border Guard rammed the tug. The tragic attempt began a spate of hijackings.[7]

Thirteen days later, hijackers took control of a ferry with eighty to one hundred people on board. The hijackers threw some of the passengers overboard and then forced the vessel out to sea. The U.S. Coast Guard intercepted the ferry before it reached Key West. At least half of the passengers chose to continue on to Florida while the remainder opted to return to Havana.[8]

On August 3 and 4, hijackers took a second and third ferry. In the latter case, a police officer died in the takeover. On August 5, crowds gathered at the ferry dock listening to rumors about another Mariel and wondering whether there would be another ferry to transport them across the harbor. A riot soon ensued. Kelly M. Greenhill states that this period proved "some of the worst civil unrest Cuba had witnessed in decades."[9]

At the same time, Castro watched as the United States welcomed those escaping his country by sea. United States–based organizations such as Brothers to the Rescue, which flew small private aircraft over the Straits of Florida looking for rafters and directing help to any Cuban in distress, helped cause some of the rise in the statistics of undocumented migrants. This particular organization gave many rafters a better sense that they might actually make a safer attempt to reach the United States. (More on Brothers to the Rescue in chapter 13.) A decline in the Cuban Border Guard abilities and resources to pursue illegal migrants also helped spur on those who wished to leave. All of these factors led to the U.S. Coast Guard intercepting 3,721 Cubans during the first six months of 1994.[10]

After the riots, Castro appeared on television. Claiming the hijackings a part of U.S. policy to foment revolution in Cuba, Castro also pointed out that the United States did not live up to its agreement on the number of visas it would issue. Furthermore, Cuba "could not continue to guard the coasts of the United States."[11] Welcoming the rafters only helped encourage Cubans to leave their country. If the U.S. policy did not change, Castro threatened to withdraw the Border Guards and allow any Cuban who wished to escape via raft to depart.

Greenhill believes that "Castro transformed an internal crisis that began with boat hijacking and a riot in Havana, into an American foreign and immigration policy crisis, in which the U.S. was forced to provide refuge to tens of thousands of Cubans it intercepted—at a cost of US$1 million per day; and he got a new U.S.-Cuban immigration accord."[12]

Three days later another hijacking took place. Leonel Macias hijacked a Cuban government vessel, shot and killed a navy lieutenant, and threw his body overboard. Macias then ordered two other navy people to swim for shore. The hijacker then took the vessel, picked up twenty-three migrants, and headed for the United States. Cuban diplomats called for the United States to return Macias and others for murdering a military officer.

On Wednesday, August 10, U.S. government officials, now clearly worrying about another Mariel, issued a warning that United States citizens who traveled to Cuba to pick up Cubans faced arrest and confiscation of their vessels. Officials also hinted that President Clinton might invoke emergency powers to deal with such attempts.

Florida politics now entered the increasingly tense Cuban situation. In the midst of an extremely tough reelection campaign, Gov. Lawton Childs knew how voters of his state felt about the immigration issue. The people of Florida had just experienced a situation with Haitian boat people, now Cuba loomed. The *Wall Street Journal* observed: "Illegal immigration is a hot button issue all around the U.S., but it is particularly so in Florida, where Mr. Childs has sued the federal government to recover costs accrued by the state for the costs of dealing with illegal immigrants."[13]

Reacting as if another Mariel appeared imminent, Childs insisted on action by the federal government. At the beginning of Clinton's presidency, his administration had drawn up a plan for mass migration dubbed Operation Distant Shore. Childs wanted the plan enacted. Such a strong stand might make a difference in the close race with Jeb Bush. The Clinton administration balked. The federal decision makers did not see a Mariel. Moreover, they claimed they had everything under control. Childs then declared a state of emergency for his state, causing the federal government to react.

Meanwhile, on Thursday, August 11, federal officials announced that, based upon testimony of the people aboard the hijacked Cuban government vessel, including Macias's 15-year-old girlfriend, they believed the hijacker shot in self-defense. The attorney general of the United States, Janet

Reno, hinted "that no legal action [would] be taken against Macias." The *Miami Herald* called Macias "a hero." On this same day, an official from the Department of State related that the U.S. Coast Guard would take a leading role in "interdicting and rescuing any influx of refugees in the Straits of Florida."[14]

Not too surprisingly, the next day Castro accused the United States of covering up a crime committed by Macias and of not enforcing the law. On this same day, the U.S. Coast Guard intercepted 158 Cubans. On Saturday, August 13, the White House received a "CIA report estimating that numbers were building toward [the] level of 1980 Mariel boatlift."[15]

On Tuesday, August 16, Castro carried through on his threat to remove the Border Guard and allow any Cuban to leave by the sea. The numbers of Cubans at sea quickly increased. Not long thereafter, at many of the beaches in Havana and Cojimar—where Ernest Hemingway kept his boat, the *Pilar*—people launched rafts in full view of cameras. Crowds on shore watched, helped, and cheered on the balseros. A study of fifty rafters at the U.S. Naval Base, Guantánamo, revealed that twelve rafters launched from Cojimar and seven from Havana. (Cojimar is approximately sixteen kilometers [ten miles] east of downtown Havana.)[16]

By Thursday, August 18, Governor Childs continued to press that Florida faced a mass migration crisis. The governor claimed that the Clinton administration was "in denial" while the federal government claimed that the situation was "manageable." Childs then declared a state immigration emergency, which allowed him to mobilize the state's National Guard and to "temporarily detain the refugees for processing."[17]

Childs's reaction forced a meeting of the Clinton administration's foreign policy advisors. Of the eight attendees, none "were considered experts on Cuba." The high-level conference came away with the recommendation that the United States needed to "demagnetize" from the constant flow of migrants, and that the country "could not be harsher on the Cubans (by sending them back to Castro) than it was on the Haitians." Anthony Lake, of the National Security Council, briefed President Clinton on the conference's advice. The president "gave his approval to the policy reversal." At the Department of State, Cuban specialists "used one word to describe their reaction to the new policy—*shocked*."[18] The new policy quickly led to what is now popularly reported in the media as the "wet foot, dry foot" policy.

(The policy allows Cubans who reach U.S. dry land to remain in the country; those who are intercepted at sea, and are not proven political refugees, will be deported.)

Four years after the change, Jonathan C. Smith, writing in the *Presidential Studies Quarterly*, discussed why President Clinton reversed this more than three-decades-long policy. Part of Smith's thesis noted that it was "likely" that Clinton's experiences with Mariel shaped his decision. According to Clinton's advisors, the president had two overriding thoughts during the 1994 incident: "No more Mariels" and "remember Fort Chaffee."[19]

As will be recalled, Mariel took place during 1980, also an election year. Many of the Cubans were placed in federal installations, including Fort Chaffee, Arkansas. At just this time, Governor Clinton of Arkansas sought reelection.

A group of about three hundred Cubans tried to escape from the Fort Chaffee installation on June 1, 1980. Most were quickly rounded up. After being placed back in the camp, they rioted. Governor Clinton put the National Guard on alert. Although the riot was quickly quelled and the rioters punished, most of the public believed that the Cubans were out of control. This reflected badly on Clinton, who was already smarting from resentment about recent state tax increases.

Clinton lost his reelection by four points. Dick Morris, a Clinton political advisor, said that this "defeat was really the seminal experience in [Clinton's] career." Clinton, according to Smith, "felt he had lost the election, in part, because of the Fort Chaffee riots."[20]

Greenhill, in her study of the 1994 incident, points out that part of Operation Distant Shore called for relieving the pressure of an influx of Cubans on Florida by shipping the migrants to different military bases throughout the United States. "Clinton reportedly 'went ballistic,' yelling 'Are you nuts? Do you think I am going to do [that] again?'"[21]

In his autobiography, Clinton wrote that while the situation concerning Cuba escalated, he attended a dinner at which the writer Gabriel Garcia Márquez attempted to convince the president to lift the embargo. Clinton asked Márquez to relay to Castro that the Cuban president had already cost Clinton "one election. He can't have two."[22]

None of the concern about reelection, of course, came out in President Clinton's press conference held on Friday, August 19, to announce the new

Cuban policy. Instead, he spoke very briefly about the Cuban situation. He categorized the Cuban government's action as "a cold-blooded attempt to maintain the Castro grip on Cuba, and to divert attention from his failed Communist policies." Clinton said that the "United States will do everything within its power to ensure that Cuban lives are saved and that the current outflow of refugees is stopped."[23]

President Clinton continued: "Today, I have ordered that the illegal refugees from Cuba will not be allowed to enter the United States. Refugees rescued at sea will be taken to our naval base at Guantánamo, while we explore the possibility of other safe havens within the region."

Clinton went on to state that he had "directed the Coast Guard to continue its expanded effort to stop any boat illegally attempting to bring Cubans to the United States. The United States will detain, investigate and, if necessary, prosecute Americans who take to the sea to pick up Cubans. Vessels used in such activities will be seized." After thanking Governor Childs, the Florida congressional delegation, the Coast Guard, and the INS for their help and efforts, the president moved on to comments concerning a crime bill.[24]

Far away from Miami, the *Seattle Times* reported that on the streets of "Little Havana in Miami," some Cubans shouted, "Down with Clinton!" while others agreed with the policy "as long as the intention is to keep Fidel Castro on the run." Some weeping relatives of Cubans in Miami "called the new policy a cruel end to three decades of special treatment."[25]

The reactions to this new policy among the Cubans in their native country seemed predictable. Maria Newman of the *New York Times* found one woman who said, "I am a Fidelista. We must have patience with him, because he will come through for us." But others took a very different view. One man said, "What do you know, my love? Do you know what it's like to live under a dictatorship? You outsiders come and stay in your hotels and you eat your food that most Cubans can't eat and you don't see that this is all a circus, a farce, a disaster." The man went on to explain to Newman why there is no protest in Cuba: "Remember that Mr. Castro is an intelligent man. He has created the most perfect system of repression in the world."[26]

By Friday, despite radio broadcasts that Cubans detained at Guantánamo would have to return home to gain entry into the United States, there "seemed to remain an article of faith along the shores east of Havana that being picked up by the United States Coast Guard and taken to Guantanamo would mean some kind of priority on the list of people seeking to immigrate."[27]

One twenty-two-year-old Cuban told Tim Golden of the *New York Times*, "I would rather be locked up in Guantanamo than here with Fidel. I love this country—I am Cuban—but you cannot live here anymore."[28]

A thirty-year-old automobile mechanic, as he prepared to shove off in a raft, proved the most prophetic. "The people who are going to get in are the ones who get to Guantanamo." As events later unfolded, he was proved correct.[29]

A cutter's crew never knew what the next case might bring, even if it meant working with a different group of undocumented migrants. Take, for example, an incident that occurred during the work of the 270-foot cutter *Seneca* (WMEC-906), commanded by Cdr. Arthur E. Brooks, USCG. Commander Brooks also held the title of Commander, Task Unit 44.7.9. His mission was to prevent undocumented Cubans from entering Florida. On Saturday, August 19, 1995, the crew of the *Seneca*, carrying out their orders, finished the work of boarding vessels between 2:00 to 4:00 a.m.[30]

Meanwhile, an early-morning U.S. Coast Guard aircraft patrol flight located a Cuban sailing vessel headed north toward Cay Sal Banks. Both *Seneca* and the 110-foot patrol boat *Monhegan* (WPB-1305) changed courses to intercept. *Seneca* had a HH-65A helicopter on board to help locate the Cuban vessel. Eventually, Commander Brooks's cutter had twenty-seven undocumented Cubans on board.

As both crews of the *Seneca* and *Monhegan* worked on the Cuban vessels, Commander Brooks learned via message traffic of a Haitian freighter in distress in the Bahamas with at least two hundred to three hundred people on board. Because the vessel remained a long distance from their operational area, the crews focused on their own cases.

Once the helicopter returned to *Seneca*, however, Coast Guard District 7 released Commander Brooks's command from its duties and diverted the cutter to the Northwest Channel, Bahamas (north of Nassau), to intercept the Haitian freighter. More information filtered to Brooks. The freighter, some 60 to 70 feet in length, had between two hundred to three hundred people on board. It had been sighted by a Bahamian mail boat, which called the Royal Bahamian Defense Force (RBDF). A RBDF patrol boat tried to intercept the Haitians, but "they did not want to be interdicted in the Bahamas because the locals treated them very badly and the crew threatened to throw babies over the side if the Bahamians came too close." The freighter proceeded out into the Northwest Channel with a fifteen-degree list. "The situation was critical because they could roll at any second, leaving all of [the] non-swimming Haitians in the water."

The U.S. Coast Guard District 7 staff made a major effort to divert units to the scene. They sent a C-130 aircraft to fly cover and ordered the patrol boats *Point Glass* (WPB-82336) and *Farallon* plus *Monhegan* to the scene. Commander Brooks shaped *Seneca*'s course to the scene with orders that he should "assume On Scene Commander and come up with a way to get all these people off safely, without rolling the boat or dumping a lot of them in the water."

Commander Brooks called a planning session. The plan that eventually developed had U.S. Coast Guard aircraft drop some deployable rafts because they held about twenty people each and would be easier for untrained people to enter or hold onto the lifelines attached to the rafts.

Meanwhile, the *Seneca*'s small rigid hulled inflatable boats (RHIB) would make the first approach to the freighter with interpreters to calm the Haitians and encourage them to sit still. Once they were calmed, the cutter's RHIBs would move in with lifejackets, floats, and life rings. The patrol boats would remain a slight distance away, ready to rush in if the freighter rolled. During the early morning hours, U.S. Coast Guard helicopters from Florida brought in the deployable rafts and two interpreters. Now everyone waited for first light.

Sometime during the night the Haitians decided to put everyone on the beach in the Bahamas. They ended up just off Hawk's Nest Cay. Commander Brooks received information "that all the Haitians were safely ashore and therefore a completely Bahamian problem." However, the U.S. Coast Guard District 7 staff told Commander Brooks "to continue in case the vessel proceeded toward Miami with some Haitians aboard."

Fourteen years later, Brooks, now an admiral, recalled, "The morning was clear and bright with a 10–12 knot northeast wind and slight northeast swell." Hawk's Nest Cay "is a fairly small rock, with a small beach, just offshore from the much larger Harbour Cay. Harbour Cay has a small town with an airport and several very large, opulent mansions. . . . The scenery was breathtaking, classic Bahamas."

By 8:30 a.m., when *Seneca* arrived and Commander Brooks took over as on-scene commander, "about 12 Haitians had managed to make it to Hawk's Nest Cay in a small skiff, but [northeast] winds and swells were dragging the [freighter] ashore. As the vessel rolled in the surf, it was very close to capsizing," with the possibility of everyone on board drowning. The RBDF vessel *Marlin* tried to pass a towline to the freighter, but Haitians jumped or fell into the sea with every effort. Commander Brooks requested the *Marlin* to stop until he could maneuver *Seneca* into position.

The cutter's RHIB started toward the freighter with interpreters and all the flotation devices the craft could carry. The Creole speakers managed to calm the Haitians. Soon afterward U.S. Coast Guard crewmembers from *Seneca* and the patrol boats passed the flotation devices—lifejackets and rafts—to the Haitians.

By the time all the Haitians had their lifejackets on, the freighter now lay a close fifty yards "off the beach and the surf line." Brooks maneuvered *Seneca* as close to the freighter as possible and started to bring the RHIBs with the Haitians in on both the port and starboard sides of the cutter. Brooks later said that the normal plan for Haitian operations is to use two boats and "approach simultaneously from opposite directions. If you approach from only one side the Haitians rush to that side and may overturn their vessel."

When the *Seneca* had about 120 Haitians aboard, Brooks recalled, "three things occurred that stymied us." First, the RHIBs brought aboard some "very, very sick people who had to be hoisted in stokes litters [a stretcher-like device]. [There were] three in three different boats." Second, the U.S. Coast Guard officer in one of the cutter's RHIB became "very concerned about the freighter going into the surf line and was anxious to tow it off." Third, the RBDF *Marlin* reported a Haitian attempting to commit suicide by jumping over the side. The RBDF craft and the patrol boats took care of the jumper while *Seneca*'s crew worked with the other Haitians. One of the emergency medical technicians (EMTs) dove "in 25 feet of water to pull the Haitian to the surface" and all the EMTs began CPR. This forced Commander Brooks into a difficult decision: the EMTs on the patrol boats requested the *Seneca*'s hospital corpsman to help them with the jumper.

"Because I knew," recalled Brooks, "that [the jumper] had been underwater for over five minutes, [and the EMTs]had been doing CPR for over 10 minutes without a response, and because we had 4–6 [Haitians] literally dying in our hanger, I told them that I couldn't give them a corpsman."

Eventually, through some very good seamanship involving a boat from the cutter, the freighter was pulled from the danger area and all the Haitians brought on board *Seneca*. Helicopters evacuated two very serious medical cases. Meanwhile, during the final stages of bringing the Haitians on board *Seneca*, the cutter drifted close to a reef in only twenty feet of water. Commander Brooks broke off operations until he maneuvered the cutter to safety.

As the freighter slowly emptied of its human cargo, a boarding team from the patrol boat *Monhegan* began to search the vessel. A grisly scene awaited the crewmembers. They found four dead Haitians below decks, each "had been apparently executed. One had his throat cut while his hands were tied behind his back. Two others had their heads crushed by blunt objects. . . . The fourth with his ear cut off and jaw broken so severely that the bone stuck out of his face, was determined to be alive. . . . The horror was compounded because several of the dead had parts missing, including one man's leg, apparently due to cannibalism." The injured man was quickly medically evacuated.

The Haitians on board the freighter said they each paid $250 for the trip, "but once underway, three enforcers began to shake everyone down for money on their persons. If you didn't pay them, nor had no money, they would hit you in the head, slash you with machetes, and throw you over the side. Up to 550 may have started the trip. Up to 100 people may have been murdered during the transit into the Bahamas." The U.S. Coast Guard crewmembers managed to capture all three of the enforcers.

Admiral Brooks recalled one surreal aspect of the case. A large cruise ship stood at anchor near Hawk's Nest Cay. "The wealthy, or relatively wealthy, were at play in the sun and on the beaches less than 10 miles from the scenes of destitution, depravity and horror that we [viewed]."

At the end of the operation, the *Seneca* had a total of 430 live migrants—403 Haitians and 27 Cubans—and 5 dead Haitians. The cutter put into Nassau to disembark its human cargo.

Admiral Brooks recalled fourteen years later, "We had literally saved 403 lives [from the freighter], and everything went like clockwork. I have rarely seen a flawless operation, but this was one. There were numerous opportunities for disaster and each was successfully averted."

Admiral Brooks also remembered that "the Haitians were in the worst condition I have ever seen: given their dehydration, the murders and torture, and the depravity." Brooks vividly recalled "one very graphic example of their state. . . . Throughout the operation, people on top of the boat were draping shirts over the side and into the water to cool themselves. There were several small holes in the bow, just above the waterline, and people below decks were threading strips of cloth out those holes and into the water—and pulling the cloth back in, in frantic attempts to cool themselves. The picture was startling."

After all the Haitians departed *Seneca*, Commander Brooks addressed his crew and told them "how proud of them I was, how magnificently they had done, that they had saved 403 lives, and they could be proud of that for the rest of their lives."

Later, a crewmember asked his commanding officer: "I wonder what conditions are like in Haiti that would force people to attempt this voyage to Miami on a boat like this?" Brooks remembers asking himself the same question on other Haitian operations. "After seeing Haiti and its absolute destitution, you'll understand," Brooks later said. "But, most Americans can't conceive of the Third World, let alone a nightmare like Haiti."

The saddest postscript to the Hawk's Nest Cay case: "The Bahamians sent the [Haitian] 'enforcers' back to Haiti for prosecution. All of their cases were dropped. There was never any accountability for their murders, theft and brutality on this voyage."

Back in Havana, Tim Golden interviewed some of those standing in line near the U.S. Special Interest Section waiting to see if they would be among the twenty thousand allowed into the United States. One thirty-year-old woman told Golden of her attempt to leave on a raft made up "of old inner tubes, plastic foam and oil drums" with her husband and eleven-year-old daughter, three nephews, and "two other friends" on Friday, August 19. Like many balseros, her husband did not know how to swim.

In three days at sea, the raft capsized five times. "At one point," the woman related in a hoarse voice, "a bag of family possessions went overboard and my husband dove after it. . . . One of the nephews [who knew how to swim] dove after [my husband] but he was not strong enough to save the larger man." Standing in line nearby, the woman's sister said, "She is hoarse because she dreams about it every night. She yells in her sleep."[31]

In 2008 a former balsero living in Havana said that he and some friends had been writing antigovernment graffiti on buildings and felt they should leave their country. He drew a diagram of his raft, which consisted of three truck inner tubes lashed together, a makeshift sail, and paddles they made themselves. The balsero pointed out the dangers of this type of craft. "One night," he said, "I was asleep and suddenly found myself underwater. I didn't know which way was up. Then I saw my flashlight tumbling downward. I quickly swam in the opposite direction." Unfortunately, this happened just after President Clinton's wet foot, dry foot policy came into effect and the man was returned to Cuba. He said he now had a family and did not care to undertake such a risky venture again.[32]

President Clinton announced the new policy toward Cuba on Friday, August 19. Thirty-four days after this major change, the U.S. Coast Guard, on Thursday, September 22, officially ended Operation Able Vigil as the number of balseros dwindled to a trickle.[33] An amazing amount of rhetoric and political maneuvering took place in this short time. Calls from the media, diplomats, politicians, and others said the solution lay in ending the embargo; others said to enforce a naval blockade while others called for relaxing the Neutrality Act and allowing exiled Cubans to invade their former home. By August 25, Castro announced willingness to enter into talks dealing with migration and did not insist that "negotiations include the embargo." The next day, Radio Marti broadcasted strong messages discouraging rafters. The talks between Cuba and the United States on migration began.

On September 9 Cuba and the United States reached an agreement on migration. The United States agreed on several points: to grant a minimum of twenty thousand visas a year with an additional forty-five hundred to sixty-five hundred granted during the first year of the agreement; to resolve the disposition of the Cubans held in detention camps; and to stop the hijacking of planes and boats. The Cuban government agreed to do what it could "to stop the exodus" and to repatriate those who asked for repatriation.

The day after the agreement, Castro announced that Cubans had seventy-two hours to remove their rafts from the beach. After that, people would be prevented from leaving.[34] Thus, one of the major maritime migrant waves from Cuba that established Operation Able Vigil lasted, officially, some thirty-six days. Despite the heated rhetoric and political machinations that took place during this brief span of time, the crisis quickly faded away.

Greenhill believes the 1994 "slow Mariel" was a deliberate move on the part of Castro not only to relieve domestic pressures but also to provide an "opportunistic attempt to coerce the U.S. to the negotiating table on immigration and a wider array of issues." Greenhill labels Castro's method "extortive engineered migration"—that is, flooding a receiving country with migrants to gain your goals. Greenhill points out that Castro's "military dictatorship allows him to undertake potential risky moves internationally with considerably less concern about possible domestic backlash." One of the main reasons Castro took this move, however, is that he had tried it two times before—during Camarioca and Mariel—and succeeded.[35]

Greenhill has pointed out that the potential numbers of the 1994 exodus might have topped Mariel. A few interesting factors worked in favor of the U.S. Coast Guard during this period, which helped hold down the number of cases. During Mariel, the U.S. Coast Guard contended with many Cubans from Miami taking their own boats into Cuba. The boaters ignored warnings of severe penalties for such actions. In the 1994 exodus, however, the Cuban community in Miami heeded these warnings, probably because many in Miami saw this new wave of immigration as economic instead of political. Secondly, after learning that Castro had put many criminals and mental patients in the boats leaving Mariel, those in the Miami Cuban community wanted no more of these people in their midst, "nor to be so explicitly used as pawns by Castro." Lastly, many came to realize that by "aiding the flight of those who opposed the regime they were deflating the pressure to remove Castro." Thus, the U.S. Coast Guard had one less source of problems—and numbers.[36]

President Clinton, in his 957-page autobiography, devoted one paragraph of sixteen lines to the period, using a dinner he attended with the writer Gabriel Garcia Márquez to illustrate the problem. There is no mention of the fact that despite the president's news conference that Cubans held in Guantánamo would be sent to safe havens in other countries, Attorney General Janet Reno allowed all the Cubans, except for criminals, to be paroled to the United States and thus come under the Cuban Adjustment Act of 1966. Thus, the Cuban automobile mechanic setting off in his flimsy raft after the Cuban-U.S. agreement proved correct about the machinations of political and international relations.[37]

12 "The Toughest Thing Is to Not Have Your Heart Broken"

Operation Able Vigil, Part 2

> Politics are irrelevant to what we're doing. We're in the business of saving lives—and business these days is good.
>
> Crewmember aboard U.S. Coast Guard 110-foot patrol boat *Nantucket*

While politicians and heads of state maneuvered, the U.S. Coast Guard, recognizing the increasing numbers of Cubans intercepted, began increasing patrols in the Florida Strait on Friday, August 12, 1994. After the announcement by President Clinton of a changed policy, the service began Operation Able Vigil on August 19. The magnitude of the coming operation caused the chairman of the Joint Chiefs of Staff, Gen. John Shalikashvili, to order the other four armed forces to support the U.S. Coast Guard in the operation. The U.S. Navy received the mission of transporting migrants to Guantánamo as well as some interception duties.[1]

During the operation, U.S. Coast Guard 110-foot patrol boats and larger cutters worked in boxed out areas on charts and worked near Cuba's twelve-mile territorial limit. Aiding the cutters, U.S. Coast Guard Falcon jets and helicopters provided aerial surveillance. The patrol boats transferred the Cubans to larger cutters or Navy ships. Smaller U.S. Coast Guard craft, largely 41-foot boats, worked the areas around the Florida Keys for any rafters that slipped through the other patrol areas.[2]

The larger cutters and naval units transported the Cubans to Guantánamo. At the beginning of the operation, the Navy used the 552-foot guided-missile cruiser USS *Vicksburg* (CG-69). The commanding officer of the warship, Capt. T. J. Wilson, said, "We're having to be very ingenious, building bathrooms, showers and medical facilities for [the Cubans] in corners of the ship." Captain Wilson went on to explain that his ship could take up to one thousand undocumented migrants. Later, the Navy again ordered the hospital ship *Comfort* to transit the Panama Canal from San Diego to be a receiving unit during this operation.[3]

The Army's duty focused on camp construction and security at the migrant camps. The U.S. Marine Corps provided security at Guantánamo and on some U.S. Coast Guard cutters. The Air Force provided transportation to Guantánamo and Panama.[4]

The beginning week of Operation Able Vigil, August 22, quickly pointed out the reason for the U.S. Coast Guard's need for this additional help. The service recorded 10,190 Cubans intercepted, more than from the years 1983–93.[5] On Tuesday, August 23, the service brought on board their cutters the record number of Cubans for one day: 3,253. Among the cases, the crew of the 110-foot cutter *Matinicus* (WPB-1302), ordered from Cape May, New Jersey, to serve in the operation, rescued a forty-seven-year-old man suffering from dehydration. The cutter's commanding officer called for a U.S. Coast Guard helicopter to airlift the man to a Key West hospital.[6]

In addition to rescuing Cubans, the crews of the cutters now had to inform the undocumented migrants of a new policy. Fourteen years after Operation Able Vigil, an officer recalled that on his cutter "we had a Spanish-speaking crewmember and he wrote up a booklet in Spanish that we had printed up that said in part, 'Welcome to the United States.' We had to quickly get rid of the booklets."[7]

As the operation proceeded, the commandant of the U.S. Coast Guard, Adm. Robert Kramek, assured the news media, "We're able to take assets from all of our other missions and meet a surge requirement like this. Obviously, if you do it for a very, very long time, it has detrimental effect on your other missions."[8]

Admiral Kramek went on to explain that the service had sixty units committed to Operation Able Vigil and that it planned "to maintain the heightened work pace for at least 30 days."[9]

The statistics of the operation give the barest idea of what took place among the crews who worked to carry out their mission. At best, U.S. Coast Guard people are reluctant to call attention to what they consider "just their job." Interestingly, very few of the print media, both of the service and of civilians, took the time to file reports of what they observed taking place. The works of a few writers, combined with the observations of some veterans from the operation, are all that exists to give a feel for the work and how it affected those who "just did their job."

Fourteen years after the beginning of Operation Able Vigil, Rear Adm. Arthur E. Brooks, recalled his experiences when he commanded the 270-foot cutter *Seneca*. At the time of his participation in the operation, his cutter had been in port resupplying at the U. S. Naval Station Roosevelt Roads, Puerto Rico. He received a message to proceed to the Straits of Florida. When he asked what he should do with the helicopter and crew attached to his cutter, U.S. Coast Guard District 7 said, "Bring it. Bring everything." And hurry.[10]

Brooks recalled that he had worked with undocumented migrants since 1988, "but I never saw anything like the first day on the raft line" north of Havana's harbor, with literally "hundreds, if not thousands, of boats, rafts, and inner tubes. [The Cubans] were crying for help. They were fifteen miles out and they had no idea of how it would be out in the Straits of Florida. They were dying when we arrived. We were not the first there, maybe a day afterwards, because we went through probably thirty miles of rafts, tubes, and other things from those that had been interdicted, or something happened to them before we got to the raft line."

The *Seneca*'s crew immediately started working the rafts. Brooks recalled that he told his crew that it appeared they might do at least twenty interdictions. "I had never done over one or two interdictions a day. To even dream of twenty interdictions was unbelievable. Everybody laughed. It was impossible to even consider doing twenty interdictions. By two o'clock the next morning, we had done forty-two! We had almost three hundred people on board."

Commander Brooks sent a message to the district with the total number of Cubans on board. Brooks recalled that the district responded that "we had too many on board, we [had] to go down to two hundred, because it was unsafe to haul that many Cubans." Brooks pointed out that "four hundred was a good, tight pack for Haitians, but two hundred Cubans were too many!" Apparently, the district felt the Haitian culture made people feel more comfortable tightly packed together than Cuban culture.

A number of patrol boats received orders to transfer many of the Cubans off the larger cutter. Once the boats removed enough Cubans to reach the two hundred mark, Brooks had his navigator shape *Seneca*'s course to Guantánamo.

Another problem developed en route to the naval base: the cutter's crew kept intercepting more and more rafters as they departed the north coast of Cuba. "We kept doing interdictions along the way and not telling the district," recalled Brooks. "The largest boat [interdicted:] a 120-foot tug [the Cubans] had stolen and brought out, with thirty to thirty-five people on board. Once on board the cutter we sank the tug. The first day was really bad."

Not only did Commander Brooks and his crew face large numbers of Cubans even as they proceeded to Guantánamo, but page seventeen of the message with the operational orders for Able Vigil contained a brief instruction: do not take any Cuban pets on board. Commander Brooks understood that "we were supposed to destroy any Cuban pets we encountered." Brooks pointed out that Haitians had consistently brought chickens and goats with them for food. "Routinely, we killed the chickens and goats before burning their vessels. The Cubans[, however,] were bringing Fluffy and Fido."

In a fine bit of understatement, Brooks said that the policy put those most closely working with Cubans—the cutter and small boat crews in "a difficult situation." If a pet came on board, the crew had to dispatch the animal with the owner watching. Other options, such as throwing the pet over the side, or just leaving the dog in the raft, all with the owners watching, seemed just as difficult. Yet Brooks realized they could not take the pets with them to the United States.

The *Seneca*'s problems with the policy began on their busiest day, August 22, 1994, "in the middle of a multiple raft interdiction." Commander Brooks noticed a Cuban come aboard with a small dog. "As the dog was already aboard, I wasn't sure what to do with him, so I ignored the issue."

The executive officer named the dog Sparky. "The crew immediately stopped processing Cubans and started to play with the dog. The Cubans on the flight deck also were very distracted, in a positive way, by the dog." Commander Brooks felt he must segregate the dog and had it placed in a little-used compartment until something could be done with Sparky.

By 2:00 a.m., Commander Brooks's crew had transferred many of the Cubans to awaiting 110-foot patrol boats. The cutter then started toward Guantánamo to off-load the remaining Cubans.

Sparky became the center of attention for most of the crew, especially an electronics technician. Commander Brooks "the next night put the issue of Sparky to the wardroom at the evening meal." A lively discussion followed. Some wanted to bring Sparky to their home port of Boston and have a member of the crew adopt him. Another option was to bring him to Key West. The executive officer pointed out that the Department of Agriculture would not permit the dog into the United States. Finally, everyone agreed to hold onto Sparky and see if the Marines at Guantánamo would take him.

Admiral Brooks recalled that as their mission continued, "the crew continued to polarize along Sparky lines." Half the crew wanted to shoot him and half the crew wanted to take him home.

The situation escalated a few days before *Seneca*'s arrival in Guantánamo. Another message arrived from District 7 that read: "It has come to our attention that some of you are picking up Cuban pets. Let us make this clear, humanely dispose of the pets!"

This called for another meeting between Commander Brooks and his executive officer. The two decided to keep Sparky on board until they arrived at Guantánamo and dispose of him after off-loading the Cuban undocumented migrants.

"Anticipating a 'Free Sparky movement'" Commander Brooks asked the engineering officer to move Sparky to another compartment and to put one of his locks on it. No one knew about the move.

Sitting in Juneau, Alaska, many years later, Admiral Brooks recalled that the *Seneca* arrived at Guantánamo around 8:00 p.m. Immediately upon securing mooring lines, the first person aboard the cutter was a U.S. Coast Guard liaison officer, and his first question was "Do you have any dogs?"

"No," said Brooks.

"Really? Do you have any dogs?"

"We're not supposed to have any dogs, so we don't have any dogs," said the commanding officer of the *Seneca*.

"You don't understand. We've set up a kennel for them here. We won't tell anyone that you gave him to us. Do you have any dogs?"

Brooks recalled that "after a moment of hesitation, I squeaked out a tentative, 'Maybe.'"

Commander Brooks then "asked the EO to bring up Sparky while all those of the 'Free Sparky movement' [among the junior officers] rushed to get him from the [compartment]. They were surprised to find that Sparky wasn't there."

The veterinarian met the cutter at the pier and "Sparky was the first one ashore." Sparky's first action ashore: to relieve himself. "All of the marines on the pier waiting to process Cubans dropped their professionalism to play with the dog."

"In discussing this policy with many of the [U.S. Coast Guard people] who responded in Able Vigil," said Admiral Brooks, "I never met one who 'humanely disposed of the pets.'"

Commander Brooks found that after the first few days, things settled into the routines similar to Haitian operations, such as what to do about food, sanitation, and protecting the Cubans from the sun. A few new twists developed, however.

In later years, some U.S. Coast Guard people claimed Cubans could be very demanding. Admiral Brooks observed that during Operation Able Vigil, Cubans "came aboard making a lot of demands. They expected to talk to the captain and to set conditions. They expected to be taken to Miami. [This even after the wet foot, dry foot policy came into effect.] They expected all these things." Some of the ships, "especially the navy ships," spent a great deal of time listening to these demands. Admiral Brooks recalled that based upon his experience with migrants, "and while I viewed myself as extremely compassionate and focused on their comfort and treatment to the best extent that conditions permitted, the reality was: one, the ship was not designed to carry passengers. Two they [aren't going] to Miami: they are going to GITMO."

Admiral Brooks recalled that he told the Cubans his philosophy on their demands: "You have the right to sit down and be quiet. You take a shower when I say and get chow when I say and you get to sit here and be quiet. That is what you have a right to do right now. That's all you have. That was the most humane way to deal with it." Brooks pointed out that the people who tried to talk with the Cuban undocumented migrants "just ended up extremely frustrated. The short answer was: the sooner the Cubans realized I was going to do everything to keep them safe, and that's all we are going to do, and we are going to GITMO it was [all] going to work out."

Later, nearing the end of Operation Able Vigil, William Booth, of the *Washington Post*, accompanied the 110-foot patrol boat *Baranof* (WPB-1318) on Thursday and Friday, August 25–26. He watched as the commanding officer, Lt. Gwen Keenan, worked her cutter close enough to Cuba to see the outline of buildings in Havana. Her crew pulled seven "waterlogged and seasick Cubans in cheap Chinese sneakers and frayed blue jeans" aboard just as a Cuban patrol boat closed, forcing them farther outside the Cuban twelve-mile territorial limit.[11]

Lieutenant Keenan noted a slight decrease in the numbers of balseros. Some on the patrol boat felt that visibility and increasing seas caused the downswing. A quartermaster, Joe Washburn, stated, "The Cubans may be eyeballing the weather and staying home, or we might be finding them in this mess."

As squalls and eight-foot seas battered the *Baranof*, the executive officer, Lt. (jg) Eric Gleason, said, "This ain't a pretty day to be a rafter." Lieutenant Keenan agreed with her executive officer, "There is no way these rafts can handle much of this."

The cutter continued to spot empty rafts, not knowing whether the balseros perished or the U.S. Coast Guard rescued them. Cutter crews usually destroyed the rafts after taking rafters aboard. On this Thursday and Friday the crews of all the cutters were so busy they could not take the time to destroy the rafts. Booth reported that the patrol boats were so busy they could not take the time to pick up a corpse.

Booth told readers that the crew of the *Baranof* had "lifted from the sea rafters so weak and dehydrated they could not stand up. One man told the crew he was so thirsty he drank his own urine, so hungry he fished with his hands and ate the catch raw. Aboard another cutter, a woman was nine months pregnant—and dilating."

On the previous two-day patrol, Tuesday and Wednesday, the crew of the 110-foot cutter rescued 718 rafters from 196 rafts. "At one point, the cutter was so overloaded the crew could feel her wallow in the waves, the decks packed with people."

During Booth's voyage on the *Baranof*, the crew took aboard thirty Cubans from eight rafts. "One raft was a homemade catamaran, its pontoons built of blue bathroom tiles, its riggings of bathroom fixtures. The others were constructed of strung-together inner tubes."

The crew threw lines to the rafters to pull them close to the cutter, then helped the Cubans aboard with "the seawater running out of their pants." Some wore "army boots and sandals and sneakers and some were barefoot."

The Cubans first received a search by Marines, "whom some of them tried to hug." One man limped away after the search, his feet swollen. The ones who rowed had bleeding blisters. "So many had bloodshot eyes, with that faraway glaze of people lost at sea. . . . They carried water-soaked bundles: photographs of girlfriends, wives and mothers. A picture of the Virgin Mary. Bayonet knives from Soviet AK-47s. Matches, aspirin, mirrors, combs, underwear, lines, compasses."

While wrapped tightly in a blanket, Carlos Hernandez, who left with six others from Santa Fe, near Havana, said, "Three days. Three storms. The sea pushed us. Where are we?"

Later Lieutenant Keenan told Booth about a previous patrol. At night the crew scanned for any type of light that might indicate balseros. "It was like chasing fireflies," Keenan said. "You know, how when you were little you ran around with a jar and caught all the fireflies you could. That's what it was like. Fireflies."

Most writers who detail operational subjects rightfully focus on units and people at the point of the spear. Those in supply make it possible for operations to continue but seldom, if ever, receive the credit they deserve. In U.S. Coast Guard District 7 headquarters, purchasing agents Georgia Coats and Joyce Lasseter faced innumerable problems of getting the right material to the right unit in the right amount. Coats said "this [was] one of first times I've had to buy 6,000 baby bottles, 10,000 cans of formula, 40,000 jars of baby food or 70,000 disposable diapers. Those items are not even in the federal supply schedule."[12]

Even when Coats and Lasseter found material in government warehouses, the stocks would not support the amount needed. When they went to vendors outside of the government, the businesses also had the same problems. Lasseter did find some help. "When we told vendors we needed 100,000 blankets in South Florida, they wondered why. I told them all of the rafters being saved by the Coast Guard are wet and cold. One vendor sold me blankets that sell in the government supply catalog for $19.13 each for $2.75."[13]

Another portion of the Operation Able Vigil that received little notice was the public information people of U.S. Coast Guard District 7. They, too, had some interesting moments. One of their duties centered on putting out press releases on the number of Cubans taken aboard cutters. This usually amounted to no more than two pages of double-spaced narrative. Interestingly, this seemingly banal duty provoked ire in the political leadership, which made its feelings known at the district level. In a message to the district public information office at 10:00 p.m. on August 24, a senior captain in Washington, D.C., said "to stop releasing those Cuban migrant numbers so fast." President Clinton was "complaining that he is tired of seeing those numbers on CNN before he reads them in his . . . [situation reports.]"[14]

Writer Allan Weisbecker accompanied the 110-foot patrol boat *Nantucket* (WPB-1316), home ported at Key West, on one day of operations during Operation Able Vigil. Early in the morning, the cutter crew pulled more than a dozen balseros from their pitching raft in the Florida Strait. Following standard procedures during the operation, members of the U.S. Coast Guard crew set fire to the abandoned raft to prevent hazards to navigation. Black smoke drifted over the deck of the *Nantucket*, enveloping both rescuers and those rescued. Weisbecker wrote the scene bordered "on the apocalyptic."[15]

No sooner had the cutter cleared the area than they sped to another raft. The balseros on deck reacted to their situation in a number of ways. A young mother clutched her infant daughter, torn between joy at the rescue and the uncertainty of her future: would she be returned to Cuba or go the United States? An older man, muttering a religious litany, went to the bridge for medical treatment. A young man claimed Russian citizenship. Two other stunned men watched their burning raft.

Weisbecker marveled at how "the calm efficiency of the *Nantucket*'s crew" kept a quiet scene on the cutter's deck, despite the "psychological turmoil" of the Cubans. The crews quickly but courteously moved the balseros to the stern of the patrol boat. The crew searched for weapons and contraband, handed out blankets and water, and attended to those needing medical attention.

Weisbecker's writing approached awe at how the cutter's crew showed no impatience or "ill temper" at the Cubans, despite working "essentially nonstop . . . for four months." Instead, he found "touching acts of kindness. A bosun's [boatswain's] mate kneels by a young woman in little more than rags and holds a seasickness bag for her. One of the two Marines on board reunites a preadolescent girl with her family after they become separated in the boarding process. One of the ship's two Spanish-speaking crew members relays a distraught woman's fear that her family's photographs remain on the raft about to be set fire, another member boards the diesel-soaked craft to find them."

The crew worked on, hardly stopping for the noon meal. Late in the afternoon, the cutter pulled near a sailboat with five men on board. These Cubans refused to give up their boat for fear of ending up in Guantánamo. They demanded a guarantee of landing in the United States. A Spanish-speaking crewman, electrician Julio Garcia, at the bow of the *Nantucket*, tried to convince the Cubans to leave their craft. Weisbecker noted that the commanding officer of the cutter might have taken the easy way out of this impasse and "deceive these people, but Captain Andy Bloome instructs Garcia to make no false promises. Eventually, Garcia persuades them to come on board."

Later, crewmen went aboard an unusual raft made of metal pipes filled with foam that proudly displayed *La Nina* engraved near the stern. Unburnable, the two crewmen from the *Nantucket* attacked the raft with axes, trying to smash the craft. A balsero rose from his location on the deck of the cutter and said in broken English: "She not sink! Never!" The raft, indeed, resisted all efforts to sink it. Recalled back to the cutter, one of the sweating crewmen approached the balsero and asked if he built the raft.

The Cuban warily nodded his head. The crewman offered his hand "in respect and admiration. For the *balsero*, stripped of his dignity by circumstances, the gesture is monumental. He sits down, vainly attempting to hold back the tears."

By 5:30 p.m. the *Nantucket*, filled to capacity, rendezvoused with a Navy boat, which took the Cubans to a Navy frigate that took the Cubans to Guantánamo. Although a routine turn over, Lt. Rich Condit made eye contact with each balsero, "offering a nod and a pat on the back" to each as they left the *Nantucket*.

Sometime during this one day, QM Jose Rosa, received an injury when some panicky balseros rushed to one side of their raft and capsized it. Rosa at just this time was reaching for a Cuban and the capsizing raft struck him in the head. He continued to pull people into the cutter's Zodiac (a rigid-hulled boat). Upon retrieving the boat, crew, and Cubans on board the *Nantucket*, Rosa passed out. Quickly evacuated to a Navy ship for medical care, Rosa was diagnosed with a mild concussion but would return in the morning.

"Acts of heroism seem all but routine on board this ship," Weisbecker noted. Ten days before the writer visited for one day, he found that the cutter had come upon a crowded raft about to sink in heavy seas. Most of the cutter's crew pointed out to Weisbecker the efforts of three of their shipmates who dove into the turbulent water near the jagged raft and pulled out drowning people. Their commanding officer wrote in his night order book: "Long after my tour aboard *Nantucket* is over, I will look back on today's events with the sinking migrant craft (it could hardly be called a vessel) and I will tell people 'I served with heroes.' In one's life, there are few moments that so immediately and truthfully test the soul as those of today. Without question, we know that MK2 [Machinery Technician Second Class] Kevin Brown, FN [Fireman] Beryl Brown, and SA Dave Ezquerra posses the selfless dedication that makes the Coast Guard the world's life-saving service without equal."

It amazed Weisbecker that the nonstop work and danger that the crew of the *Nantucket* faced did not seem "to cause any resentment or intolerance on board the ship." When the writer asked about the politics of the situation, one crewman responded: "Politics are irrelevant to what we're doing.

We're in the business of saving lives—and business these days is good." Another, with a lump in his throat, said, "The toughest thing out here is to not have your heart broken."

The new Cuban policy made it difficult for many U.S. Coast Guard people, after they saw the condition of some of the Cubans, to return the undocumented migrants to Guantánamo. This proved especially hard for Ens. Jorge Garrido, serving on the 270-foot cutter *Mohawk*. Ensign Garrido recalled his hometown of Santiago, Cuba, 860 kilometers (533 miles) east of Havana. His mother took him out of school, telling the teacher "he had a dentist appointment." Instead, eight-year-old Garrido left his country during Mariel. Garrido remembered the trip across the Florida Strait in a shrimp boat that ran into trouble in rough seas. Then he "saw a white ship with a red stripe: the U.S. Coast Guard had arrived to tow the sinking ship to Key West."[16]

Fourteen years later, Ensign Garrido still experienced the same situation, except from the side of the enforcer/rescuer. "I wish I could bring them into my state room and feed them," Garrido said. "But you can't. There's too many of them."

When the Cuban policy changed, Ensign Garrido said, "At first I was like, 'I don't want to do this, I don't want to pick them up and bring them back to Guantanamo.'" But he understood his duty: "I joined the Coast Guard to save lives, not to make policies."

Garrido observed that most of the undocumented Cubans did not know about being sent to Guantánamo. "Before Guantanamo, they [the migrants] would ask me how (pro baseball players) José Canseco and René Arocha were doing and how the Yankees were doing."

For the crews of the U.S. Coast Guard, the new policy of wet foot, dry foot put into place by President Clinton meant something other than returning the undocumented migrants to Cuba. Wet foot, dry foot eventually added an additional danger to an already dangerous mission.[17]

13 The Dance

> I feel for those at the stations. Usually, they are young people, plus they must literally make life-and-death decisions quickly without consulting anyone. When, as a young ensign, I went on a boarding party in the cutter's small boat, I had with me a Chief Petty Officer with years of experience, plus I knew the captain was on the wing of the bridge. The young people at the stations do not always have this benefit.
>
> Cdr. Robert J. Klapproth, commanding officer, USCG cutter *Active* (2006)

The establishment of the 1994 migrant policy dubbed "wet foot, dry foot" meant the Cuban policy moved closer to equable treatment of Cubans and Haitians, it also brought additional problems for U.S. Coast Guard crews. In the words of many in the U.S. Coast Guard, when the "Cubans had a free ride" into this country, they welcomed the sight of the white U.S. Coast Guard cutters and small boats. It meant the end of their perilous journey. Wet foot, dry foot changed this. Now the sight of a white cutter might mean a return to Cuba. The undocumented Cuban migrants know they must make it above the water line before they could be accepted into the United

States. This has led to another twist in the history of Cubans attempting to leave their country: the rise of human smuggling operations from U.S.-based smugglers.

In 1998 Dan Geoghegan, assistant chief of the U.S. Border Patrol in Florida, remarked that the "idea is not to get caught by the [U.S.] Coast Guard. The idea is not to leave Cuba in a raft, but to leave it in a fast boat. . . . One theory for the activity is that the Cubans who came here in 1994 have been [making enough] . . . money . . . [so that it] is not inconceivable that they could be funding relatives to come here too."[1]

U.S. Coast Guard petty officer Jeff Murphy reported "seeing more and more smugglers bringing human cargo" into Florida. The boats ranged from homemade to "sophisticated speedboats."[2] Within a decade after Geoghegan's and Murphy's comments, human smugglers had established a regular route and routine for moving human cargo from the Florida Keys into Cuba and return.

Smugglers normally operated out of a marina near, for example, Marathon. A ride in 2007 with U.S. Coast Guard Station Marathon's crew to patrol a "hot spot" marina proved enlightening. When coming through the entrance from the sea, one immediately observed people carefully watching the U.S. Coast Guard boat. No friendly waves, as normal when entering a marina, just long, steady stares. This continued as the boat made its way slowly through the marina. A calm day usually means that smugglers might be out earlier to check sea conditions. The boat crew tied up and approached a Cuban American boat just in from the sea.[3]

"Been out this morning?" said the leading petty officer of the U.S. Coast Guard boat to the Cuban American boat owner.

"Yes, we've been fishing."

"Where are your fishing poles?"

A smile was the only answer from the owner; the normal reply to any U.S. Coast Guard crew coming upon a suspect boat at sea in the Florida Keys was "just fishing." As the U.S. Coast Guard boat left the marina, the scene resembled a prison's yard area: groups of people standing around doing a poor job of looking innocent but always watching the officers until they depart.

Once the human smugglers decide to make their run to Cuba, they usually do it in three stages. The first is the departure at night from the Florida

Keys. Smugglers in their center-console, fast fishing craft with at least two outboard engines of between 200–300 hp for each engine, usually run to the Cay Sal Banks area in Bahamian waters, approximately eighty miles to the southeast of Station Marathon and almost the same distance due south of Station Islamorada. At Cay Sal Banks, the boats, which carry additional water, food, extra oil, gas, life jackets, and, of course, fishing poles, wait throughout the day until night before beginning the second stage in the operation.

The second phase of the human smuggling routine begins as the boats depart Cay Sal Banks en route to the north coast of Cuba at locations such as Bahía Honda for their loads of people. The smugglers at times will cram an amazing number of Cubans into their boats, which slows the boat but makes more money for the smuggler. In 2006 smugglers charged approximately US$10,000 per person upon successful delivery into the United States. The third phase is trying to bring the human cargo into Florida.[4]

Part of the agreement between Cuba and the United States during the Clinton administration's shift to wet foot, dry foot stated that Cuba would also try to stop the flow of undocumented migrants. The Cuban Border Guard has the same problems as the U.S. Coast Guard in trying to stop the smugglers. In one case, for example, Cuban American smuggler twenty-nine-year-old Joel Dorta Garcia, in his 32-foot Scorpion boat with fourteen people on board, tried to outrun the Cuban Border Guard patrol boat. Dorta raced through the dark, moonless night in rough seas. A cap to a spare two-hundred-gallon gas tank on deck blew off, dousing the passenger's legs in gasoline. "The Border Guard officers . . . were shouting for Dorta to stop, to save the men, women and children on board from almost-certain disaster."

Later, Dorta said to reporter Mark Fineman, "I'm not stopping. I didn't force these people to get on the boat. And I thought, 'If I stop, we'll capsize, and I'll never get home.'"

The boat did capsize, killing forty-seven-year-old Sergio Maurilio Martinez. Dorta sat in confinement in "the forbidding compound of Cuba's Department of State Security, [showing] little remorse while describing the journey that killed a man."

In 2001 the Cuban Border Guard, operating under the Ministry of the Interior, had an "aging naval fleet." The Border Guard allowed reporter

Mark Fineman to accompany a patrol in "a speedboat confiscated from Florida smugglers." In 2008 captured go-fast boats (high-powered speedboats) could be seen at the Cuban Border Guards headquarters near Havana. Using captured smuggler's boats is nothing new, especially with law enforcement agencies that do not have large budgets. The U.S. Coast Guard, for example, during the Prohibition Era, used many of the faster rum-running boats to pursue smugglers of illegal liquor.

Fineman felt that his "unique access" resulted from a desire "to show Cuba's commitment" to stopping the human smuggling. Fineman interviewed many Border Guard commanders "along the island's northern coast . . . [and] they echoed the frustration of many U.S. Border Patrol and Coast Guard officers responsible for stopping the smugglers after they leave Cuban waters but before they reach the Florida coast."[5]

If the Cuban Border Guard receives intelligence of a smuggler's departure, or if they have chased a smuggler out to their twelve-mile limit, they contact the U.S. Coast Guard with the location or locations. This starts what now retired U.S. Coast Guard District 7 commander Rear Adm. David W. Kunkel called the "dance."[6] The smuggler's boat is spotted by aircraft of the U.S. Coast Guard, Customs and Border Patrol (CBP), or Immigration and Customs Enforcement (ICE), or by a surface unit of the U.S. Coast Guard. Large cutters or patrol boats begin the chase, keeping in constant radio communication. As they near the Keys, the fast boats from one of the U.S. Coast Guard stations or from CBP join to make the capture.

In the past, the U.S. Coast Guard seemed never to have fast enough craft to overtake those who were breaking the law. Beginning in 2002, however, the service obtained the 25-foot Defender-class boats, with speeds up to 45+ knots per hour (51.8+ miles per hour). Since then, the service has obtained two other classes, the Response Boat, Medium and the Special Purpose Craft, Law Enforcement, with speeds in excess of 50 knots (57.6+ miles per hour).[7]

A daylight ride on one of the U.S. Coast Guard's Special Law Enforcement boats in the Florida Keys proved interesting to one who was used to older boats of the service. It also hinted at what took place during the pursuit of human smugglers.

Casting off from the dock at Station Marathon, Florida, MCPO Charles W. "Skip" Bowen, the officer in charge of the unit, sat in a seat behind the coxswain of the boat. He leaned across the seat, smiled, and said, "You'd better strap yourself in." This hinted at coming events.[8]

Once clear of the harbor and into open water, the coxswain pushed the throttles open and the three high-powered outboard engines quickly brought the boat up to 50+ knots. Shock absorbing seats took care of some of the jarring of the craft as it hit the choppy seas. The coxswain, BM1 Scott Foster, glanced over and said, "I'll show you some tactical turns." The Disney Corporation should use such turns on their rides!

Coming back up to 50+ knots again, Master Chief Bowen pointed out, "Imagine it is very dark, with no moon. Smugglers will take their boats at this speed and aim their craft at us."

The U.S. Coast Guard has employed a number of tactics to slow a smuggler's boat, one of which is a device to foul the screws (propellers) of the outboard engines. Probably the most misunderstood tactic used since 2005 is firing at the boats. This caused some raised eyebrows in the pleasure-boating community. Some wondered if a service known for maritime rescue had now abandoned that reputation for a police-like force. Many perceive that if a boat refuses to stop, the service fires at will. What actually happens during a pursuit does not live up to the popularly held perception.

In U.S. Coast Guard District 7, when the service cannot overtake a smuggler's boat, the coxswain of the boat informs his commanding officer via radio and they discuss the situation. The commanding officer then informs the sector commander of his recommendation to shoot. If the sector commander agrees with the decision, the sector officer then contacts the district commander, an admiral. The admiral is the person who gives the order for shooting. In the lexicon of the service, the decision is briefed up the chain of command before a shot is fired.[9]

On board the pursuing U.S. Coast Guard boat, only a qualified crew member does the shooting. First a warning shot is fired across the bow. If this fails to stop the boat, the gunner aims for one of the outboard engines of the fleeing boat and fires a copper slug. Putting one engine out of commission slows the craft so the Defender-class boat can "easily" come alongside. In certain situations, the gunner may be cleared to use rubber bullets on the person at the wheel of the pursued boat.

Late one evening in 2007, Station Islamorada received information that a pursuit had started and the station crew should remain ready if the smuggler could not be overtaken because the boat was headed toward the station's area of operations. Shortly thereafter, the boat crew received their orders to get under way. The designated shooter drew his weapon and, like most in this situation, one could see the adrenaline level increasing.[10]

As the chase continued through the night, the radio traffic of the pursuit boat was more exciting than any television program or movie. A customs service boat joined in the pursuit. The smuggler's boat raced toward an area of the coast dotted with reefs. At the speed of the smuggler's boat, should it hit one of the reefs, there could be a large loss of life. The commanding officer of Station Islamorada, CWO Robert C. Schmidt, recommended to the sector commander to fire at the engines. Chief Warrant Officer Schmidt, however, felt by the time the decision from the district reached him, the smuggler would be in the area where they could be in danger of running aground. He radioed his boat coxswain "to let customs take the shot."

The U.S. Coast Guard boat dropped back slightly and customs moved closer to the smuggler's boat. Shortly after this, the radio crackled with the U.S. Coast Guard coxswain's voice: "They're holding a baby near the engines!" Eventually, the customs boat fired six shots, with at least one disabling an engine.

Next came one of the most hazardous of the operations in stopping a smuggler's boat: boarding it. Not only does the U.S. Coast Guard crew have to worry about choppy seas in the dark but there are also people who may oppose them as they board. The boarding party must quickly board and take control. Even for those who have not had to perform this operation, it is not hard to envision the adrenaline pumping just before boarding. One U.S. Coast Guardsman said, "I call jumping from our boat to theirs my 'leap of faith.' I have to have faith that I can do it. I have to have faith in my fellow crew members. I have to have faith in my coxswain." The crewman admitted, "It does give me an adrenaline rush."[11]

When the crew of Islamorada returned from their pursuit, they reported twenty-eight undocumented migrants and two smugglers, all transferred to a patrol boat. After the boat crew returned to Islamorada in the early hours of the morning, Capt. Scott A. Buschman, commanding officer of Sector Key West, called to congratulate them. The night's work by Station Islamorada garnered no headlines.

Later in the day, an examination of the smuggler's boat tied up at Station

Islamorada revealed Cuban biscuits, water, extra lifejackets, and extra motor oil scattered about the deck. This boat had removed most of the windshield to make a poor radar target. An examination of the engines revealed in one an almost neat hole where a round disabled it.

To train for shooting situations, Station Islamorada uses an old boat "fitted with wooden targets shaped like men and an old outboard motor." The boat is towed out to sea, and the gunners practice shooting at the motor. MK3 Joe Tankersly pointed out to reporter Carmen Gentile, "Not one hole in any [of the targets that are shaped like men.]"

Gentile also witnessed the questioning of a smuggler by the station. With weapons stashed aboard the smuggler's craft, "not to mention the 27 Cubans crammed into his small, rickety speedboat," the smuggler claimed "he's part of a revolutionary group hoping to topple the Castro regime."[12] PO John Fleming, "a veteran of numerous interdiction missions," remarked to Gentile, "That's a new one. Usually, the people we pick up on suspicion of smuggling say they were just fishing."[13]

Some chases seem almost scripted for a movie. One crew member recalled that they came upon a boat with three people in it. "They gave us a gesture and started off. We gave chase. We had maybe a half knot more speed, but we could not get permission to fire." The chase continued. The fleeing boat throttled back. The operator then actually "drove across us, almost hitting our gunner and did break [one crew member's] arm."

The chase continued. Now the pursuit moved into Station Marathon's area of operation. The operator did the same maneuver to Marathon's boat and managed to disable one of the station boat's engines.

The chase continued. "Custom's aircraft were pointing their weapons, [but] nothing slowed the boat. The boat [then] ran aground and the three people in the boat jumped out and ran. [Three of us] chased one [who turned out to be the operator], and drug him out from under a house. He fought the three of us."[14]

Others examined the grounded boat and found at least eight badly beaten up migrants under the center console. The smugglers went to trial, and the operator received a twelve-year sentence and the other two received six years.

Sometimes a chase can almost seem comical. A former crew member of a patrol boat recalled a chase that began near Cuban waters. "The smugglers had the right angle to make it into Cuban waters. Then [the operator] sees a white yacht in the distance and thinks it is a Coast Guard cutter, so he changes course, which makes him head right back at us, and almost has a head on [collision] with us. He was eventually caught by a station boat."[15]

As with the U.S. Coast Guard people on patrol boats and larger cutters, the crews at stations also are subjected to sights that can make one wonder about the human condition. One station crew member recalled that he had just reported into his unit from another far away from Florida. The first night on board he found himself on a boat in pursuit of a smuggler. As the U.S. Coast Guard boat drew near, the smugglers grabbed a child and put it near the side of the boat, trying to keep the U.S. Coast Guard boat from coming alongside. "The people in the smuggler's boat were screaming at the smugglers. I wondered, 'What is going on down here?'"[16]

Most of the crews of the U.S. Coast Guard stations, patrol boats, and cutters all say they feel sorry for the migrants. The only time there is any sympathy for the smugglers is when it is proved that the boat owner is going after a family member. Most of the smuggling, however, is done to make money for the smugglers.

A Cuban American crew member said, "I feel for the migrants. Sometimes it makes my heart cry to know they have to be sent back, especially the rafters." The crewman went on to say,

> My parents came here in 1961. In 1980, my father took his own boat to bring out his mother. My father worked hard to get ahead in this country. I thank God my parents came here and allowed me to be born here. I have no respect for the smugglers. Most are Cubans who have only recently come here and find out that, unlike a Communist country, they have to work. They can make $10,000 [per] person [smuggling]. Even then they get greedy. They could haul smaller amounts of people and maybe go undetected, but the more they can squeeze in, the more they make.[17]

Once interdicted at sea by station boats, the undocumented Cuban migrants, move to a patrol boat. The patrol boat usually hands them off to a larger cutter—a buoy tender or a medium- to high-endurance cutter—because they have more room. On board the larger cutters, the Cubans receive a screening to determine if they are refugees or economic migrants. Refugees are then transported to Guantánamo for further processing, and the other Cubans are placed aboard another patrol boat and repatriated. Normally the patrol boats bring the Cubans into Bahía de Cabañas, to the west of Havana. In 1851 Venezuelan-born Gen. Narciso López led an army made up of men recruited from the Southeastern United States to free Cuba from Spain. The force landed in a small town in Bahía de Cabañas. The Spanish quickly defeated and executed many of the invaders.[18]

The wet foot, dry foot policy causes yet another problem for U.S. Coast Guard crews. As Master Chief Bowen put it, "The policy means that now if the illegal migrants see shore they start to become agitated. If there is going to be violence, it will happen within sight of the beach."[19]

To reinforce the master chief's observation, Lt. Scott Sharp, the commanding officer of the 110-foot patrol boat *Matagorda*, commented, "We're [now] going into a combat situation at sea. Migrant interdiction used to be routine. Now [when] you come upon a migrant vessel, you have to determine whether they're going to attack you. That translates into a very dangerous and volatile situation for us."[20]

In May 2000 the *Matagorda*'s crew rescued fourteen Cubans who had drifted without water for more than a week; eight of the fourteen on board were unconscious and needed immediate medical evacuation. "Less than three weeks later, the same [U.S. Coast Guard] crewmen were fending off attacks from another boatload of healthy Cubans." Another U.S. Coast Guard boarding party faced eight "migrants, who threatened to eat rat poison, doused themselves in gasoline and tried to set fire to everyone on scene." Lieutenant Sharp at one point said that sometimes the crews had "to use hand-to-hand combat." This is illustrated in yet another incident when Gunner's Mate First Class (GM1) Ronald Scoggin boarded a Cuban migrant craft from another cutter's small boat. Scoggin recalled, "I got hit with a hose in the face and had an oar swung at me. That was after we were doused with gasoline. We had the gas, salt water and [pepper spray] on us, in our eyes. One migrant had a lighter with him that he was trying to light as we were bringing him across to the [cutter's small boat.] We got the lighter away from him after a couple of quick flicks." Other migrants have slit their stomachs, and in one case a migrant swallowed broken glass.[21]

As with pursuit, there are times when some of the U.S. Coast Guard people actually smile while making these decisions. One crewman many miles from the beach tried to talk a Cuban into letting him bring him aboard the boat. The Cuban gasped that he was a professional swimmer and could make the beach. "I could see the man did not have the endurance for another mile, but said, 'Okay, I will give you another mile. We moved the boat slowly near him and I watched him until he could go no farther, and then took him aboard."[22]

Wet foot, dry foot led to human smuggling and possible violence, and to the chance for Cubans to inflict self-injury so they could be medically evacuated to shore. In recent years, this self-inflicted harm has caused the service to carefully search each Cuban they intercept. Crew members on larger cutters have mentioned that they must watch Cubans carefully so that they do not obtain anything from the ship that could be made into something that could harm them. An officer recalled that Cubans even filed the buckles on the lifejackets to make a weapon to injure themselves. The officer pointed out that many Cubans who did not know about other migrants who impaled themselves did not understand why they were being searched; "they felt the U.S. was rude to them. The Cubans perceived you are taking everything away from [them] and telling [them] we are going to get it back. It was tough, even for the [U.S. Coast Guard people], who are a pretty compassionate group."[23]

Near Key West, a smuggler's boat containing twenty-nine undocumented Cubans raced through a summer's night in 2006, pursued by two U.S. Coast Guard boats and a helicopter. When the boat failed to stop, despite sirens and flashing blue lights, two shots were fired into one of the smuggler's outboard engines, causing the boat to veer sharply. The sudden movement threw Anay Machado Gonzalez head first into the side of the craft. As usual, when there is an injury involving Cuban undocumented migrants, decisions had to be reached: if Machado needed to be evacuated to a hospital, she could claim "dry foot." By the time she reached the hospital two hours later, she was dead. "She was the third Cuban migrant in just over a year to die of traumatic head injuries." Agustin Uralde, Machado's husband, who rode in the same boat, told reporter Block that he placed equal blame on America's policy and the methods employed by the U.S. Coast Guard. "It's madness," said Uralde, who now lives legally in the United States. Even years later, it is not entirely clear if the death came about because of the interdiction itself or the smuggling event in and of itself. The Machado case is only one example of the problems facing U.S. Coast Guard people trying to enforce policies concerning Cubans after the implementation of wet foot, dry foot.[24]

The decision to evacuate Cubans is something not taken lightly. One of the reasons for the hesitation is largely because of the legal ramifications. At one station, a coxswain said, "Sometimes I have to make a decision of whether to take a [Cuban] to the beach because of a medical problem instead of [to] a cutter. It is a hard decision."[25] The case that received extended coverage came in 1999 with the decision to evacuate the six-year-old Elian Gonzalez (see chapter 14).

The high-speed chases are inherently dangerous to the U.S. Coast Guard crews and the Cuban undocumented migrants. Robert Block, writing in the *Wall Street Journal* in 2007, stated that since March 2003, "half of the estimated 50 cases of customs agents shooting out engines of fleeing boats . . . involved illegal-alien smuggling from Cuba. . . . [A U.S.] Coast Guard report shows that four of the eight deaths and all of the 13 injuries to Cubans who tried to enter Florida illegally in 2005 and 2006 involved high-speed chases with Coast Guard or Customs Service and Border Protection vessels." Block does point out that "in some cases, enforcement agents were also hurt."[26]

Anyone who works in law enforcement will quickly explain how chases and confrontations can cause the adrenaline to kick in. There is always a danger that the situation can lead to deadly results. Some people can master this situation. Take, for example, a case that took place near Station Marathon in the fall of 2004. Previously, a U.S. Coast Guard boat from Key West stopped a boat with undocumented migrants and found a gun in the boat. Coupled with the growing cases of boat crews attacked with sticks with nails in them and with machetes, the new intelligence of a weapon now added an additional factor that boarding crews had to keep in mind. On the day of the Marathon case, the station received information of a chug [motorized raft] near shore. The first boat on scene had a Cuban American U.S. Coast Guard petty officer as the coxswain in charge of the craft.

One of the Cuban undocumented migrants held up an opaque bag and screamed that he had a gun in it and would shoot if anyone approached the boat. Master Chief Bowen, then the officer-in-charge of Station Marathon, later recalled that the situation had all the elements for the U.S. Coast Guard policy to shoot. The petty officer had been threatened by a man claiming to have a gun, a gun had been found on a migrant boat, there was no real place to take cover, and he was close to the boat.

The petty officer did not shoot. At just about this time, Master Chief Bowen arrived in the station's second boat. Both boats came "in fast on both sides of the chug and we started to pull people off. The Cubans brandished sticks. They had smeared themselves with Vaseline so they would be slick. We used pepper spray and got them off the chug and put them into flex cuffs."

It turned out that the Cuban did not have a weapon. Later Bowen recalled, "If a Cuban American U.S. Coast Guard petty officer had shot and killed an unarmed Cuban undocumented migrant, the political implications in South Florida just before the presidential election would have been incredible. It is an extremely difficult mission and even more for Cuban Americans. Some have criticized the petty officer for not shooting, even though legally he had the right to do so. I'm glad he didn't."[27]

At midnight on January 4, 2006, after the dangerous twenty-seven-hour voyage across the Florida Strait, the outboard engine on a chug stopped. Junior Blanco, his wife, his two-year-old son, and twelve other Cubans clambered onto an abutment of the abandoned old seven-mile bridge in the Florida Keys. Blanco, a quarry worker, later said, "We knew that according to the law we were safe. By law they couldn't return us to Cuba because we had dry feet." Thus began another case study of the 1994 wet foot, dry foot policy.

Two years later the officer in charge of the nearest U.S. Coast Guard Station at Marathon, Master Chief Bowen, recalled, "I had always wondered about that old abandoned seven-mile bridge. What would happen if someone landed on it? The bridge had gaps in it and did not connect to shore. The wet foot, dry foot policy as we practiced it stated that if an undocumented migrant made it to a lighthouse, that was considered wet foot; they had to actually make it to land."

Master Chief Bowen remembered that he received the call early in the morning that undocumented migrants had landed on the abutment below the old seven-mile bridge section that did not attach to land. The station's ready boat reached the scene first, followed by the unit's 41-footer and by Master Chief Bowen in a smaller fast boat.

"I called Group [Key West] and told them the [exact] location of the Cubans. The decision came back: [the undocumented Cubans were] dry feet. So, we loaded them, men, women, and children onto the 41-footer. These people were not in very good shape. It was one of those heart wrenching groups."

The 41-footer drew close to mooring at the station. "My cell phone rings. It was [the Joint Forces] lawyers calling me directly. They said, 'We've rethought this.' They're telling me [the Cubans are] wet foot. I got really upset. [The Cubans] are cheering, they can see the station. I said, 'You know what happens when they are that close—they bail off.' There were a lot of little kids" on the boat and Bowen worried about their safety.

"I had to think really quickly," recalled Bowen. "I told the coxswain to quietly turn around and go back out. I'm not too sure whether I should have just said, 'Screw it, there's so much risk of these Cubans going overboard and getting hurt if they realized we were taking them out.'"

The boat turned around and started out. Bowen followed in his boat in case anyone jumped overboard. "Safety of life is always paramount," said Master Chief Bowen. "I am not sure I made the right decision." Later a federal judge declared the U.S. Coast Guard lawyers wrong in their decision and ruled that the Cubans were dry feet. District judge Federico Moreno called "the administration's decision to repatriate the Cubans unreasonable and demanded that the Department of Homeland Security make its best efforts to bring the Cubans back to the United States." Most of the Cubans managed to make it back to the United States.

The difficult decision forced upon Master Chief Bowen is but one example of what the policy means to those enforcing the law. If Master Chief Bowen had put the undocumented migrants ashore, he could have faced charges of disobeying an order. As it was, Bowen and his station crew had to face angry media and Cuban American activists. Master Chief said that he always told his crews "we are always fifteen minutes from an international incident." His observation proved correct at the old seven-mile bridge.[28]

In addition to the dangers brought about by the wet foot, dry foot policy, the crews sometimes felt frustration. An incident at Station Islamorada beginning on May 6, 2003, is a case in point. A petty officer third class and his three crew members received orders to proceed to the area of Key Largo, in the Florida Keys, to intercept Cubans in a makeshift sailing craft. The coxswain of the U.S. Coast Guard boat recalled, "These guys were two miles from shore; we knew they would be determined to make it, but we still didn't approach . . . [the case] any different than usual."[29]

The wind worked in favor of the Cubans, pushing them toward shore and dry foot. The petty officer ordered the four Cubans to lower their sail. They refused three times. The boarding party then decided to cut the line controlling the sail. Over the next few minutes things became hectic. A Cuban took down the six-foot mast and, using it as a spear, lunged at the petty officer, who drew his sidearm and aimed it at the undocumented migrant, while another Cuban brandished a knife. Two members of the boarding party then sprayed the Cuban holding the spear-like pole with pepper spray. The boarding party then retreated to their craft to regroup and call for backup.

A boarding party member yelled to the Cubans in Spanish, "Drop your weapons!" The two Cubans threw their weapons over the side of their craft. To be safe, the petty officer had his Spanish-speaking crew member tell the Cubans to throw "every single thing off the raft to ensure we could see the deck. That's when we saw a machete go overboard, another knife, fishing gear, a compass and clothing."

The U.S. Coast Guard crew members watched as the Cubans threw off their clothing and doused themselves with salt water. This would make it difficult to bring them on board the U.S. Coast Guard boat.

About this time, the inevitable news helicopter crews began filming the drama that was taking place. The petty officer tried to take the Cuban craft under tow. A boarding team member was hit by a Cuban, who in turn received a dose of pepper spray.

Soon thereafter the Cubans jumped into the water. The petty officer ordered the tow line cast off so he could maneuver to pick up the undocumented migrants. Once cast loose, the Cubans climbed back into their craft. The petty officer again ordered the Cuban boat taken in tow. Once the towline was secured, the Cubans went back into the water.

"We threw lifejackets to them; they threw them back at us. They threw lines off our stern to try to foul up our propellers. They spat at us, they threatened to swim under my engines," recalled the petty officer. "I even had to pull the engine kill switch a couple of time."

As the petty officer began to reposition his boat between the undocumented migrants in the water and the beach, he received a message from U.S. Coast Guard District 7 Command Center to allow any undocumented Cuban who wanted to be picked up on board the boat, and if the others refused, they should be allowed to swim to shore. Other law enforcement people awaited them on the beach. Only one Cuban willingly climbed on board the U.S. Coast Guard boat. Later, ABC World Nightly News newscaster Peter Jennings said the U.S. Coast Guard crew exercised "remarkable restraint" throughout the incident. The Cuban undocumented migrant who voluntarily gave up was transported to Guantánamo and accepted asylum in Panama. Two of the three remaining Cubans faced trial on charges of assaulting federal officers.

On April 5, 2004, the two Cuban undocumented migrants went to trial. Their defense attorney said the U.S. Coast Guard boarding party overreacted, that the Cubans did not understand the commands. Furthermore, there was no physical evidence of any weapons. (Recall that the U.S. Coast Guard boarding party had the Cubans throw everything that could be considered a weapon into the sea out of concern for the safety of the boarding party.) Three days later, on April 8, the jury ruled in favor of the Cubans. They were "welcomed to America by the jury's foreman . . . in front of cameras which rolled outside the courtroom."

Because of the nature of their work, the U.S. Coast Guard has had some form of communications with Cuba since Fidel Castro came to power. Capt. Randy Beardsworth, USCG (Ret.) writes that the service's communication with Castro's regime remains "one of the most well-established functional relationship between the two countries" and the longest between the Cuban Border Guard. The relationship, beginning with teletype communications, focused quite naturally on search and rescue. However, "between the late 1970s and 2000 there have been at least four meetings between the U.S. government and the Cuban government for ironing out protocols for communication." As the War on Drugs escalated, the need for better operational information between Castro's regime and the U.S. Coast Guard arose. The Department of State in the 1990s gave its permission for the service to communicate with Cuba on drug smuggling.[30]

During the increase of undocumented Cubans to the United States, a volunteer rescue organization known as Brothers to the Rescue came into being. The volunteers flew aircraft to help guide rafters to safety in Florida. In 1996 Cuban fighter aircraft attacked and shot down two of the organization's airplanes in the straits "for allegedly violating Cuban airspace."[31]

Cuban Americans began organizing "freedom flotillas" of private craft to approach Cuban waters and conduct demonstrations, including dropping flowers in memory of the deceased pilots of Brothers to the Rescue. Quite naturally, both Cuba and the United States worried that such activities so near Cuban territorial waters might lead to an international incident. The U.S. Coast Guard became the lead federal agency in trying to work with both the Cuban government and the freedom flotillas. Officers consulted with the organizers, coordinated U.S. resources, and sent a U.S. Coast Guard officer to the Special Interest Section in Havana to "coordinate with the Cuban Border Guard. In the process, the professional relationships between the two operational organizations, the U.S. Coast Guard and the Cuban Border Guard, was strengthened."[32]

The drug issue, the case of the flotillas, and migration all led the U.S. Coast Guard to propose to the Department of State that a meeting with Castro's government would help the communications between the service and the Border Guard. In 1999 Captain Beardsworth attended meetings in Havana in which the Cuban government agreed to allow telephone communications between the Border Guard and the U.S. Coast Guard and "protocols for the two agencies' vessels to communicate by radio at sea, and for the U.S. to assist the Border Guard in certain drug cases."[33]

One part of this 1999 agreement that Captain Beardsworth helped negotiate is little known, even within the service. There is a U.S. Coast Guard liaison officer stationed in Havana at the U.S. Special Interest Section. The genesis of this position began when Beardsworth attended Harvard as a National Security Fellow in 1995–96. Most of the attendees' interest focused on Korea, Russia, and Eastern Europe. Beardsworth felt those fields were crowded, so he pursued the Caribbean. Rafael Hernandez, a visiting scholar from Cuba, held a seminar. Beardsworth said he "would go over every other week for the seminar and sit in the back. I didn't know much about Cuba."[34]

As it turned out, the only people to attend the seminar the first week were a *New York Times* reporter, Beardsworth, a retired faculty member, and the head of the department. "I got forced into having a conversation," recalled Beardsworth. The "conversation" between Beardsworth and Hernandez "developed into a series of conversations focused" on building confidence between Cuba and the United States "if the relationships between our governments changed. We looked at things like pollution, counter narcotics, and migration."[35]

The conversations moved to jointly writing a paper. In 2006, after the shooting down of the Brothers to the Rescue aircraft, Rafael went back to Cuba. "Rafael actually wrote an article, but shortly after that Raúl [Castro] condemned the academics and expelled a number from their posts, including Rafael, who went into internal exile. So the collaboration on the article went down the drain."[36]

Later, stationed in Miami as the chief of law enforcement for U.S. Coast Guard District 7, Beardsworth "took some of the ideas and we created a planning document for the U.S. Coast Guard of things we could do with Cuba. That managed to make it somehow to the National Security Council." The document also reached the State Department.[37]

Beardsworth recalled that "one day in 1998 I got a call to meet Adm. Ray Riutta, head of operations in headquarters, at the Department of State. We got in an elevator and Ray says, 'Randy do you know why you are here?'"

"I don't have any idea."

"We're going to talk about Cuba."

Those attending the meeting were Riutta, Beardsworth, the Department of State assistant secretary for International Narcotics and Law Enforcement, Rand Beers, one of Beers's staff, and a person from the Western Hemisphere Affairs at the White House.

Beardsworth remembered that "the assistant secretary turns to Ray and says, 'Tell us your ideas about Cuba.'"

The admiral replied, "I'll have Randy tell you about it."

Many years later, Captain Beardsworth recalled, "I hadn't thought about this in about six months. I didn't know I was going to be asked to explain the ideas." Beers said to Beardsworth, "What are the three or four things we could do?"

Beardsworth recalled, "Literally, off the top of my head I reached out and pulled out three or four things." Beers said, "Thank you, Admiral."

After the meeting, the Admiral Riutta said to Beardsworth, "Give me a white paper by tomorrow." Beardsworth said, "Ultimately, I went to Cuba in 1999 and negotiated these four points. We got all four, one of which was the liaison billet."[38]

One U.S. Coast Guard officer assigned to Havana said, "For me, it was a fascinating job. . . . I was in the Embassy in Costa Rica before coming to Cuba. I got to see firsthand what happens when you are a top ally of the United States. Going to Cuba was the opposite, to see the confrontational efforts."[39]

The officers in Havana found themselves "in a catch-22 situation." Interestingly, one U.S. Coast Guard officer said,

> You have to understand that the Cubans more than anything else want to reestablish military to military relations with the U.S. government. They see this Border Guard-U.S. Coast Guard relationship as the model and they want it to work. They want the positive relationship to be reverberated in Washington. By working with the Border Guard, the Cubans are sending signals that they wish full-blown military-to-military relationships. We had several [U.S.] retired four star [officers] out of U.S. Southern Command come down to Cuba and say we should be working with the Cubans, that's the path to getting relations going with the Cubans.

Another officer stationed in Havana said, "Current U.S. policy [2008] does not allow for normalization of relations." The officer went on to point out that prior to any relaxation of relations, the Helms-Burton Act requires the president to submit a determination to Congress that a 'transition government' is in power in Cuba.[40] What constitutes "a 'transition government' has been defined in the Act . . . For example, a specification that such a government may not include Fidel Castro or his brother, Raúl Castro, in an active or inactive role or position."

Most of the U.S. Coast Guard officers said the assignment placed an officer "in a very precarious situation." Both the U.S. Coast Guard officer and

Border Guard wanted the relationship to work. However, a Coast Guard officer "does not get many points for working with the enemy and vice versa." The officers of both nations found themselves "in a very unique situation." Furthermore, Cuban and U.S. officers had to be very careful how close they got to each other. Yet both knew their most important mission focused on preventing international incidents. "We had this understanding that you could call on me 24/7 and I could call on you whenever there was a situation on our level to keep it out of escalation, with the Cuban Missile Crisis being the ultimate level of escalation. We both had a desire to work through our differences, very respectfully."

On the political level, each Cuban and U.S. officer quite naturally "saw things very differently. We didn't call it cooperation; we called it a case-by-case activity. There were some cases the Cubans wanted to work well with us on, there were some cases there was no working with."

Another officer related, "Everything the Cubans do is very calculative and required us to stay a couple of steps ahead of them to achieve a desirable outcome." One officer related the story of a strange case. A U.S. Coast Guard auxiliarist near Marathon Key was working on his boat while the engine was running and on autopilot. A wave struck the 27-foot Boston Whaler and threw the man over the side while the boat continued on a preset course. The auxiliarist spent twenty-hours in the water before being safely rescued.

Later, the U.S. Coast Guard officer at that time assigned to Havana received a call from a Border Guard official saying, "We got this boat that says 'Coast Guard Auxiliary' on the side. It just showed up on our shore with no one in it." They brought the U.S. Coast Guard officer pictures of the boat. The U.S. officer received the boat's number from the Cubans and then contacted U.S. Coast Guard District 7 for information on the case. He then briefed the Cuban Border Guard.

Next, "of course, the insurance company contacted me right away and said we would like to have that boat back; otherwise they had to pay the guy off." The officer then started "a formal diplomatic request to the Cuban government to return the vessel. They wouldn't do it, even though there was this special relationship. I thought that if there was ever a gimme, this was it. I knew you couldn't bring anyone into the country. I even volunteered to run it back. But they would not return the boat."

Ironically, the Cuban Border Guard base in Havana is between the Hemingway Marina and the old Biltmore Country Club. The U.S. Coast Guard officer could see the former auxiliarist's boat tied up at the Border Guard's pier, now with the Border Guard's distinguishing stripe on it. As the U.S. Coast Guard officer mentioned, this case illustrates "there were times when the Cubans were very forthright on casework and other times not so helpful."

The U.S. Coast Guard officers in Havana constantly faced one of the major sticking points between Cuba and the United States. One officer said, "The Cuban government calls wet foot, dry foot, and the Cuban Adjustment Act, *la ley de los asesinos* [the assassins' law]."

"The Cubans accuse the U.S. government of being hypocritical," pointed out another officer. "On one hand [they say your government tells] the U.S. Coast Guard [to] do everything you can to prevent these illegal migrants from coming in, but on the other hand they reward the Cuban migrant the second they make landfall."

Still another officer pointed out that the "Cuban government says, 'We can down play this migration, if you would just change your law. If the Cubans knew even if they got into the United States, they would be repatriated, just like the Haitians; there would be a tremendous disincentive.'"

In rebuttal, the U.S. Coast Guard officers "would tell them, wet foot, dry foot is a policy decision and [the Cuban Adjustment Act is a law.] The U.S. Coast Guard is not going to be able to change [this]." The officers also added that Cuba's "poor economical conditions and repressive political environment force Cubans to migrate."

The U.S. officers pointed out that the migration accords state that the Border Guard will notify the U.S. Coast Guard whenever they observe a raft leaving. "You are doing a good job of telling us when the go fast [boats] are coming in," the officers would tell the Cuban Border Guards, "but rather than just telling us when they are in your territorial waters, we need you to intercept them and take them into custody. Don't just go and see them and notify us. Do something. Act."

The Cuban officials responded:

> Listen, when you guys receive [the undocumented migrants], it is five hours [after they have left], or three days, when they're weathered, tired and hun-

> gry. They're a lot less feisty. When we get them, they're fresh in their voyage. When we come alongside in our patrol boats—they don't have the fancy boarding platforms that we do—they are hitting us with oars, throwing things at us. With the amount of force we are going to have to use, people are going to get hurt. If you didn't have the Cuban Adjustment Act, maybe they wouldn't be going out.

As pointed out by the U.S. Coast Guard officers, the Cubans were not going to put their people "in harm's way [in order to take the undocumented migrants] off their rafts, or shoot at them in go fast boats, for that is the only way you can stop a go fast." What they would do was notify the U.S. Coast Guard.

In general, most of the U.S. Coast Guard officers noted that the system "works very well." Part of the reason for the U.S. Coast Guard's success in intercepting undocumented migrants is because of the Cuban's notification.

Most officers found the duty "fascinating." At first officers could travel anywhere in Cuba; then, after an amendment to the Helms-Burton Act restricting the movement of Cuban diplomats in the United States, officers by 2005 were restricted to a twenty-six mile radius around Havana, unless they were escorted by a Cuban official. This restriction applied to all U.S. diplomats assigned to the U.S. Special Interest Section in Havana. Nevertheless, one officer said he "found the simplicity of life and lack of technological gadgetry to be a refreshing change." The officer enjoyed shopping in the open-air markets. He admired the Cuban people's innovation, as evidenced by their ability to keep things running long past their normal shelf time.

Most officers did not like the "fish bowl" environment. One officer said of being stationed in Havana: "I wish every American could experience living in Cuba, if only to appreciate our freedom and the quality of life we have." Furthermore, the officer felt a part "of an exclusive fraternity tied together by our unique experience to operate under the watchful eye of the Cuban government in an environment which outsiders could neither fathom to understand nor were permitted to visit."

Captain Beardsworth, who negotiated the billet for a U.S. Coast Guard officer in Havana, wrote that through 2009 "there have been five consecutive [U.S. Coast Guard Liaison Officers] posted to the U.S. Interests Section. . . . By all accounts, this particular operational relationship is fulfilling expectations and meeting both countries' national interests."[41] Of the officers who had served in Havana, all proved to possess outstanding abilities for the assignment.

In 2006, when Fidel Castro seemed on the verge of death, many hoped that his brother, Raúl, who took over as president that year, might bring about changes to the island. A 2007 increase in undocumented migrants, however, is seen by some as disillusionment in the new president. Others point out the movement is economic.

By 2007 the *New York Times* reported that Cubans were migrating to the United States "in the greatest numbers in over a decade, and for most of them the new way to get north is first head west—to Mexico—in a convoluted route that avoids the United States Coast Guard."[42]

Even prior to 2007, Cubans began seeking a less risky and less expensive route to the United States instead of traveling directly to Florida. The Cubans ran into problems when trying a new route to Central America:

> The government of Honduras at the time had a policy that they would put into detention camps any Cubans that would arrive, while Nicaragua and Guatemala would take care of any that arrived. The thinking [among the Cubans] was that you didn't want to arrive in Honduras. So, what the Cubans would do when they thought they were off [their destination], they would take the [raft into] about 500 meters off the beach and send in their best swimmer in [to] find out where they were at. If they found out they were in [Honduran waters], they would go further south.[43]

Obviously, the longer voyage to Mexico in unseaworthy craft greatly increases the danger. The risky sea voyage, however, is only the beginning of the hazards of this route. Jose Luis Savater took four days to reach Isla Mujeres, Mexico. Along with fourteen others, including one woman, Savater's transportation was a "rickety boat made of wood, fiberglass and aluminum and powered by a jury-rigged motor used for irrigating fields." The Cubans took turns bailing the craft. In a bit of understatement, Savater reported, "It's extremely dangerous. I saw myself dead. I suffered a lot."

The next leg of the journey for Savater proved easier. He obtained an airline ticket, with money wired from relatives in Florida, to Matamoros,

Mexico, just across from Brownsville, Texas. Because of poor border security, Savater had only to walk across the border and tell U.S. officials that he sought political asylum. In short, he is now considered "dry foot." Some now call this the "dusty foot" route.[44]

One former official at the U.S. Special Interest Section in Havana said that the Mexican route began because of economic and risk factors. That is, the costs and risks of traveling from Cuba directly to the Florida Keys became too high. Cubans explored another way. Because many could not afford the high cost of the Cuba-Florida route, they cobbled together homemade craft and propulsion, including "in at least one case, a weed trimmer."[45]

When migrants forged a new route, smugglers soon followed. Some smugglers now operate out of Miami with people in place on the coasts of Cuba and Mexico. They have set up safe houses on the Mexican coast. This has led to gang rivalry and, in some cases, murder. Problems began when rival smugglers clashed over territory. For example, the bodies of three people "suspected of smuggling Cubans . . . through Mexico were found gagged and blindfolded . . . near Cancun." By early 2008, many Cubans still used the makeshift form of transportation on the Mexican route, but now smugglers added high-powered go-fast boats and charged US$10,000 per person.[46]

Cuban authorities have large stretches of isolated beaches to patrol, with not much in the way of equipment. They attempt to close off portions of beaches. If they manage to spot a boatload of undocumented migrants leaving, they use a loud speaker to warn them of the dangers and try to persuade them to return; the migrants rarely, if ever, turn around. If "a boat seems headed for Florida, they radio the United States Coast Guard. If it seems on course to Mexico, they throw up their arms."[47]

In the last quarter of 2008, Mexico and Cuba entered into an agreement "to deport Cubans smuggled into the country on their way to the United States." Cuban foreign minister Felipe Pérez Roque said at the signing of the agreement that the pact "will be a decisive tool for preventing and confronting illegal immigration, human trafficking and other related crimes."[48] Pacts between countries and the enforcement work of the U.S. Coast Guard and others, however, does not spell the end of undocumented Cubans trying to reach the United States—far from it.

14 Something Different Happening Every Day

> A picture does not tell the whole story.
>
> Capt. Thomas C. Paar, USCG (1999)

The effects of the wet foot, dry foot policy for those in the U.S. Coast Guard at sea, small boat stations, and air stations of the service have been discussed in previous chapters. Not too surprisingly, the policy also causes challenges for those at the senior levels of the service. In a narrow space of time in 1999 there occurred a series of events for the commander of U.S. Coast Guard District 7. How then–Rear Adm. Thad W. Allen, U.S. Coast Guard, dealt with these cases and their aftermath graphically illustrates what "wet foot, dry foot" can mean for those who lead the service. A decade later, now commandant of the U.S. Coast Guard, Admiral Allen, recalled the period as "something different happening every day."[1]

On Tuesday, June 29, 1999, Allen had held command of the district for two weeks. His schedule for this Tuesday called for him to fly to Puerto Rico for the change of command of the commanding officer of the Marine Safety Office (MSO) at San Juan. "Just as the door of the aircraft was closing," he received a message saying that U.S. Coast Guard Station Miami Beach had a case in progress involving Cuban undocumented migrants four hundred yards off Surfside, a town just north of Miami Beach. While the Cubans tried to get around the station's boats, television news helicopters hovered over the area. "Then the aircraft doors closed." Admiral Allen explained that "we had had a lot of migrant cases and a lot of television videotaping cases." The situation did not seem in itself a reason to cancel his appearance at the ceremony.

Upon his arrival in San Juan, about two and one-half hours later, the commanding officer of the MSO met him and told him there were telephone calls waiting for him. "I learned that my chief of staff, Capt. Greg Sutton, was trying to get to Miami Beach to hold a press conference." Allen also learned that demonstrators had stopped the outbound traffic on the MacArthur Causeway, a major link between Miami and Miami Beach, and the island on which U.S. Coast Guard Station Miami Beach is located. "There were traffic slowdowns all around town."

What Admiral Allen faced became known as the "Surfside 6" incident. Six Cubans in a 15-foot wooden boat managed to reach within four hundred yards of the beach at Surfside. The U.S. Coast Guard Command Center in Miami dispatched a 41-foot boat from U.S. Coast Guard Station Miami Beach to intercept the Cubans. The ubiquitous television news helicopter also arrived on scene and began to broadcast live what unfolded below. The news helicopters recorded a U.S. Coast Guard helicopter using its rotor wash (wind from the rotor blades) to push the Cuban boat back. The undocumented migrants refused to stop and eventually entered the water.[2]

The crew of the U.S. Coast Guard craft tried to pull the Cubans from the water while the undocumented migrants attempted to evade them and make it to the beach, thus becoming "dry foot." More U.S. Coast Guard units arrived. Three boats from Station Miami Beach, one North Miami Police boat, and a U.S. Coast Guard helicopter naturally attracted attention. More news helicopters arrived, and people gathered on the beach.[3]

The situation escalated. Television viewers and the growing crowds on the beach watched as the U.S. Coast Guard boat crews used streams of water from fire hoses—described as "water cannons" by some of the media—to force the swimmers to give up. Because the streams of water were not working, a crewman on one of the boats pepper-sprayed an undocumented migrant while he swam near a U.S. Coast Guard 41-footer. This was all broadcast live throughout the Miami area. As is normal with such television reporting during a news event, viewers saw constant replays of the water and pepper-spraying, and they listened to commentators give their version of what was taking place at Surfside.[4] Admiral Allen later related, "The switchboards of the Hispanic talk radio stations of Miami lit up" with heated comments from indignant and angry callers.

Two of the undocumented Cubans somehow managed to make it to shore, where police promptly arrested them, prompting many irate comments from the onlookers. The other four undocumented migrants eventually gave up. Boat crew members placed them into a 41-foot U.S. Coast Guard boat and transported the undocumented migrants to a 110-foot patrol boat off shore to begin the normal procedures of questioning and possible repatriation.

By that evening, furious protestors blocked the MacArthur Causeway highway. Demonstrations broke out through the Miami area. The calls to the talk radio stations continued. Callers began demanding that the four Cubans be allowed to remain in the United States. Demonstrators in the street also continued this demand.

Meanwhile, back at San Juan, after finishing his telephone call from his chief of staff, Admiral Allen prepared to return immediately to Miami. The next call came from Adm. James Loy, the commandant of the U.S. Coast Guard and the senior officer of the service. Rear Admiral Allen explained to Admiral Loy what he knew of the situation in Miami.

Admiral Loy then said, "What are you going to do?"

"Get on the plane and go back to Miami."

"That sounds like a good idea."

By the time Admiral Allen arrived back in Miami, around 9:00 p.m., "basically everything had happened." The media frenzy continued while Allen and his staff tried "to figure out what happens next."

The service held the four undocumented migrants offshore and out of sight of land. Normally, "we would have repatriated [the Cubans], but with the political volatility of the incident," said Admiral Allen, it made the situation uncertain. Eventually "a deal was cut with the White House that we [the U.S. Coast Guard] weren't even involved in" and the four migrants were brought ashore. Admiral Allen recalled that this happened by 10:00 p.m.

The indignation from the public and media did not slacken the next day. Admiral Allen received a telephone call the next morning that "Governor

[John E. "Jeb"] Bush wants to see you in Tallahassee immediately." The national news media carried harsh words from President Clinton on the U.S. Coast Guard's actions at Surfside.[5]

A decade later Admiral Allen said, "Moving away from the tactical problems of the incident, how do you handle this incident as a senior leader?" Allen's first action was to call together his staff and inform them he would hold a press conference. "I needed to explain where I was at during the incident—in an airplane—and what I intended to do." Admiral Allen explained that rumors had circulated that he was hiding during the confrontation.

Allen wanted his actions to be "transparent." At the press conference he explained that he would "convene an investigation." The investigation would "measure the conduct of our people and how we conducted the operation against our [own] standards." Admiral Allen went on to explain that if the service's standards were not met, he would apply appropriate action to those responsible. Conversely, "if the standards were met and there is a problem with the standards, then we need to change the policy of what they did at Surfside."

Admiral Allen also did something unusual for the U.S. Coast Guard: he removed the people involved in the case from law enforcement duties during the investigation. "I [thought] it best not to subject them to anything while we were trying to figure out what happened." Understandably, this announcement did not go over well with the crew at Station Miami Beach. Some thought they were "going to be the scapegoats for the Admiral." Admiral Allen sent MCPO Charles W. Bowen, who was at the time the command master chief for District 7, to explain to the crews that he was thinking of the crew and the "integrity of the U.S. Coast Guard . . . and they should not take it as a loss of faith [in them]." The admiral also visited the station with the same message.

Admiral Allen also pointed out at the press conference that the captain selected would not be under his command, thus disputing any comments that the investigating officer had to worry about repercussions from the admiral. Capt. Thomas C. Paar, USCG, assistant superintendent of the U.S. Coast Guard Academy, received the assignment. Captain Paar had previously served as the commanding officer of Group Miami Beach.

Admiral Allen told the media that after the completion of the investigation, he would hold another press conference and release the report without them having to file a Freedom of Information Act request to read the results. "This made my lawyers apoplectic when I stated that," recalled Admiral Allen.

Captain Paar's investigation began on Tuesday, July 6, 1999. Before the investigation concluded, another event took place that brought additional problems for Admiral Allen. "In the second week of July we had a [Cuban American] flotilla heading south to make a statement," recalled Allen.

The Cuban Americans left in their craft during the night. At some point during that night a confrontation occurred with a rustic Cuban boat of undocumented migrants and the U.S. Coast Guard 82-foot patrol boat *Point Glass* (WPB-82336). The patrol boat and the rustic shouldered each other (hit a glancing blow). The first reports did not make clear who hit who, but in any case the Cuban boat flipped over. Everyone got out, except one woman who could not swim. She was sitting in the bow and had an inner tube around her. When the boat went over, the tube prevented her from getting out. "Now, we have another incident," recalled Admiral Allen.

After the Surfside case, many questions about the U.S. Coast Guard began circulating around Miami, one of which stated that if what happened at Surfside took place in daylight close to shore, what were they doing at night offshore and out of sight? Now a Cuban woman died offshore at night.

Admiral Allen recalled that he immediately informed Governor Bush of the incident. "We decided not to release the information until after the Cuban American [flotilla] left its demonstration. We thought that if they heard the news, it might affect their behavior and put people at risk. We announced about noon the next day. The reaction was: 'What in hell is the Coast Guard doing?'"

Admiral Allen brought in Capt. Timothy Doherty to conduct an investigation, "with pretty much the same results. The whole issue focused on how the two boats came into contact." Did the U.S. Coast Guard patrol boat hit the Cuban American boat, or vice versa? The investigation showed that the Cuban American boat had tried to get under the bow of the patrol boat, and this caused the contact, which caused the boat to flip. To obtain this information, Admiral Allen had Spanish-speaking investigators interview the Cuban undocumented migrants on the patrol boat. He also later sent Spanish-speaking investigators to Cuba to do follow-up interviews.

Shortly thereafter Admiral Allen called a press conference and released Captain Paar's report concerning the Surfside case. Captain Paar accomplished an amazingly thorough investigation in a short time.

For those who observed the incident on television, the pepper-spraying and the spraying of water remained the most troubling acts. Captain Paar approached these subjects head-on. The use of pepper spray remained within the U.S. Coast Guard's policy of use of force. That is, if a boarding officer feels in danger, or to protect someone else in danger, then the service authorizes the use of pepper spray. Unknown to most viewers of the event, an undocumented migrant had threatened to swim into the propellers of the 41-foot boat. Furthermore, earlier one of the Cubans had swung a board with a nail in it at the U.S. Coast Guardsmen. Moreover, at this time, the violence level caused by the wet foot, dry foot policy had increased among the Cuban undocumented migrants. As Captain Paar pointed out, all of these reasons explained the use of the pepper spray.

After ruling that the boat crew followed policy, Captain Paar interrupted his narrative and wrote, "I would like to draw a 'line of safety' in the sand, and with the benefit of eight days vice eight minutes of thought and analysis, address some safety issues with respect to the [U.S.] Coast Guard's actions." Paar "had no objection to [the use of pepper spray] while the migrants were in the boat. . . . However, with the respect to the line of safety, I question its use while once the migrants were in the water." Captain Paar also noted that when a petty officer first class arrived to become the on-scene commander, he ordered the crew to stop using the spray.[6]

On the use of the helicopter and fire hoses, Captain Paar found their uses within policy but again over "the line of safety." In addition, Paar pointed out that before "the use of fire hoses against people [there needs an] understanding of the cultural meaning/history for this action."[7]

The investigation revealed that part of the problem stemmed from an almost tunnel-vision mindset in the leadership at the Group and District 7 Command Center in Miami that they had to stop the undocumented migrants at all coasts. The first class petty officer who became the on-scene commander at one point over the radio recommended that they should back off and let the Cubans swim to shore. Higher authority refused and ordered the continued effort, so the drama continued to play out.

Captain Paar clearly felt that the boat crews never intended "to hurt or harm the Cuban migrants." He pointed out that actions of the senior petty officer illustrate this fact.[8] As Captain Paar noted, what eventually ended the confrontation with the remaining four Cubans was that one gave up and a member of a boat crew entered the water and brought the other two into the boat. While not exactly finding anything wrong with this, Captain Paar felt that the entering of a boat crew into the water crossed the line of safety. He felt this should be accomplished only by those who had received extensive training in rescue swimming.

In the eighth and last of his opinions in the report, Captain Paar wrote: "The view from the news camera at several hundred feet in the air gave a very limited look at this situation. It did not capture the sound or dialogue, nor did it convey an appreciation for the meaning/threat of a raised paddle that a law enforcement officer observed up close and personal. Consequently, to the viewer, the response to actions appear disconnected or unexpected." He closed with what many who have been exposed to video television coverage might say: "A picture does not tell the whole story."[9]

After receiving the report and releasing it, Admiral Allen notified the media that he had set into motion certain recommendations based upon Captain Paar's investigation, and that the commandant of the U.S. Coast Guard had accepted the recommendations. Pepper spray could no longer be used on migrants in the water "unless they pose a threat to officer safety." He emphasized that "safety is of paramount concern in migrant law enforcement." Boarding parties should consider that using pepper spray on undocumented migrants in an open boat might cause them to leap into the water. He further noted that before water streams are directed at a boat, the stability of the craft must be considered. Allen said, "I am now well aware of the sensitivities to using firehoses on people. Accordingly, directing solid steady streams of water directly on passengers is neither appropriate, nor authorized except against violent or unruly crowds."[10] Much later Admiral Allen added that another factor had entered into the angst of the Cuban Americans. At one point, the Cuban Border Guard had used a steady stream of water to stop undocumented migrants. The volume of water eventually caused the sinking of the craft, leading to the deaths of a number of Cubans.

Admiral Allen also considered dangerous the use of untrained swimmers in the water to recover undocumented migrants. A struggling undocumented migrant might cause both to drown. Allen said that unless "there is a concern for safety of life at sea," boat crews should not enter the water.

Lastly, Admiral Allen noted that policy needed change, and the Surfside case proved the catalyst for this change. However, the boat crews of Station Miami Beach at the time followed the policy of the service. Allen wrote that the responsibility for the "inappropriate use of pepper spray lies with me as the District Commander, and with the entire Service, rather than the individuals involved. Accordingly, I do not contemplate taking administrative or disciplinary actions against the Coast Guard personnel who were involved."[11] Much later, and after some further changes in policy, Admiral Allen remarked that he wanted to "subtly" tell those working with undocumented migrants that "safety of life is the number one goal . . . that we may have to accept that people may make it ashore" if it means putting either the crew or the undocumented migrant at risk in trying to stop them.

The investigation and Admiral Allen's actions, plus the release of the report on the woman's death, helped hold things down in the Miami area.

The Surfside and the *Point Glass* cases, and others, happened during the first few months of Admiral Allen's tenure as commander of U.S. Coast Guard District 7. Admiral Allen said a decade later, "Then the coup de grâce happened."

On the Sunday before Thanksgiving, District 7 received a report from the Cuban Border Guard of a northbound craft with a number of people in it. Admiral Allen pointed out that "the families [waiting in Florida] will never tell you that [any boat] is overdue until they panic." This means that any search is already at least twenty-four hours late.

In this case, the U.S. Coast Guard searched for the overdue boat on Monday and Tuesday, with no results. "At some point," said Allen, "you assume that they made it [into the United States.]" After the two-day search, the case was closed.

On Thursday, Thanksgiving Day, Admiral Allen received a call at his home in Miami from the district command center. The center reported that two Cuban adults had come ashore on Key Biscayne and said they had become separated from a larger boat of undocumented migrants that sank.

"We immediately concluded it was the boat we were looking for and launched a massive search," Admiral Allen recalled. The search continued throughout the day.

"I am eating a turkey sandwich and watching the Dallas Cowboys on television," recalled Allen. "I get a telephone call from the command center. 'Admiral, Station Fort Lauderdale came upon a boat with two fishermen that found a five-year-old boy in an inner tube. We figured it might be connected to the case.'"

"I asked, 'What is his condition?'"

Admiral Allen learned the boy did not speak English. He appeared hypothermic even in 70-degree water. "I didn't even hesitate at that point and said, 'Bring him in and get him seen by a doctor.' After that, I had no control over what happened."

The boy's name was Elian Gonzalez. The question of who should have custody over the small boy—his father in Cuba or relatives in the United States—launched a national and international media frenzy. As the battle continued into 2000, an amazing amount of ink, movie film, video, and photographs chronicled the legal and verbal battles. Politicians of both parties entered the fray.

The dispute ended with dramatic and wrenching photographs of a raid by armed federal law enforcers taking the boy from the house where he resided in Florida to be delivered to his father in Cuba. On June 28, 2000, Elian returned to Cuba.

As Admiral Allen pointed out, once Elian reached shore, the matter no longer rested with the U.S. Coast Guard, and it is not the purpose of this work to show the twisted path of this story. Richard Cohen, writing in the *Washington Post*, perhaps best sums up this story: "Elian and Juan Miguel Gonzalez, son and father. The former is an innocent child, the latter a man whose boy was taken from him. Elian has behaved like a typical 6-year-old, Juan Miguel like a typical father. And most of the politicians like typical fools."[12]

Admiral Allen related that because of his position in the law enforcement community, "I knew about the raid." The Gonzalez incident, combined with the Surfside and *Point Glass* cases plus other incidents, made him "realize there is something fundamentally wrong with our [the U.S. Coast Guard's] Cuban American relationship and we can't live like this." He felt that, as the senior leader of the service in Florida, it was his "responsibility to redefine what the U.S. Coast Guard is and what they do in the community of South Florida."

He began by obtaining a list of "up to twelve people who represented broad-based viewpoints of the Cuban American community." He then invited these people to a personal two-hour meeting with him at district headquarters. Later, Admiral Allen recalled that "I set up the room with traditional Cuban pastries and Cuban coffee—*café con leche*." He later learned that "this little gesture" paid great dividends, for the invited people realized the admiral was respectful of them and their culture.

He spoke to the meeting participants about their perceptions of wet foot, dry foot and other matters. Allen realized that he had to reach out to the community and explain to them what the U.S. Coast Guard is and what they do. Allen volunteered to be area chairman of the Combined Federal Campaign for Southern Florida. This allowed him an entry to an even larger base of people.

Admiral Allen then approached the publisher of the *Miami Herald* newspaper. He wanted the paper to show U.S. Coast Guard people as a part of the fabric of the community. The publisher agreed.

From the Surfside case onward, Admiral Allen realized that, along with broadening his base with the community, he needed to include "local politicians and make sure they understood our mission." What helped greatly in this part of his plan came from a call from a woman from the Cuban American community who worked as the public affairs officer for Secretary of State Madeleine Albright. The public affairs officer told Allen that she was coming down to Miami to see him, and she was bringing with her someone from the Cuban Affairs, Western Hemisphere desk of the State Department. She wanted to introduce Allen to a number of influential people in the Miami area and have him explain his mission to these people.

Admiral Allen recalled that near the end of his two-year tenure as the commander of District 7, there occurred a case in which the service rescued two young boys from their capsized boat. The father of one the boys was the treasurer for the state Republican Party. The boy's father came down to thank the crew and the local congressional representative came also and "embraced the guys at the station." Admiral Allen then realized "things were back to where they should be."

Years later, during an interview, Admiral Allen said of his former command at Miami that "every day something new was happening and tactics were evolving because you never knew what you would be presented the next day." Despite the hectic pace, when asked if, in the middle of everything, he might have regretted his assignment to U.S. Coast Guard District 7. Admiral Allen replied emphatically, "Oh, no! This was one of the greatest jobs in the Coast Guard!"

15 Summing Up

> Migrant operations [proved] the hardest, nastiest Coast Guard mission I have ever done.
>
> U.S. Coast Guard officer

Beginning in the latter part of the eighteenth century and continuing for the next 214 years, the U.S. Coast Guard has worked to prevent undocumented migrants from entering the United States via the sea. In this mission, they have performed a credible job, considering a shortage of resources and personnel. For the first 186 years, the mission continued as a "tack-on" assignment. They did have one advantage over the crews of the last two decades of the twentieth century: a consistent political policy. In general, the U.S. policy toward undocumented migrants presented a clear guideline for the U.S. Coast Guard. All of this began changing during the Cuban Camarioca Boatlift in 1965, but the Cuban Mariel Boatlift in 1980 effectively changed an established U.S. Coast Guard mission from part time to full time.

Mariel also had other ramifications that affected how the men and women of the U.S. Coast Guard conducted their mission. Beginning with President Jimmy Carter's poor attempt at handling the 1980 boatlift through President Bill Clinton's vacillating attempts to come to grips with large numbers of Haitians and Cubans, a single phrase sums up these fourteen years: inconsistency in political leadership. Unpreparedness of the service and other federal agencies that deal with undocumented migrants provided a subtext for working with undocumented migrants.

When speaking of their experiences during Mariel, Operation Able Manner, and Operation Able Vigil, many U.S. Coast Guard people spoke of having little or no training for what they faced. One retired officer stated that the service was "rudderless" during Operation Able Manner.[1] Much of this unpreparedness can be laid at the doorstep of Congress: traditionally underfunded and understaffed, the multitasked service can only prepare for so many eventualities.

The question of funding is very important, but equally important is the lack of strong civilian political leadership. The simple fact is that, as far as now can be determined, no one in the civilian or service's leadership expected such an event as Mariel. Part of this is simply because of poor understanding of the country involved.

Contributing to part of the problem, the political leaders also had other international events on their minds and failed to heed the situation at their own doorstep. This is amply illustrated in the three important periods of Cuban undocumented migrant work for the U.S. Coast Guard. Kelley M. Greenhill points out that the Johnson administration struggled with Vietnam and, fearing a tragedy in the Florida Straits, quickly came to an agreement with Castro over Camarioca. Castro, "who is known to be a keen observer of U.S. politics," learned that "the appearance of loss of control over U.S. borders, coupled with the perception inside the U.S. that Florida might be overrun, would be viewed by U.S. leaders as politically costlier than the alternative of dealing with him. Thus if Castro could transform his own domestic problems into the U.S.'s problems via the exploitation of refugees, he could coerce its leaders into helping him solve them."[2]

Greenhill notes that because "so few policymakers in the Carter Administration knew of the Camarioca crisis, they ignored repeated warnings that Castro was considering reopening one of his ports." Another scholar added, "The word 'Camarioca' had no meaning to them. It set off no alarms." Carter at the time struggled with an Iranian crisis plus a heated reelection campaign.

Clinton's conflicting policies can be best summed up by Robert Pastor: "If a crisis did not engage the public or attract the media or an interest group, it was ignored. The administration, however, could not afford to ignore intense objections from a core constituency group . . . [and] it was wary of antagonizing a Florida ethnic group . . . unless a broader national domestic interest (e.g., halting an influx of refugees) forced a recalculation."[3]

It is easy to see why the U.S. Coast Guard operated under such conflicting policies. The service, however, is not entirely blameless for not being prepared. The latest plan for increases in undocumented migrants from Cuba, Operation Plan Vigilant Sentry, states that planners looked at data from Mariel and Operation Able Vigil but did not consider Camarioca. It appears from the written evidence available that Camarioca, as in the Carter administration, is a forgotten word in the service's corporate memory. Even a short fourteen years after Camarioca, there is no evidence that the service had any plans based upon that crisis. Anecdotal evidence indicates that preparedness for Operation Able Vigil also lacked lessons learned from Mariel.[4]

Operation Plan Vigilant Sentry did have a test in 2004 when another increase in Haitian undocumented migrants occurred. All written reports seem to indicate a successful conclusion.

While Operation Plan Vigilant Sentry is a step in the right direction and seems to have the blessing of favorable media coverage, there are still questions. For example, the plan indicates a need for focused civilian political leadership. While this is the U.S. form of government, the political leadership in the past has been anything but focused and consistent. Another aspect not covered is where the undocumented migrants are held until the determination of repatriation or asylum is granted.

Since the 1990s, the service has pointed out the resistance and increasing danger of violence among undocumented migrants, especially Cubans and Chinese. In the case of Cubans, some of this comes from the wet foot, dry foot policy. However, a senior officer pointed out that he believes many of the confrontations from both groups result from language differences. The language confusion could be ameliorated by the service sending more of its officers and enlisted force to language training in at least Spanish, French (preferably Creole), and Chinese (Mandarin). The U.S. Coast Guard Academy does not currently grant majors in any language to its officers. There is a program to certify language proficiency in the enlisted force. However, formal training at the Defense Language Institute in Monterey, California, or other approved language training schools should be undertaken so there is a large pool of trained people on hand. Ideally, there should be at least one Chinese speaker as a boarding team member on every cutter in the Pacific, and cutters in the Atlantic should have at least one Spanish speaker and one French Creole speaker. Shore stations in U.S. Coast Guard District 7 should have the same requirements. Not only should there be language training but also an understanding servicewide of the cultures of the major undocumented migrant groups.[5]

The results of understanding the cultures of the groups of undocumented migrants with whom the service most often works is best illustrated by the work of Adm. Thad W. Allen (see chapter 14). One wonders why such work was not accomplished previously, or why it is not carried out at every district.

Despite a lack of proper funding, a lack of personnel, and in some cases a lack of training, it is amazing how quickly the crews of the U.S. Coast Guard who most closely work with the undocumented migrants react to new and dangerous aspects of a traditional mission. As the people at sea and stations encounter problems, they quickly, and with little or no direction from higher command, solve the difficulties with their own intelligence and experience. In the story of the U.S. Coast Guard's role in attempting to stop the flow of undocumented migrants from the sea, the people on the cutters and stations made the mission work. Recall twenty-two-year-old Lt. (jg) Robert Borowczak, of the cutter *Munro*, who prevented problems with Chinese undocumented migrants with the idea of starting an intravenous line on a sick migrant. For those who study the history of the U.S. Coast Guard, this quick reaction to a new situation with intelligence and inventiveness continues to the present day as the hallmarks of the service. In other words, the people in field carried the mission until the staff and policy could catch up with the situation.

From the time of the immigration accords reached between Cuba and the United States in 1994—popularly known as the wet foot, dry foot policy—there has followed a relatively stable period of fifteen years. Haitian and Chinese policy has remained fairly steady from 1980 onward, with minor changes brought because of periods of unusual numbers of undocumented migrants. The former policy for both countries resumed as soon as events normalized. This has made the duties of the service somewhat easier. Capt.

Bernard Moreland, however, has rightfully pointed out that policymakers should "expect [Chinese undocumented] migration from Fujian to continue, with occasional spikes when U.S. policy makes open loopholes," such as happened at Guam.[6]

It seems evident that two things would immediately help the U.S. Coast Guard in their mission to intercept undocumented migrants: repealing the wet foot, dry foot policy and having a consistent policy for all migrants. A ranking officer in the Border Patrol offered two simple solutions to the problem. First, secure the borders of the United States. Second, change the immigration laws.

The comments proclaiming what is needed to help the U.S. Coast Guard's mission and those of the Border Patrol officer are easier said than done. One major question emerges: setting aside the southwestern border, how do you secure thousands of miles of U.S. coastline? In the final analysis, the borders can be secured and a new immigration policy put into place *if* there is a national and political will plus a will to spend national treasure.

Ideally, the only solution to prevent desperate undocumented migrants from trying to reach the United States is to stop the extreme economic differences between nations. How this can come about is for another book, but as long as these differences continue, there will always be those who are willing to risk even their lives to seek a better way of life. And as long as there are people who are willing to risk their lives for a better life, there will always be those who wish to prey upon these desperate people. Therefore, there will always be a need for the U.S. Coast Guard to perform its mission.

The focus of this examination of the U.S. Coast Guard's role in preventing undocumented migrants from reaching the United States via the maritime route is to show how the mission affects the people who must enforce a political policy. Put another way, this is how the enforcers see what is taking place far from the view of most Americans.

Anyone who wishes to tell the story of the U.S. Coast Guard and its mission of attempting to stop the flow of undocumented migrants from the sea is brought up against a number of amazing stories within the main story. In all of the material in newspapers, journals, and magazines on Haitians, Cuban, and Chinese undocumented migrants, there is a dearth of material on U.S. Coast Guard people and what they accomplish. If they are mentioned at all, it is only a few lines of print. Most of the reason for this lack of information is that reporters focus on the plight of the migrants. One can understand this approach. Very few journalists chose to accompany the cutters and small boats as they worked closely with the undocumented migrants. However, when writers did spend time with a U.S. Coast Guard crew, most wrote a sympathetic view of the enforcers. In fact, they detailed two other important stories concerning the U.S. Coast Guard and its mission. The journalists wrote how most U.S. Coast Guard people had great sympathy for the undocumented migrants but still carried out their mission, not blindly following orders but after understanding both sides of the situation.

There are a number of cases of the humane and compassionate treatment of the undocumented migrants by U.S. Coast Guard people. The example of one officer will suffice. In 2002, Cdr. Randy Beardsworth commanded the cutter *Mohawk*. He also held the title of senior U.S. Coast Guard officer present at Guantánamo. He received an invitation to attend a meeting of high-level officers briefing the chairman of the Joint Chiefs of Staff, Gen. Colin Powell.[7]

Prior to the meeting, the Haitians were screened at Guantánamo to determine if they had legitimate claims for asylum in the United States. Seventeen years later, now retired Captain Beardsworth recalled that the Haitians had figured out how to answer the questions to make their claim. The statistics showed an upward swing in the number of cases with enough legitimacy to proceed to the United States and seek asylum. Someone in the bureaucracy then decided to change to another set of questions. "I didn't have an issue with that" decision, recalled Beardsworth. However, along with the new questions came the decision to make the questions retroactive. In other words, those Haitians who had notified their families or friends in the United States that they had been authorized to come to the States now had to respond to additional questions.

Beardsworth recalled, "That decision was eating at me." Meanwhile, back at the meeting of the senior officers, the officer presiding had just said, "I think that is about it; any other issues?" Feeling there could not be anything else, the officers prepared to leave.

"I hesitated for a minute," remembered Beardsworth.

Then I raised my hand. "General, I have a concern." You could see all the senior leaders go, "Who is this guy? What's the issue he's going to raise?" It was clear from the body language that everyone was not happy with me.

"General, I buy U.S. savings bonds because I believe what the U.S. government tells me—that they are safe and secure and I believe that when the government tells me they are going to pay the bonds, they're going to pay the bonds."

"We have screened these Haitians and told them that they are going to the United States. I don't think that these new procedures should be retroactive. I think we should be going forward, not backward."

Beardsworth recalled, "Everyone gasped."

General Powell said, "Randy, I agree with that and I am going to tell the President that."

Beardsworth said that ultimately the new questions were not retroactive. "I am not sure whether it was my recommendation that caused General Powell to suggest this to the president, but at least General Powell listened to what a much more junior officer had to say."

Beardsworth also recalled another incident on the *Mohawk* while transporting a large number of Haitians back to Haiti. During the night run from Guantánamo to Port au Prince, a message arrived "that there were two families that should not have been sent back to Haiti." Beardsworth had the families separated from the other Haitians and moved to another location on the cutter.

After the other Haitians had been off-loaded in Port au Prince and the cutter started back to Guantánamo, the only passengers on the cutter were the two Haitian families. Beardsworth found that one man was an artist, an oil painter. He recalled, "I felt badly that the government had made this mistake. Of course, none of these Haitians had anything with them. I happened to have a set of oil paints. I was obviously never going to be capable of using them in any manner resembling art, so I gave the set of oil paints to the man. On the way back to Guantánamo, he painted me a picture which still hangs in my bedroom."

During an interview, Beardsworth pointed out a wrenching photograph hanging in his office of a young Haitian girl with tears streaming down her cheeks. He revealed that while working undocumented migrant operations, "I kept it hanging in my cabin to remind me what we are doing."

During another interview, Captain Beardsworth noted that two of his four command philosophies were do what is morally right and treat everyone with respect and dignity, whether your shipmates, prisoners, or migrants.[8]

The humane treatment of the undocumented migrants reached every level of those who worked most closely with the Chinese, Cubans, and Haitians, from commanding officers, such as Commander Beardsworth, to the lowest ranked people on the cutters and stations. This exhibited itself in such things as U.S. Coast Guard people spending their own money to give something to the undocumented migrants in their custody and to going back to a raft to retrieve family photographs for a Cuban family. One of the largest examples of this treatment came on September 11, 1993, when seamen apprentices Lance R. Manno and Patrick L. Richmond, who served on the cutter *Mohawk*, entered the sea on a dark, moonless night "fighting adverse conditions" and swam numerous times to rescue more than twenty migrants after their *yola* capsized. For their work, both received the Coast Guard Medal, the highest award a cutter crew member may receive for heroism during peace time.[9]

It is understandable that the U.S. Coast Guard's public affairs organization and the leadership strongly focus on the success of the mission. In general, considering that the service had fewer people than the New York City police department to undertake its duties throughout the world during the period covered in this work, it can rightfully call attention to its success. What is not understandable is that the leadership never focused on putting a human face on the people who successfully carried out the missions. Vincent C. Thomas Jr., a contributing editor for *Sea Power* magazine, in 1984 derided the "ineffective way in which the Coast Guard communicates to the media and general public the accomplishments of its people. Heroics at sea by Coast Guard personnel are an everyday occurrence; those accomplishments should be communicated routinely to higher authority as a matter of practice, so that the information is at least available for release to the public. That simply is not happening now; as a result, a horrendous vacuum of newsworthy information exists."[10] One also can add that few people in the United States understand not only the heroics of the people in the service but also their compassion. Thomas's comments hold true twenty-five years later.

The genesis of this work came from a remark by MCPOCG Charles W. "Skip" Bowen, at the time the officer-in-charge of Station Marathon in the Florida Keys. After explaining the duties of his station in intercepting undocumented migrants, Master Chief Bowen added, "The story of migrant work is more than an account of legal policies, politics or tactics. It is a human story both from the perspectives of the migrants involved and the men and women charged with stopping them."[11]

A reaction by Rear Adm. Arthur Brooks during an interview with a cynic best sums up how working with migrants affects those at the working level. The comment and question put forth to the admiral was, "The U.S. Coast Guard claims Haitian and Cuban operations are lifesaving missions or search and rescue (SAR) cases, they do not stress it is part of stopping undocumented migrants. By calling it 'a lifesaving mission,' is this not a way to disguise what is actually taking place, making it more palatable to the crews?" Admiral Brooks's reply is revealing.

> If you had been there and seen the Haitians dead on the beach at Fort Lauderdale and encountered these [overcrowded] vessels with bodies [on board], if you had seen [the Cubans] on the first day of the raft line north of Havana crying for help and dying when we arrived, [then] it feels like SAR. And so, if you told a crew this was a SAR case in reality they believed you, but it felt an awful lot like SAR case[s].
>
> When we worked the Hawk's Nest Cove case, [chapter 11] it was touch and go. For seven hours I did not know whether four hundred people were going to die. That feels a lot like a SAR case. I will go to my grave remembering the cloths [on the Haitian vessel during] the Hawk's Nest Cove case. As we approached, there were all these openings in the hull and people sticking shirts and other things out into the water and pulling them back to cool themselves. It was an amazing visual image.[12]

A U.S. Coast Guard officer said it best:

> Migrant operations [proved] the hardest, nastiest Coast Guard mission I have ever done. The hardest thing about it is that you understand, mainly with the Haitians, but to some extent the Cubans, they have given up ev-

> erything they have to buy a ticket on this death trap to take one long shot to have what every American has: an opportunity at the golden mountain. While you saved their lives because most of them underestimated the risks and dangers of a sea voyage, [as] most had no idea of how to get to Miami, you took away hopes and dreams. The hardest thing that we did was to dash hopes and dreams. That was the job; that was what the United States required you to do: take away their hopes and dreams. That was the hardest things for me personally. We did it. That was the mission, but it was the hardest part of the mission.[13]

Interviewing U.S. Coast Guard people who put up a gruff "Old Guard," no-nonsense, only-the-mission-matters exteriors, most let the mask slip when speaking about dealing with undocumented migrants. A crew member on the cutter *Nantucket*, for example, remarked, "The toughest thing out here is to not have your heart broken." Combine this with Capt. Michael Inman's emotional recounting of seeing the blanket-covered bodies of dead Haitians on the flight deck of a cutter, Admiral Brooks's statements, Captain Beardsworth's comments, and many others all give a graphic illustration of just how much migrant operations affect those who must enforce political policies.

The U.S. Coast Guard has carried out its mission of intercepting undocumented migrants from the sea route and has done so in a humane way, despite a vacillating political policy concerning undocumented migrants. In the process, the crews of the service saved literally thousands of lives. This is something that is little known by most Americans. It is time that the work of these men and women is recognized by the people they serve.

Acknowledgments

I received grants from the Foundation for Coast Guard History, the Naval Historical Foundation, and the Marine Corps Historical Foundation to help defray some of the costs for research.

I heard many stories and events during the research and writing of this book. Unfortunately, I could not include all of them, but even if they do not appear within the narrative, they helped me through the journey.

I owe a great deal of gratitude to many people. I would like to single out the following people who allowed me to take up much of their valuable time or contributed a great deal of support:

Adm. Thad W. Allen, commandant of the U.S. Coast Guard, who not only supported me in this project but also spent a great deal of time explaining the undocumented migrant situation earlier in his career.

MCPOCG Charles W. Bowen, who started me on this voyage and paved the way when the path became muddled, provided me with much information on his long experience in dealing with undocumented migrants, and read the work in manuscript form.

MCPOCG Vincent W. Patton III, Ed.D., (Ret.) provided me valuable information and support. Although very busy with his own work, he always had time to help.

Capt. Randy Beardsworth, USCG (Ret.) provided me with much valuable information on every trip to the Washington, D.C., area. His expertise is amazing, and it is a source of wonder to me that he spent so much of his valuable time answering my questions.

Rear Adm. Arthur E. Brooks, USCG, took time out of his busy schedule to relate valuable information from early in his career, as did Rear Adm. Wayne Justice.

Cdr. Michael F. White, USCG, proved a very great help, from paving the way for interviews and supplying information based upon his knowledge of AMIO, to providing a wonderful place to stay while researching in Miami.

Lt. Cdr. Rodrigo Rojas, USCG, exhibited his large amount of knowledge on Cuba and policies relating to that country during our many visits and e-mails.

Loren A. Noble read the manuscript many times and put up with my travels to unusual places, plus my frustration—also known as tantrums—when the manuscript was not going the way I wanted.

I am grateful for the following people who took time out of their own busy schedules to respond to my questions: Dr. Ko-lin Chin, Dr. Kelly Greenhill, and Mirta Ojito.

Peggy Norris read the manuscript. Readers should appreciate her abilities to spot mistakes and ask questions. Truman R. Strobridge listened to my comments and gave advice as I made my way through the project. Robin Smith, of Robin Smith, Ink, provided invaluable editorial advice.

Mark C. Mollan, archivist of the National Archives and Records Administration, went out of his way to provide me information and records, especially in the period prior to Mariel.

Tracy Ellen Smith, of Creative Design Resources, Inc., produced the outstanding maps for this work.

In Cuba, I appreciated the work of my guide and interpreter, whose name I will not mention because he had nothing to do with what I wrote about Cuba. He opened many doors for me and gave me good lessons on Cuban culture. Michael Parmly, head of the Special Interest Section in Havana, took time out from his busy schedule to discuss my project. Merri Ansara of Common Ground Education & Travel Services arranged the many things needed for my research in Cuba.

The following people, arranged alphabetically, helped a great deal. Unless otherwise mentioned, all are in the U.S. Coast Guard as active or retired military or civilian employees of the service. OSC James Armstrong III; Kirsten L. Arnold, U.S. Navy Historical Foundation, U.S. Navy History and Heritage Command; Dr. Gena Atkins, Operational Archives, U.S. Naval

History and Heritage Command; HSC Paul Battenfeld (Ret.); CMC Bruce Bradley; Cdr. Donald Brown; Capt. Peter Brown; BMC William E. Bulman; Lt. Eric Burley; Capt Scott Bushman; CMC Leilani Cale-Jones; Lt. Raymond Caro; Steven C. Carrier; BMC Raymond Codd; Eric Driggs; CWO3 Morgan Dudley; MK1 Joe Eick; Lt. R. A. Ellerbe; Lt. W. J. George; CWO4 Robert Gesking (Ret.); Capt. Robert C. Grant; Ens. Karl Hansen; Timothy Hecht; Angela Hirsch; CWO3 Michael B. Hoag; PA1 Jennifer Johnson; Daniel Jones, Naval History and Heritage Command; BMCM Phil Jordan (Ret.); CWO3 Brian Klimeck; Lt. Cdr. Fritz Kuebler; Lt. Cdr. Robert Landolfi; Dana Lewis; John Long; CWO4 Rick Loster; GMC Jory Luchsinger (Ret.); BM2 James Madsen; MKCM Tim Maleport—"If you don't make the ship's wheels move, you're just ballast"; Capt. James F. McEntire, USCG(Ret.); CMC Sean McPhilamy; Jason Molinari; Lt. Matthew Moorlag; Lt. Cdr. Cris Nettles(Ret.); Cdr. Kim Nettles (Ret.); Tom Nies; Donald O'Brien; Louis Orsini; Capt. Thomas Paar (Ret.); Lt. Cdr. Ronald Pailliotet; Tim Pettit, Operational Archives, U.S. Navy Heritage Center; BMC Joel Pribek; Capt. James E. Rendon; SSC Martin Risard; CMC Kurt Rugenius; Jeffery S. Ryan; Lt. Cdr Harry Schmidt; CWO2 Robert C. Schmidt; Capt. Karl L. Schultz; Lt. Robert Shaye; CWO4 Cliff Simonsen (Ret.); BMCS Stuart Slesh; BMCM Robert Sloan (Ret.); MCPOCG (Reserve Force) Jeffery Smith, who made sure I did not get lost; MK1 Charles Sowers; BMCS Chris Swiatek; Pat Szarek, CIS Historical Library; Michael Thomas; CWO Justin O. Vanden Heuvel, for his talk and film; Capt. Darrel V. Walraven, U.S. Customs and Border Protection; Edward Ward; Cdr. R. B. Watts; CWO2 Todd Weimorts; BMCM Chad Wendt; Cdr. Howard R. White; Marian White, CIS Historical Library; Lt. Cdr. Matthew White; Zack Wilske, CIS Historical Library; Capt. Marcus Woodring; CPO's Mess at Key West, Florida; crew of Station Islamorada, Florida; crew of Station Key West, Florida; officers and crew of Sector Key West, Florida; crew of Station Marathon, Florida; officers and crew of Sector Miami Beach, Florida; and to all those who wished to remain anonymous. Others who helped are listed within the narrative and notes.

I am grateful to the following people at the University Press of Florida: Gene Allen Smith and James Bradford, editors of the *New Perspectives on Maritime History and Nautical Archaeology* series; and Meredith Morris-

Babb, director of the Press; as well as countless others in the editorial, design and production, and marketing departments who have had a hand in bringing this book to fruition.

Writing this book was an experience akin to being in a U.S. Coast Guard *Defender*-class boat going forty knots in a three-foot sea for more than four hours. I could not have done it without the help of all those mentioned here, and the help of many others who go unmentioned who, I hope, will excuse the oversight. Where the book has merit, it is because I listened to the people who helped me. Where the book falters, it is because I ignored their advice.

Appendix

Numbers of Undocumented Migrants Intercepted by the U.S. Coast Guard from 1982 to 2009

Year	Chinese	Cuban	Haitian
1982	0	0	171
1983	0	44	511
1984	0	7	1,581
1985	12	51	3,721
1986	11	28	3,422
1987	0	46	2,866
1988	0	60	4,262
1989	5	257	4,902
1990	0	453	871
1991	138	1,722	2,065
1992	181	2,066	37,618
1993	2,511	2,882	4,270
1994	291	38,560	25,302
1995	509	525	909
1996	61	411	2,295
1997	240	421	288
1998	212	903	1,369
1999	1,092	1,619	1,039
2000	261	1,000	1,113
2001	53	777	1,391
2002	80	666	1,486
2003	15	1,555	2,013
2004	68	1,225	3,229
2005	32	2,712	1,850
2006	31	2,810	1,198
2007	73	2,868	1,610
2008	1	2,199	1,582
2009	35	799	1,782
TOTAL	5,912	66,666	114,716

Source: Data from U.S. Coast Guard, "Alien Migrant Interdiction," http://www.uscg.mil/hq/cg5/cg531/AMIO/FlowStats/FY.asp.

Notes

Abbreviations Used in the Notes

CIS	Citizenship and Immigration Service
Historian	Historian of the U.S. Coast Guard, U.S. Coast Guard Headquarters, Washington, D.C.
INS	Immigration and Naturalization Service
NARA	National Archives and Records Administration, Washington, D.C.
USCG	U.S. Coast Guard

Introduction

1. Interview, U.S. Coast Guard petty officer, who wishes to remain anonymous, with Dennis L. Noble, April 20, 2006.

2. Trebilcock, "The Myth of Posse Comitatus."

3. Chin, *Smuggled Chinese*, 28.

4. Reagan, "Address Accepting the Presidential Nomination."

5. Larzelere, *1980 Cuban Boatlift*, xxii. Captain Larzelere has not only written the best detailed study of the U.S. Coast Guard's role in Mariel but has also looked at the events, the social and, to some extent, the cultural aspects of events leading up to Mariel. Larzelere's work, as of this writing, is also the most detailed of any work on the service's role in interdicting undocumented migrants. I have borrowed heavily from his work.

6. Ford, *The Good Soldier*, 11.

7. *San Francisco Chronicle*, April 27, 1993.

8. Interview, Bowen.

Chapter 1. From Operación Pedro Pan to "Machine Gun Alley"

1. Larzelere, *1980 Cuban Boatlift*, 42.

2. Quoted in ibid., 63.

3. Unless otherwise noted, the early history of Cuba is found in, Roorda, *Cuba, America, and the Sea*, chs. 2 and 3.

4. The period leading up to and including the War of 1898 is found in "The World of 1898: The Spanish-American War," Library of Congress, http://www.loc.gov/rr/hispanic/1898, accessed August 3, 2009.

5. "The United States, Cuba, and the Platt Amendment, 1901," U.S. Department of State, Office of the Historian, http://www.state.gov/r/pa/ho/time/ip86557.htm, accessed August 3, 2009.

6. "Treaty Relations between the United States and Cuba, Signed May 29, 1934," http://www.latinamericanstudies.org/us-cuba/treaty-5-29-34.htm, accessed August 3, 2009.

7. Material on Batista is in Jerry A. Sierra, "Batista," http://www.historyofcuba.com/history/batista.htm.

8. "To Cuba," "Semper Paratus," "For Cuba," all in *Coast Guard Magazine* (1933): 12; USCG, *Record of Movements*, "Cuban Expedition (1933)," 359; and Walker, "Cuban Cruise of the Coast Guard," 7–9.

9. Quoted in Larzelere, *1980 Cuban Boatlift*, 58.

10. Ibid.

11. Ibid., 65.

12. Ibid., 55.

13. Ibid., 68.

14. Ibid., 66–74.

15. Ibid., 75–84.

16. Masud-Piloto, *From Welcomed Exiles*, 33–34.

17. Torres, "Peter Pan Operation," 6.

18. Ibid., 3.

19. Ibid.

20. Triay, *Fleeing Castro*, 2, 15–17, 27–28.

21. Torres, "Peter Pan Operation," 4.

22. Triay, *Fleeing Castro*, 16–23, 27–28.

23. Torres, "Peter Pan Operation," 17.

24. Johnson, "Children of 'Operation Pedro Pan,'" A10.

25. Ibid.

26. Ibid.

27. Ibid.

28. Ibid.

29. Triay, *Fleeing Castro*, ix.

30. Torres, "Peter Pan Operation," 1.

31. Larzeler, *1980 Cuban Boatlift*, 117n; and Zucker and Zucker, *Desperate Crossings*, 32.

32. Zucker and Zucker, *Desperate Crossings*, 32; and various newspaper clippings from, "General File, Miscellaneous Info," Migrant Files of the Historian of the U.S. Coast Guard, U.S. Coast Guard Headquarters, Washington, D.C., hereafter, Migrant Files.

33. Migrants Files.

34. Ibid.

35. Kaplan, "The Coast Guard and the Cuban Exodus," 2–3; and Migrant Files.

36. H. R. Kaplan, "The Coast Guard's Cuban Patrol," typescript, 10, undated [1965?], located in "General File, Miscellaneous Info" file, in Migrants—Cuba box, located in Historian, USCG office, hereafter Kaplan typsecript, "Cuban Patrol."

37. E-mail, Rear Adm. David W. Kunkel to Dennis L. Noble, August 19, 2007, copy in author's files.

38. Kaplan typsecript, "Cuban Patrol," 12.

39. Don Bedwell, "Drama's the Rule for Coast Guard since Castro," photocopy of an unidentified and undated article, Migrant Files.

40. Ibid.

41. Kaplan, "The Coast Guard and the Cuban Exodus," 5–6.

42. Ibid., 7.

43. Ibid., 7–8.

44. Ibid., 15.

45. Larzelere gives the number as 2,979; Larzelere, *1980 Cuban Boatlift*, 117n; Roorda places the number at 5,000; Roorda, *Cuba, America and the Sea*, 119.

46. Zucker and Zucker, *Desperate Crossings*, 33–34; Franklin states that when the boatlift became "a nuisance for the U.S. Coast Guard," the United States proposed an airlift. Franklin reports that as many as "3,000, perhaps as many as 5,000 Cubans came by sea." Franklin gives the date of November 6 as to when the flights came into being and states "more than 200,000" left by aircraft. Franklin, *Cuba and the United States*, 79.

47. Zucker and Zucker, *Desperate Crossings*, 33–34. See also, Woylych, "Cuban Refugee," 15–21; and Woolwine, "Conditional Entrants," 21–23.

48. Masud-Piloto, *From Welcomed Exiles*, 68.

49. All quoted material in this paragraph comes from photocopies located in the folder, "Immigration—1960s—26 de Julio Stand Off, Portsmouth, VA," in Box, "Immigration, Cuba, 1960s," Historian.

50. File 3721-66, S&R [SAR] Case Files Relating to Cuban Refugees, 1965–70, U.S. Coast Guard Office of Operations, Security and Intelligence Division, Entry 422, 20 September 1966, Box 3, Record Group 26, Records of the USCG, NARA.

51. File I-418-67 Law Enforcement, S&R [SAR] Case Files Relating to Cuban

Refugees, 1965–70, U.S. Coast Guard Office of Operations, Security and Intelligence Division, Entry 422, 8 September 1967, Box 6, Record Group 26, Records of the USCG, NARA.

52. Fall, *Street without Joy*, 291.

53. All quoted material on the *26 de Julio* case comes from photocopies located in folder "Immigration—1960s—26 de Julio Stand Off, Portsmouth, VA," in Box, "Immigration, Cuba, 1960s," Historian.

54. Formal Board of Investigation, File 5830, 17 December 1970, 71–63, located in "Simas Kurdirka," File, Historian. Other works on the subject include Ruksenas, *Day of Shame*; and Kurdirka and Eichel, *For Those Still at Sea*.

55. Meade, "'Vigilant' Revisited," 42.

56. Kaplan, "Coast Guard and the Cuban Exodus," 15.

Chapter 2. Opening the Floodgates

1. Franklin, *Cuba and the United States*, 68.
2. Ibid.
3. Ibid., 95.
4. Quoted in Larzelere, *1980 Cuban Boatlift*, 85.
5. Franklin, *Cuba and the United States*, 91.
6. Ibid., 93.
7. Ibid., 101–2.
8. Quoted in Larzelere, *1980 Cuban Boatlift*, 97.
9. Ojito, *Finding Mañana*, 28–29.
10. Larzelere, *1980 Cuban Boatlift*, 97.
11. Ibid., 105; and Ojito, *Finding Mañana*, 15.
12. Larzelere, *1980 Cuban Boatlift*, 100.
13. Ojito, *Finding Mañana*, 5.
14. Smith, *Closest of Enemies*, 198.
15. Quoted in, Larzelere, *1980 Cuban Boatlift*, 113.
16. Ibid.
17. Smith, *Closest of Enemies*, 199.
18. Quoted in, Larzelere, *1980 Cuban Boatlift*, 115.
19. Ibid., 467n3; and Smith, *Closest of Enemies*, 202–3.
20. Larzelere, *1980 Cuban Boatlift*, 4; and Ojito, *Finding Mañana*, 80–81, 85–93, 100–102.
21. Larzelere, *1980 Cuban Boatlift*, 120.
22. Ibid.
23. Quoted in Larzelere, *1980 Cuban Boatlift*, 3; and Ojito, *Finding Mañana*, 104.
24. Ojito, *Finding Mañana*, 105.
25. Ibid.
26. Smith, *Closest of Enemies*, 206.

27. Ojito, *Finding Mañana*, 114.
28. Quoted in Larzelere, *1980 Cuban Boatlift*, 27.
29. Ibid., 28.
30. Ibid., 39.
31. Quoted in ibid., 123.

Chapter 3. It's a Zoo Out There

Epigraph: Quoted in Greenhill, "People Pressure," 9.

1. Copeland, " 1980 Cuban Crisis," 139, 140.
2. Scheina, "Cuban Exodus of 1980," 44.
3. "Narrative Summary," in "Coast Guard District 7, Lessons Learned," Box "Cuba—1980—Mariel Boatlift, 1980," located in Historian, 5. Hereafter "Narrative Summary."
4. Ibid.
5. Stabile and Scheina, *USCG Operations*, 2.
6. Larzelere, *1980 Cuban Boatlift*, 141–43.
7. Ibid.
8. Stabile and Scheina, *USCG Operations*, 2–3.
9. Larzelere, 1980 Cuban Boatlift, 133–37.
10. Ibid., 142–44.
11. Ojito, *Finding Mañana*, 170.
12. Ibid., 164–65.
13. Larzelere, *1980 Cuban Boatlift*, 145.
14. "Cuban Boatlift from Mariel, Cuba to Key West, Florida: Chronology from April 21, 1980, to June 30, 1980, with an after summary up to Sept. 28, 1980," 2–3, in file "Immigration—Cuba—1980. Mariel Boatlift: All Official Press Releases (USCG)," in Box "Cuba—1980—Mariel Boatlift." Hereafter, "Chronology," USCG.
15. Brogdon, "Patrolling the Boatlift," 17; and Stabile and Scheina, *USCG Operations*, 4.
16. Stabile and Scheina, *USCG Operations*, 5–7.
17. Brogdon, "Patrolling the Boatlift," 16.
18. Malone, "Boat-Filled Florida Straits a 'Zoo,'" 17A.
19. Ojito, *Finding Mañana*, 200–201.
20. Brogdon, "Patrolling the Boatlift," 16. See also Silverstein, "Memories of Mariel," 32–35.
21. Brogdon, "Patrolling the Boatlift," 16; and Scheina, "Cuban Exodus of 1980," 46.
22. Narrative Summary, 6.
23. Brogdon, "Patrolling the Boatlift," 17.
24. Ibid., 18.
25. Ibid.

26. Ibid.
27. Quoted in, ibid.
28. "Chronology," USCG, 7.
29. Stabile and Scheina, *USCG Operations*, 8.
30. Franklin, *Cuba and the United States*, 28.

Chapter 4. A Liking for These People

1. "Cuban Boatlift from Mariel, Cuba to Key West, Florida: Chronology from April 21, 1980, to June 30, 1980, with an after summary up to Sept. 28, 1980," 8, in file "Immigration—Cuba—1980. Mariel Boatlift: All Official Press Releases (USCG)," in Box "Cuba—1980—Mariel Boatlift." Hereafter, "Chronology," USCG.
2. Stabile and Scheina, *USCG Operations*, 8–9.
3. Scheina, "Cuban Exodus of 1980," 47.
4. "League of Women Voters Remarks and a Question-and-Answer Session at the League's Biennial National Convention." May 5, 1980, http://www.presidency.ucsb.edu/ws/index.php?pid=33365.
5. Ibid.
6. Scheina, "Cuban Exodus of 1980," 47.
7. Ibid.
8. Ibid.
9. Stabile and Scheina, *USCG Operations*, 12.
10. Ibid., 13.
11. Ibid.; and Scheina, "Cuban Exodus of 1980," 48.
12. Larzelere, *1980 Cuban Boatlift*, 172.
13. Ibid.
14. "Chronology," USCG, 11.
15. Ibid.
16. Ibid., 12.
17. "Chronology," USCG, 12; Quoted in, Stabile and Scheina, *USCG Operations*, 14.
18. Unless otherwise noted, all material on Admiral Kunkel's experiences with the Cuban MiG jet fighter and the rescue of the woman from the cruise ship comes from an interview with Rear Adm. David W. Kunkel by Dennis L. Noble, April 17, 2009, and from photocopies of newspapers and the admiral's flight log. Tape recording and photocopies in author's files, hereafter Kunkel materials. The Navy's comment is in CNO/Flag Plot, OPREPORT 7 Subject Files, Operational Archives, Naval Heritage Center, Washington, D.C.
19. "Chronology," USCG, 13–14.
20. Ibid.
21. Stabile and Scheina, *USCG Operations*, 15.

22. Ibid.

23. Ibid., 16.

24. Stabile and Scheina, *USCG Operations*, 18; and Miller, *Olo Yumi* Incident. 51.

25. Stabile and Scheina, *USCG Operations*, 20.

26. Kunkel materials.

27. Stabile and Scheina, *USCG Operations*, 20.

28. Chief of Naval Operations (CNO)/Flag Plot, Operations Report and Subject Files, Folder 3, Naval Operational Archives, Naval Heritage Center, Washington, D.C.

29. Clark, Lasaga, and Reque, *1980 Mariel Exodus*, 14.

30. Stabile and Scheina, *USCG Operations*, 21.

31. Ibid., 22–23.

32. Ibid., 23.

33. Ibid., 24–25.

34. Ojito, *Finding Mañana*, 1–2.

35. Ibid., 175–76.

36. Ibid., 177.

37. Ibid., 178.

38. Ibid., 180–83.

39. Ibid., 184.

40. Ibid.

41. Ibid., 189–90, 207–11, 212–13.

42. Ibid., 211–13.

43. Ibid., 222.

44. Ibid., 217–29.

45. U.S. Coast Guard Auxiliary, "Operation Key Chain—Mariel Boat Lift," n.d., n.p., in author's files.

46. Stabile and Scheina, *USCG Operations*, 23.

47. Ibid., 24.

48. Scheina, "Cuban Exodus of 1980," 49; and "Coast Guard Callup of 900 Reservists," Coast Guard News Release, 94-80, June 5, 1980," 1–3, in "General File, Miscellaneous Info" file, in Migrants—Cuba box, located in Historian.

49. Scheina, "Cuban Exodus of 1980," 50.

50. Ibid., 26. Doss, *Let the Bastards Go*, gives a full account of the effort by the church group and the *God's Mercy*.

51. Rivera, *Decision and Structure*, 11.

52. Ibid., 21.

53. Ibid., 20.

54. Ojito, *Finding Mañana*, 263–64.

55. Clark, *1980 Mariel Exodus*, 14.

56. Parker, "Did the USCG Use the Lessons Learned," 25, 27.

Chapter 5. Dying to Get Here

1. Henriksen, *Clinton's Foreign Policy*, 21.

2. The 2009 United Nations Human Development Reports can viewed at http://hdr.undp.org/en/statistics; see also Diamond, *Collapse*, 329–357.

3. Henriksen, *Clinton's Foreign Policy*, 21.

4. Ibid., 22.

5. Stepick, "Unintended Consequences," 125.

6. INS, *1991 Statistical Yearbook*, tab 2, 29–30; see also, table in Stepick, "Unintended Consequences," 130.

7. Mitchell, "U.S. Policy toward Haitian Boat People," 70n.

8. Henriksen, *Clinton's Foreign Policy*, 22.

9. Mitchell, "U.S. Policy toward Haitian Boat People," 72.

10. Interview, Marshall; copy of notes in author's files.

11. Stepick, "Unintended Consequences," 137–41.

12. Mitchell, "U.S. Policy toward Haitian Boat People," 71.

13. Unless otherwise noted, all quotes concerning the *Hamilton*'s case are in Thomas, "Search and Interdict," 35–43.

14. Henriksen, *Clinton's Foreign Policy*, 22.

15. Ibid., 22.

16. All material on the *Northland* is from, "Phone Log," April 1991, and unclassified message O 022300Z May 91, located in "Haiti" Box, Historian.

17. Mitchell, "U.S. Policy toward Haitian Boat People," 74.

18. Ibid., 75.

19. Interview, Inman, November 4, 2008; notes in author's files.

20. Ibid.

21. Henriksen, *Clinton's Foreign Policy*, 22.

22. Unless otherwise noted, all quotes on Chauvel's attempts to sail with the Haitian boat people are from Chauvel, "Voyage of the Doomed," 9, 14–18, 22.

23. Interview, Bowen, 2006.

24. Thomas, "Search and Interdict," 40.

25. Interview, Brooks, November 4–5, 2008; copy of audio tape in author's files.

Chapter 6. To the Golden Mountain

1. Gordon Mezies is one of the latest authors to put forth this theory in his book *1421*.

2. Chin, *Smuggled Chinese*, 28.

3. Campbell, "Tribeca Review: Golden Venture."

4. Banister, Harbaugh, and Jamison, *Population and Migration Characteristics*, 1; and Hood, "Sourcing the Problem," 77.

5. Hood, "Sourcing the Problem," 77.

6. Zai and Wenzhen, "From Fujian to New York," 194–96
7. Ibid., 197–98.
8. Hood, "Sourcing the Problem," 79.
9. Chin, *Smuggled Chinese*, 9.
10. Hood, "Sourcing the Problem," 80.
11. Chin, *Smuggled Chinese*, 29.
12. Ibid.
13. Ibid., 32.
14. Ibid., 36.
15. Ibid., 33.
16. Ibid.
17. Ibid., 37–38.
18. Ibid., 66.
19. Ibid., 67.
20. Ibid., 69–70.
21. Ibid., 70–72.
22. Ibid., 73.
23. Ibid.
24. Hood, "Sourcing the Problem," 82.
25. Chin, *Smuggled Chinese*, 78.
26. David, *Our Coast Guard*, 92.
27. "Disaster at Sea," 34–36.
28. David, *Our Coast Guard*, 91–92.
29. Ibid., 92.
30. Ibid.
31. Ibid., 92–95.
32. Willoughby, *Rum War at Sea*, 77.
33. Photocopy of unidentified newspaper in Box "Chinese Migrants," Historian.
34. E-mail, Dr. Robert M. Browning Jr., Historian of the U.S. Coast Guard to Dennis L. Noble, February 18, 2009; and Dr. David S. Rosen, U.S. Coast Guard Historian, U.S. Coast Guard Pacific Area, to Dennis L. Noble, June 15, 2009. There were six 378-foot cutters in California, two in Washington State, and two in Hawaii.
35. Photocopy of unidentified newspaper in Box "Chinese Migrants," Historian.
36. Telephone conversation S/A Gene Chacon with Dennis L. Noble, April 21, 2010. Notes in author's files.
37. Burdman, "Huge Boom in Human Smuggling."
38. Unless otherwise noted, all material on the *Liberated Lady* and the *Jinn Yin No. 1* is contained in photocopies of the case in the personal file of Cdr. Michael F. White, USCG. I thank Commander White for allowing me to view the file and for further personal information concerning the at sea operations aspect of the case.
39. E-mail from U.S. Army officer who wishes to remain anonymous to Dennis L. Noble, April 15, 2010.

40. Burdman, "Huge Boom in Human Smuggling."

41. Ibid.

42. Mann, "Chinese Refugees."

43. Crossette, "Vessel Puts 150 Asian Migrants."

44. Ibid.

45. Photocopy of article, "Crew of Trawler Carrying Chinese May Face Charges," from unidentified newspaper and undated, in "Chin Wing" file, in Chinese, Historian.

46. Hardy, "Tale of the *East Wood*," 2–4.

47. Ibid., 3.

48. Ibid.

49. Ibid.

50. Ibid.

51. U.S. Coast Guard News Release 005Q-3, 2/6/93, page 3, obtained under a Freedom of Information Act (FOIA), response file 5720, February 18, 2009, copy in author's files.

52. Hardy, "Tale of the *East Wood*," 3.

53. Burdman, "Huge Boom in Chinese Smuggling."

54. Except where noted, all material on the *Pai Sheng* incident comes from photocopies of unidentified and undated newspapers located in the *Pai Sheng* file, Chinese, Historian.

55. Johnson, "Smuggling Ship Puzzled Coast Guard," A-7.

56. E-mail from U.S. Army officer who wishes to remain anonymous to Dennis L. Noble, April 15, 2010.

Chapter 7. The *Golden Venture*

1. C. T. O'Neil, "Golden Venture," [U.S. Coast Guard] Atlantic Public Affairs, an undated typescript manuscript located in Golden Venture file in Chinese Migrants, 1, in Historian, hereafter, O'Neil, "Golden Venture."

2. Ibid., 1–2.

3. Ibid., 2.

4. Ibid., 3.

5. Quote from photocopy of an unidentified newspaper located in "Golden Venture File," Historian.

6. Quote from a photocopied article from the *Washington Post*, June 7, 1993, n.p., clipping located in ibid.

7. Quote from photocopy of an unidentified newspaper located in ibid.

8. O'Neil, "Golden Venture," 5.

9. Quote from photocopy of an unidentified newspaper located in "Golden Venture File," Historian.

10. See, for example, Chin, *Smuggled Chinese*, 62.

11. The best source on the entire complicated story of the *Golden Venture*, especially the activities of "Sister Ping," is contained in Keefe, "Snakehead." Unless otherwise noted, all quoted material on the machinations and trial of Sister Ping and the *Golden Venture* are from this source.

12. U.S. Coast Guard unclassified message O 061710Z Jun 93, located in "Golden Venture File," Historian.

13. Keefe, "Snakehead"; and Murray, "Illegals Slip through the Cracks."

14. Dugger, "Dozens of Chinese."

15. Keefe, "Snakehead"; Chen, "People-Smuggling Suspect Is Held"; Preston, "Trial Starts with Details"; Preston, "Prosecutors Say Defendant"; and Feuer, "U.S. Tells of Ocean Transfer."

16. Halbfinger, "Landing Creates Stir," B6.

17. Ibid.

18. Chen, "Chinese Man Released," B5.

19. Ibid.

20. Ibid.

21. Ibid.

22. Ibid.

23. Westerman, *Fly to Freedom*, 23.

24. Director's statement, www.goldenventuremovie.com/HTM/statement.htm. See also, Campbell, "Tribeca Review: Golden Venture."

25. Waldman, "Smuggling Ship," B-3.

26. Ibid.

27. Moreland, "Stealing Passage to America," 33.

Chapter 8. Escaping the Dragon

Epigraph: Roberto Suro, "Smuggling Patrols Face Violence at Sea," *Washington Post*, January 27, 2000, A1.

1. Ting, "Door Stays Closed for Chinese," 2.

2. Ibid.

3. Sengupta, "Crackdowns Have Smugglers."

4. "174 Chinese Migrants."

5. Unless otherwise noted, all material on the Guam Boatlift is found in Moreland, "Stealing Passage to America," 42–50.

6. Ibid., 26.

7. Sundae, "19 Chinese Caught," A1.

8. Moreland, "Stealing Passage to America," 37.

9. Sundae, "19 Chinese Caught," A1.

10. Offley and Connelly, "U.S., Canada Track Smugglers' Ships," A1.

11. Verhovek, "Deadly Choice of Stowaways," A1.

12. Sanchez, "For Stowaways, Perilous Passage," A1.

13. Suro, "Smuggling Patrols Face Violence," A1.

14. Notes on the case are found in U.S. Coast Guard PACAREA/DISTRICT 11, Command Center, at 1126 (time), obtained by Freedom of Information Act (FOIA), hereafter, Command Center, [time]. All material obtained via FOIA in this and other notes are located in author's files.

15. Ibid., 2055; and interview, Justice; tape in author's files.

16. Situation Report (SITREP) 1, U.S. Coast Guard message O 072300Z DEC 99, obtained through a FOIA.

17. Interview, Justice; and Command Center, 0457.

18. Command Center, 0929, 0950.

19. SITREP 3, U.S. Coast Guard message O 100019Z DEC 99.

20. Ibid.; and interview, Justice.

21. Suro, "Smuggling Patrols Face Violence," A1.

22. Quoted in ibid.

23. Interview, Justice.

24. Ibid.

25. Suro, "Smuggling Patrols Face Violence," A1.

26. Interview, Justice.

27. Suro, "Smuggling Patrols Face Violence," A1.

28. Quoted in ibid.

29. Interview, Justice; and Suro, "Smuggling Patrols Face Violence," A1.

30. Suro, "Smuggling Patrols Face Violence," A1.

31. Interview, Justice.

32. Quoted in Suro, "Smuggling Patrols Face Violence," A1.

33. Ibid.

34. Interview, Justice; and "*United States of America v. Hsin-Yung Yeh, a/k/a Yeh Hsin Yung*, No. 00-3093, *United States of America v. Jian Zhou Li*," http://www.ll.georgetown.edu/federal/judicial/dc/opinions/00opinions/00-3092a.html.

35. Zhang and Chin, "Enter the Dragon," 738–39. Anyone interested in the organization of Chinese human smugglers should closely study this article.

36. Ibid., 739.

37. Quoted in Sanchez, "For Stowaways, Perilous Passage," A2.

38. Quoted in Zhang and Chin, "Enter the Dragon," 749.

Chapter 9. A War without Bullets

Epigraph: Quoted in Greenhill, "People Pressure," 229.

1. Henriksen, *Clinton's Foreign Policy*, 6.

2. Interview, Klapproth; notes in author's files.

3. Photocopy of newspaper in Able Manner File, Historian.

4. "Haitians Ready to Flee," B2; "Coast Guard Intercepts 640 Haitians," A18; and "Clinton Team Faces Test."

5. Marcus, "Clinton Beseiged," A1; and Kamen, and Marcus, "Clinton to Continue," A16.

6. Quoted in Travis, "Operation Able Manner," 1.

7. Ibid., 1–2.

8. Booth, "Navy, Coast Guard to Surround Haiti," A1.

9. "U.S. Sets Up Sea Barricade," A15.

10. Booth, "Navy, Coast Guard to Surround Haiti," A1.

11. Greenhill, "People Pressure," 237.

12. Beard, "Haitian 'Exodus' Discounted," A9.

13. Ibid.

14. Farah, "Coast Guard Patrols," A14.

15. Newspaper clipping in "Operation Able Manner" file, Historian.

16. Henriksen, *Clinton's Foreign Policy*, 23.

17. Ibid.

18. Ibid., 24.

19. Ibid.

20. Ibid., 25.

21. Ibid., 27.

22. Interview, senior U.S. Coast Guard officer who wishes to remain anonymous, April 2008, notes in author's files.

23. U.S. Coast Guard, Alien Migrant Interdiction, "Operation Able Manner," http://www.uscg.mil/hq/cg5/cg531/amio/AbM.asp.

24. Statistics are found in "Operation Able Manner" file, Historian.

25. Waldschmidt, "Haitian Rescues Illustrate," 1.

26. Clary, "Bodies of Four Haitians Wash Ashore," A12.

Chapter 10. The Human Factor

1. Interview with senior enlisted person who wishes to remain anonymous, with Dennis L. Noble, May 4, 2006; notes in author's files.

2. All materials on the *Neptune* case are in interview, Inman, November 5, 2008; e-mail, Capt. Michael D. Inman, to Dennis L. Noble, November 17,2008; notes and e-mail in author's files; Norton, "Ferry Sinking Survivor," A2; and "Of 800 to 1,200 Aboard Ferry, 285 Lived," 1.

3. Waldschmidt, "411 Haitians Rescued," 1.

4. Ibid., 1, 6.

5. Reynolds, *Skilful Show of Strength*, 23–24.

6. Ibid., 24.

7. Ibid.

8. Ibid., 25.

9. Ibid., 25–26.

10. Ibid., 26.

11. Ibid., 27.
12. Ibid.
13. Ibid., 29.
14. Ibid.
15. Ibid., 30–31.
16. Ibid., 31.
17. Vest, "Haitians Flood U.S. Fleet," A3.
18. Ibid.
19. Rey, "Voodou, Water, and Exile," 206.
20. Ibid.
21. Ibid., 206–7.
22. Ibid., 207.
23. Ibid., 212n31.
24. Vest, "In Windward Passage," A17.
25. Ibid.
26. Dorsey, "Coast Guard's Busiest Period," A1.
27. Quoted in ibid.

Chapter 11. Balseros

1. U.S. Coast Guard, "Alien Migrant Interdiction," http://www.uscg.mil/hq/cg5/cg531/AMIO/FlowStats/FY.asp, hereinafter "Alien Migrant Interdiction."
2. U.S. Coast Guard unclassified messages P041916Z May 91; P041437Z May 91; P0140616Z MAY 91 and statistics are found in Box Immigration, Cuba—1991, Historian.
3. Booth, and Williams, "Mixed Signals at Sea," A. 1.
4. "Alien Migrant Interdiction."
5. Greenhill, "Engineered Migration," 43.
6. Masud-Pilo, *From Welcomed Exiles*, 137.
7. Franklin, *Cuba and the United States*, 338; and Masud-Pilo, *From Welcomed Exiles*, 137.
8. Franklin, *Cuba and the United States*, 339.
9. Greenhill, "Engineered Migration," 40.
10. "1994 Migration Crisis—Chronology," 1, copy supplied to author from a former official at the U.S. Special Interests, Havana, Cuba; hereafter "1994 Chronology"; Newspaper clipping, "How the Cuban Crisis Unfolded," *Washington Post*, September 1, 1994, located in "Cubans-United States (1994 Sept. 1)," CIS Library, hereinafter cited as, "Clipping," CIS.
11. "1994 Chronology," 1.
12. Greenhill, "Engineered Migration," 40.
13. Quoted in, Smith, "Foreign Policy for Sale?" 212.
14. "1994 Chronology," 2.

15. "Clipping," CIS.

16. Copy of, "Intelligence Bulletin: Cuban Interviews, Part 1," September 1, 1994, 3, located in, "Cubans—United States (1994 Sept. 1)," CIS Library.

17. Smith, "Foreign Policy for Sale?" 212.

18. Ibid., 212–13.

19. Ibid., 213.

20. Ibid., 213–14.

21. Greenhill, "Engineered Migration," 53.

22. Clinton, *My Life*, 614–15.

23. Copy of, "Press Conference by the President," August 19, 1994, located in Box, "Cuba—1995," Historian.

24. Ibid.

25. Booth, "Cubans in U.S. Divided," A1.

26. Newman, "Flight from Cuba," A1.

27. Golden, "U.S.-Cuba Accord," A1

28. Ibid.

29. Ibid.

30. Interview, Brooks; e-mail, Brooks to Noble, June 8, 2009.

31. Golden, "With High Winds," A1.

32. Interview with a Cuban who wishes to remain unidentified, with Dennis L. Noble in La Habana Vieja (Old Havana), January 23, 2008. He also requested that Noble destroy the diagram while in Cuba.

33. U.S. Coast Guard, "Alien Migrant Interdiction," http://www.uscg.mil/hq/cg5/cg531/amio.asp.

34. "1994 Chronology," 4; Franklin, *Cuba and the United States*, 351; and Clinton, *My Life*, 614–15.

35. Greenhill, "Engineered Migration," 42.

36. Ibid., 61–62.

37. Sawczyn, "The United States Immigration Policy toward Cuba," 348–49.

Chapter 12. "The Toughest Thing Is to Not Have Your Heart Broken"

1. U.S. Coast Guard, "Alien Migrant Interdiction," http://www.uscg.mil/hq/cg5/cg531/amio.asp.

2. Nordheimer, "Flight from Cuba," A1.

3. Schmitt, "Flight from Cuba," A-18.

4. "Operation Able Vigil."

5. Ibid.

6. "Coast Guard News Release, 08-52," Box, Cuba—1995, Historian.

7. Interview, Rendon.

8. Quoted in Schmitt, "Flight from Cuba," A-18.

9. Ibid.

10. Interview, Brooks. Unless otherwise noted, all material on Sparky is contained in an e-mail attachment from Rear Admiral Arthur E. Brooks, USCG, to Dennis L. Noble, dated September 20, 2008. A copy is in the author's files.

11. Unless otherwise noted, all quotations concerning activities on the cutter *Baranof* are from Booth, "Latter-Day Boat Lift," A1.

12. Quoted in Waldschmidt, "Operation Able Vigil," 5.

13. Ibid.

14. Photocopy of teletype message AMR-00013359, August 24, 1994, Box, Cuba—1995, Historian.

15. Unless otherwise noted, all quotations concerning activities on the cutter *Nantucket* are from Wiesbecker, "Los Balseros."

16. Photocopy of AP story by Karen Testa, "Refugee Now Helps Rescue Countrymen with Coast Guard," September 15, 1994, Box, Cuba—1995, Historian.

17. Cihelka, "Desperation + Determination = Danger."

Chapter 13. The Dance

1. Pressley, "Faster Boats Carry Cubans," A2.

2. Ibid.

3. Personal observations and notes during a patrol with boat crew from Station Marathon, June 15, 2007.

4. Interviews with various station members and officers in the Florida Keys during June 2007.

5. Fineman, "Human Tidal Wave," A16.

6. Interview, Kunkel; notes in author's files.

7. For Defender Class boats, see U.S. Coast Guard, "Aircraft and Cutters: 25-foot Defender Class Boat (RB-HS/RB-S)," www.uscg.mil/datasheet/25rbs.asp; and for Special Purpose boats, see "Coast Guard Takes Delivery of 33-Foot Special Purpose Boat," *Coast Guard News*, July 24, 2007, www.coastguardnews.com/coast-guard-takes-delivery-of-33-foot-special-purpose boat/2007.

8. Interview, Bowen, 2006, and personal observations, Station Marathon, June 17, 2007.

9. Interview, Bowen; notes in author's files.

10. Personal observations and notes, Station Islamorada, June 13, 2007.

11. Interview with boat crew member who wishes to remain anonymous, with Dennis L. Noble, June 15, 2007; notes in author's files.

12. Gentile, "'Coasties' vs. Cubans," A2.

13. Ibid.

14. Interview with a boat crew member who wishes to remain anonymous, with Dennis L. Noble, June 15, 2007; notes in author's files.

15. Ibid.

16. Ibid.

17. Ibid.

18. For information on López's invasions, see May, *Manifest Destiny's Underworld*, 1, 23–28, 29–32, 83, 96, 126, 137–38, 163, 169, 171, 173, 190–91, 227, 228, 229, 273, 376n38.

19. Interview, Bowen, 2006.

20. Cihelka, "Desperation + Determination = Danger.

21. Ibid.

22. Interview, with a station member who wishes to remain anonymous, with Dennis L. Noble, June 17, 2007; copies of notes in author's files.

23. Interview, with U.S. Coast Guard officer who wishes to remain anonymous, by Dennis L. Noble, September 22, 2008; audio tape in author's files.

24. Block, "Blood and Water," A1.

25. Lacey, "For Cubans Fleeing," A1; interview, U.S. Coast Guard boarding officer who wishes to remain anonymous, with Dennis L. Noble, June 18, 2007; notes in author's files.

26. Block, "Blood and Water," A1.

27. Interview, Bowen, April 9, 2009.

28. Ibid.; Blum and Diaz, "Return 15 Cubans," 1A; Lopez, "Migrants say Cuba Slow," 1; and Marx, "Cubans' Case Stirs Passions," 10.

29. All material on the Station Islamorada case is found at Bartlett, "The Verdict."

30. Beardsworth, "9 Ways for US to Talk to Cuba," 27–28. The other government entities in communication with Cuba are the Federal Aviation Administration, the National Weather Service, and the "monthly military Guantanamo fence line talks"; and interview, Beardsworth, April 16, 2009; audio tape in author's files.

31. Beardsworth, "U.S.-Cuba Functional Relationships," 28–29.

32. Ibid., 29.

33. Ibid.

34. Ibid., 29–30; Interview, Beardsworth.

35. Interview, Beardsworth.

36. Ibid.

37. Ibid.

38. Ibid.; The points covered were law enforcement, port security, environment, and the establishment of a U.S. Coast Guard officer as liaison officer in the U.S. Special Interests Section, Havana.

39. Three former U.S. Coast Guard liaison officers in Havana were interviewed. All wished to remain anonymous. Unless otherwise noted, all quotes in the section on the liaison officers are from these sources. Audio tapes, e-mails, and notes from the sources are in the author's files.

40. Officially titled, The Cuban Liberty and Democratic Solidarity (LIBERTAD) Act of 1996, Pub. L. 104-114, the act—usually referred to as the Helms-Burton Act, named for Sen. Jesse Helms (R-NC) and Rep. Dan Burton (R-IN)—strengthened the U.S. embargo of Cuba. As pointed out in the narrative, among its many provi-

sions is the prohibition of Fidel or Raúl Castro in any "transitional government." See, http://www.treas.gov/offices/enforcement/ofac/legal/statutes/libertad.pdf. For a discussion of the act, see, Roland Estevez, "Modern Application."

41. Beardsworth, "U.S.-Cuba Functional Relationships," 30.

42. Roig-Franzia, "Smuggling of Cubans," A11.

43. Information supplied by a former official at the U.S. Special Interests Section, Havana, who wishes to remain anonymous; audio tape in author's files. See also, Jordan, "Risky Route to Freedom," A1.

44. Lacey, "For Cubans Fleeing," A1.

45. Ibid.; and information supplied by a former official at the U.S. Special Interests Section, Havana, who wishes to remain anonymous; audio tape in author's files.

46. Roig-Franzia, "Smuggling of Cubans," A11.

47. Lacy, "For Cubans Fleeing," A1.

48. Quoted in Ellingwood, "Mexico and Cuba Agree," A3. See also Watson, "Mexico Is Returning Migrants," A13.

Chapter 14. Something Different Happening Every Day

1. Interview, Allen; audio tape in author's files. All quotes, unless otherwise noted, are from this interview.

2. "Investigation into the Circumstances Surrounding the Use of Force and the Interdiction of Six Cuban Migrants in the Vicinity of Miami Beach, FL, on Tuesday, June 29, 1999," Serial 5830, with enclosures, dated July 14, July 22, July 27, and August 9, 1999, obtained under a Freedom of Information Act (FOIA) request; copy in author's files. Hereafter, Investigation, with date and page number(s).

3. Ibid., July 14, 2–6.

4. Comments on videotape of news reports provided in ibid.

5. The amount of newsprint on Surfside 6 almost equals the amount of television time. The following is a sampling: Clary, "Coast Guard Forcibly Halts," 1; "Clinton Condemns Coast Guard Action," A20; "Miami Protests Capture," A3; Mercer, "Miami Cubans Are Outraged," A14; "No End to This Mistake," 2E; and "Re-Examine U.S. Policy," 20A.

6. Investigation, 9–11, July 22, 1999.

7. Ibid.

8. Ibid.

9. Ibid., 11.

10. Ibid., 22 July 1999, 1–2.

11. Ibid.

12. Cohen, "Fools for Elian," A23. The amount of material on this case is voluminous. A Google search of Elian Gonzalez on June 19, 2009, for example, revealed 172,000 entries, while a Google Scholar search revealed 4,150 entries.

Chapter 15. Summing Up

1. Interview with a retired U.S. Coast Guard officer who wishes to remain anonymous, with Dennis L. Noble, April 13, 2007; notes in author's files.

2. Greenhill, "Engineered Migration," 48.

3. Quoted in ibid., 42.

4. "OPLAN VIGLANT SENTRY (OVS) Mass Migration Plan," an unclassified briefing in the Office of Law Enforcement, U.S. Coast Guard Headquarters, Washington, D.C.

5. Interview with senior officer who wishes to remain anonymous, with Dennis L. Noble, February 30, 2009; notes in author's files; and e-mail, Dr. Alex Wald, associate professor of Spanish, U.S. Coast Guard Academy, to Dennis L. Noble, March 17, 2009; copy in author's files.

6. Moreland, "Stealing Passage to America," 50.

7. Interview, Beardsworth, April 15, 2009; e-mail, Beardsworth to Noble, June 13, 2009; all material in author's files.

8. The other two philosophies were always strive to become a true professional and have fun.

9. See Coast Guard Medal Award Citations, R-S, http://www.uscg.mil/history/awards/CGMedal_Citations_R_S.asp, and e-mail, Lance R. Manno to Dennis L. Noble, April 9, 2009; in author's files.

10. Thomas, "Search and Interdict," 40.

11. Interview, Bowen.

12. Interview, Brooks.

13. E-mail from officer who wishes to remain anonymous, to Dennis L. Noble, June 5, 2009; copy in author's files.

Selected Bibliography

Archives

Historian of the U.S. Coast Guard, Washington, D.C.
Library, Citizenship, Immigration Service, Washington, D.C.
National Archives and Records Administration, Washington, D.C.
Naval Heritage Center, Washington, D.C.
Naval Operational Archives, Naval Heritage Center, Washington, D.C.

Interviews and Questionnaires

Allen, Adm. Thad, Commandant of the U.S. Coast Guard, April 7, 2009, Washington, D.C.

Beardsworth, Capt. Randy, USCG (Ret.), Catalyst Partners, various dates, 2006–9, Washington, D.C.

Brooks, Rear Adm. Arthur E., Commander, Coast Guard District 17, November 4–5, 2008, Juneau, Alaska.

Brown, Capt. Peter, Chief of Law Enforcement, Coast Guard District 7, January 29, 2009.

Bowen, Charles W., Master Chief Petty Officer of the U.S. Coast Guard, various dates, 2006–9, Washington, D.C.

Inman, Capt. Michael D., Chief of Response, Coast Guard District 17, November 4–5, 2008, Juneau, Alaska.

Justice, Rear Adm. Wayne J., USCG, Assistant Commandant for Capability, U.S. Coast Guard Headquarters, April 13, 2009, Washington, D.C.

Klapproth, Cdr. Robert J., USCG, Commanding Officer, U.S. Coast Guard Cutter *Active*, December 28, 2006, Port Angeles, Washington.

Kunkel, Rear Adm. David, USCG (Ret.), Commander, Coast Guard District 7, June 19, 2007, and April 17, 2009, Miami, Florida.

Marshall, BMCS Wayne, USCG (Ret.), August 10, 2009, Silverdale, Washington.
Orsini, Louis, head of the Alien Migration Interdiction Office, Office of Law Enforcement, U.S. Coast Guard Headquarters, April 13, 2009, Washington, D.C.
Patton, Vincent E., III, Ed.D., Master Chief Petty Officer of the U.S. Coast Guard, Ret., various dates 2006–9, Miami, Florida, and Washington, D.C.
Rendon, Capt. James E., USCG, September 25, 2008, Washington, D.C.

Newspapers

Key West Citizen
Miami Herald
New York Times
San Francisco Chronicle
Seattle Post-Intelligencer
Seattle Times
Washington (D.C.)*Post*

Articles, Books, Dissertations, Theses, and Unpublished Papers

Ackerman, Holly. "The Balsero Phenomenon, 1991–1994." *Cuban Studies* 26 (1996): 169.
———. "The Cuban Rafter Phenomenon: A Unique Sea Experience." *Latino Studies* 3 (2005): 417–20.
———. "Mass Migration, Nonviolent Social Action, and the Cuban Raft Exodus, 1959–1994: An Analysis of Citizen Motivation and International Politics." Ph.D. diss., University of Miami, 1996.
Ackerman, Holly, and Juan M. Clark. *The Cuban Balseros: Voyage of Uncertainty*. Miami: The Policy Center of the Cuban-American National Council, 1995.
Anker, Deborah. "The Forty Year Crisis: A Legislative History of the Refugee Act of 1980." *San Diego Law Review* 19, no. 9 (1981): 30–33.
Atkinson, William. "Fate of the Xin Ji Li Hou." *Commandant's Bulletin* (July 1995): 6–8.
Banet-Weiser, Sarah. "Elian Gonzales and the Purpose of America, Nation, Family, and the Child-Citizen." *American Quarterly* 55, no. 2 (June 2003): 149–78.
Banister, Judith, Christina Wu Harbaugh, and Ellen Jamison. *Population and Migration Characteristics of Fujian Province, China*. Washington, D.C.: Center for International Research, U.S. Bureau of the Census, November 1993.
Bartlett, Sandra. "The Verdict: Station Islamorada Faces Crucial Test." U.S. Coast Guard Web site, http://www.piersystem.com/go/doc/586/38018.
Beard, David. "Haitian 'Exodus' Discounted—Coast Guard Expects a Short-Term Surge, But Not a Flood of Refugees." *Seattle Times*, January 17, 1993, A9.
Beardsworth, Randy. "U.S.-Cuba Functional Relationships: A Security Imperative."

In *9 Ways For U.S. to Talk to Cuba and For Cuba to Talk U.S.*, 27–32. Washington, D.C.: The Center for Democracy in the Americas, 2009.

Billeaudeaux, Andre. "Changing Tactics in the Mona Pass." *Commandant's Bulletin*, February 1996, 4–5.

Block, Robert. "Blood and Water: Cuban Migrants Confront Harsher U.S. Tactics at Sea; Colliding Policies Feed Speedboats, Shootings; Treating Ms. Machado." *Wall Street Journal*, July 23, 2007, A1.

Blum, Vanessa, and Madeline Baro Diaz. "Return 15 Cubans to United States, Federal Judge Rules." *South Florida Sun-Sentinel*, March 1, 2008, 1A.

Bockley, Kathryn M. "Comment: A Historical Overview of Refugee Legislation: The Deception of Foreign Policy in the Land of Promise." *North Carolina Journal of International Law and Commercial Regulation* 21 (1995–1996): 253–91.

Bond, George D. "Stemming the Haitian Tide." U.S. Naval Institute *Proceedings* 112 (August 1986): 104–6.

Booth, William. "Cubans in U.S. Divided on New Policy." *Seattle Times*, August 20, 1994, A1.

———. "Latter-Day Boat Lift Tests Rescue Fleet; Record Numbers of Cubans Try to Cross Florida Straits." *Washington Post*, August 27, 1994, A1.

———. "Navy, Coast Guard to Surround Haiti; U.S. Seeks to Stop Expected Exodus at Sea." *Washington Post*, January 16, 1993, A1.

Booth, William, and Daniel Williams, "Mixed Signals at Sea; U.S. Opening Lures Desperate Cubans to Boats." *Washington Post*, August 18, 1994, A1.

Brannan, Liz. "CG Ends Chinese Passage." *Commandant's Bulletin*, July 1994, 2–3.

———. "Migrant-Smuggling Voyage Comes to an End." *Commandant's Bulletin*, June 1995, 2–5.

Brogdon, W. J. "Patrolling the Boatlift." U.S. Coast Guard Academy Alumni *Bulletin*, September–October 1980, 16–21.

Brown, Donald. "Crooked Straits: Maritime Smuggling of Humans from Cuba to the United States." *Inter-American Law Review* 33, nos. 2&3 (Summer–Fall 2002): 273–93.

Burdman, Pamela. "Huge Boom in Human Smuggling." *San Francisco Chronicle*, April 27, 1993, A1.

Calvo, Dana. "Coast Guard Suspends 8 Officers Fire Hose, Pepper Spray Used on Cubans at Sea." *Sun Sentinel* (Fort Lauderdale, FL), July 9, 1999, 1B.

Campbell, Christopher. "Tribeca Review: Golden Venture," April 17, 2006, http://www.cinematical.com/2006/04/17/tribeca-review-golden-venture/.

Carter, Jimmy. *Keeping Faith: Memoirs of a President*. New York: Bantam Books, 1982.

Castro, Max J. "The New Cuban Immigration in Context." In *The North-South Agenda Papers*, 3–12. Miami: North-South Center, 2002.

Celeste, Manoucheka. "Media Portrayals of Cubans and Hatitians: A Comparative Study of *The New York Times*." Thesis, University of Florida, 2005.

Charles, Carolle. "Politicial Refugees or Economic Immigrants? A New 'Old Debate' within the Haitian Immigrant Communities but with Contestants and Divisions." *Journal of American Ethnic History* 25, nos. 2–3 (Winter–Spring 2008): 190–208.

Chauvel, Patrick. "Voyage of the Doomed." *Miami Herald*, March 1, 1992.

Chen, David W. "Chinese Man Released Ends a Five-Year Tale of Misfortune." *New York Times*, September 10, 1998, B5.

———. "People-Smuggling Suspect Is Held after 5-Year Hunt." *New York Times*, April 21, 2000, B3.

Chin, Ko-Lin. *Chinatown Gangs: Extortion, Enterprise, and Ethnicity*. New York: Oxford University Press, 1996.

———. *Smuggled Chinese: Clandestine Immigration to the United States*. Philadelphia: Temple University Press, 1994.

———. "The Social Organization of Chinese Human Smuggling." In *Global Human Smuggling: Comparative Perspectives*, edited by David Kyle and Rey Koslowski, 216–33. Baltimore, Md.: Johns Hopkins University Press, 2001.

Churgin, Michael J. "Mass Exodus: The Response of the United States." *International Migration Review* 30, no. 1 (1996): 310–24.

Cihelka, Carolyn. "Desperation + Determination = Danger: Violent Behavior of Cuban Migrants Resisting Interdiction Endangers Rescuers and Rescuees Alike," *Coast Guard Magazine*, October 2000.

Clark, Juan M. "The Exodus from Revolutionary Cuba (1959–1974): A Sociological Analysis." Ph.D. dissertation, University of Florida, 1975.

Clark, Juan M., Jose I. Lasaga, and Rose S. Reque. *The 1980 Mariel Exodus: An Assesment and Prospect*. Washington, D.C.: The Council for Inter-American Security, 1981.

Clary, Mike. "Bodies of Four Haitians Wash Ashore in Florida." *Los Angeles Times*, February 12, 1994, A12.

———. "Coast Guard Forcibly Halts Cuban Refugees." *Los Angeles Times*, June 30, 1999, 1.

Clinton, Bill. *My Life*. New York: Alfred A. Knopf, 2004.

"Clinton Condemns Coast Guard Action on Cubans." *New York Times*, July 14, 1999, A20.

"Clinton Team Faces Test in Forming New Policy on Haiti: Haiti's Political Stalemate." Op-ed, *Christian Science Monitor*, December 3, 1992.

"Coast Guard Intercepts 640 Haitians." *Washington Post*, December 3, 1992, A18.

Cohen, Richard. "Fools for Elian." *Washington Post*, April 6, 2000, A23.

Conde, Yvonne M. *Operation Pedro Pan: The Untold Exodus of 14,048 Cuban Children*. New York: Routledge, 1999.

Copeland, Ronald. "The 1980 Cuban Crisis: Some Observations." *Journal of Refugee Resettlement*, August 1981, 22–32.

———. "The Cuban Boatlift of 1980: Strategies in Federal Crisis Management."

Annals of the American Academy of Political and Social Science 467, no. 1 (1983): 138–50.

Cornelius, Wayne A. *Illegal Migration to the United States: Recent Research Findings, Policy Implications, and Research Priorities.* Cambridge: Center for International Studies, Massachusetts Institute of Technology, 1977.

Crossette, Barbara. "Vessel Puts 150 Asian Migrants Ashore in Haiti." *New York Times*, August 18, 1992, A3.

Cushman, John H. "For 6 Haitians, Last-Minute Reprieve." *The New York Times*, February 14, 1992, A12.

David, Evan J. *Our Coast Guard: High Adventure with the Watchers of Our Shores.* New York: D. Appleton-Century Company, 1937.

Demo, Anne Teresa. "The After Image: Immigration Policy after Elian." *Rhetoric & Public Affairs* 10 (Spring 2007): 27–49.

DeWind, Josh. "Alien Justice: The Exclusion of Haitian Refugees." *Journal of Social Issues* 46, no. 1 (1990): 121–32.

Diamond, Jared. *Collapse: How Societies Choose to Fail or Succeed.* New York: Penguin, 2005.

"Disaster at Sea." *U.S. Coast Guard Magazine*, December 1932, 34–36.

Dominguez, Jorge I. "U.S.-Cuban Relations: From the Cold War to the Colder War." *Journal of Interamerican Studies and World Affairs* 39, no. 3 (1997): 49.

Dominguez, Virginia R. *From Neighbor to Stranger: The Dilemma of Caribbean People in the United States.* ARP Occasional Papers, 5. New Haven, Conn.: Antilles Research Program, Yale University Press, 1975.

Dorsey, Jack. "Coast Guard's Busiest Period: 9,697 Haitians Saved in 4 Days." *The Viginia-Pilot*, July 9 1994, A1.

Doss, Joe Morris. *Let the Bastards Go: From Cuba to Freedom on God's Mercy.* Baton Rouge: Louisiana State University Press, 2003.

Dugger, Celia W. "Dozens of Chinese from 1993 Still in Jail." *New York Times*, February 3, 1997, A1.

Ellingwood, Ken. "Mexico and Cuba Agree on Migrants; Mexico Will Deport Cubans Who Cross Its Border Illegally in a Bid to Reach the U.S. The Number Has Soared." *Los Angeles Times*, October 21, 2008, A3.

Engerstrom, David Wells. *Presidential Decision Making Adrift: The Carter Administration and the Muriel Boatlift.* Lanham, Md.: Rowman & Littlefield, 1997.

Estevez, Roland. "Modern Application of the Cuban Adjustment Act of 1966 and Helms-Burton: Adding Insult to Injury." *Hofstra Law Review* 30 (2002): 1273–98.

Fall, Bernard B. *Street without Joy: The French Debacle in Indochina.* Mechanicsburg, PA: Stackpole, 1961.

Farah, Douglas. "Coast Guard Patrols, Clinton's Switch on Repatriation Delay Haitian Exodus." *Washington Post*, January 21, 1993, A14.

Faust, Allen. "Patrolling the Freedom Flotilla." *Commandant's Bulletin*, July 7, 1980, 6–14.

Fedarko, Kevin. "Haiti: Policy at Sea." *Time*, July 18, 1994, 20–24.

Ferguson, James. *Papa Doc, Baby Doc: Haiti and the Duvaliers*. New York: Basil Blackwell, 1987.

Fernandez, Gaston A. "The Freedom Flotilla: A Legitimacy Crisis of Cuban Socialism?" *Journal of Internamerican Studies and World Affairs* 24, no. 2 (May 1982): 183–209.

———. *The Mariel Exodus: Twenty Years Later: A Study on the Politics of Stigma and a Research Bibliography*. Miami: Ediciones Universal, 2002.

Feuer, Alan. "U.S. Tells of Ocean Transfer in Smuggling of Immigrants." *New York Times*, June 14, 2005, B-3.

Fineman, Mark. "Human Tidal Wave on the Rise." *Seattle Times*, January 7, 2001, A16.

Finkel, Michael. "Desperate Passage." *New York Times Magazine*, June 18, 2000.

Ford, Ford Madox. *The Good Soldier: A Tale of Passion*. London: Penguin, 1946.

Fragomen, Austin T., Jr. *The Illegal Alien: Criminal or Economic Refugee?* Staten Island, N.Y.: Center for Migration Studies, 1973.

Franklin, Jane. *Cuba and the United States: A Chronological History*. New York: Ocean Press, 1997.

Frelick, Bill. "Haitian Boat Interdiction and Return: First Asylum and First Principles of Refugee Protection." *Cornell International Law Journal* 26, no. 3 (1993): 675–94.

French, Dave. "Standoff at Sea: An Increasing Number of Illegal Migrants Are Resorting to Violence to Earn Passage to the United States." *Coast Guard*, September 1999, 12–15.

Garcia, Maria Cristina. *Havana USA: Cuban Exiles and Cuban Americans in South Florida, 1959–1994*. Berkeley: University of California Press, 1996.

Gay, Kathlyn. *Leaving Cuba: From Operation Pedro Pan to Elian*. Brookfield, Calif.: Twenty-first Century Books, 2000.

Gentile, Carmen. "'Coasties' vs. Cubans." *Washington Post*, July 4, 2007, A2.

George, Evan. "U.S. Refugee Policy: A Comparison of Haiti and Cuba during the Cold War and Post-Cold War Periods." Thesis, University of Florida, 2004.

Girard, Philippe R. *Clinton in Haiti: The 1994 Invasion of Haiti*. New York: Palgrave Macmillan, 2004.

———. *Paradise Lost: Haiti's Tumultuous Journey from Pearl of the Caribbean to Third World Hot Spot*. New York: Palgrave Macmillan, 2005.

Golden, Tim. "U.S.-Cuba Accord Sets off a Surge of New Refugees." *New York Times*, September 11, 1994, A1.

———. "With High Winds, Cubans' Exodus Appears to End." *New York Times*, September 13, 1994, A1.

Goldstone, Jack A. "A Tsunami on the Horizon? The Potential for International Migration from the People's Republic of China." In *Human Smuggling: Chinese Migrant Trafficking and the Challenge to America's Immigration Tradition*, edited by Paul J. Smith, 48–75. Washington, D.C.: Center for Strategic & International Studies, 1997.

Greenhill, Kelly M. "Engineered Migration and the Use of Refugees as Political Weapons: A Case Study of the 1994 Cuban *Balseros* Crisis." *International Migration* 40 (2002): 39–74.

———. "People Pressure: Strategic Engineered Migration as an Instrument of Statecraft and the Rise of the Human Rights Regime." Ph.D. dissertation, Massachusetts Institute of Technology, 2004.

"Haitians Ready to Flee to U.S. They Expect the Clinton Administration Will Welcome Them Here with Open Arms." *Seattle Post-Intelligencer*, November 27, 1992, B2.

Halbfinger, David M. "Landing Creates Stir in a Seaside Town." New York Times, June 1, 1998, B1.

Hardy, Cameron. "Tale of *East Wood*," *Commandant's Bulletin*, April 1993: 2–5.

Henriksen, Thomas H. *Clinton's Foreign Policy in Somalia, Bosnia, Haiti, and Korea*. Stanford, Calif.: Hoover Institution on War, Revolution and Peace, 1996.

Herrera, Andrea O. *Remembering Cuba: Legacy of a Diaspora*. Austin: University of Texas Press, 2001.

Hood, Marlow. "Sourcing the Problem: Why Fuzhou?" In *Human Smuggling: Chinese Migrant Trafficking and the Challenge to America's Immigration*, edited by Paul J. Smith, 4–92. Washington, D.C.: The Center for Strategic and International Studies, 1997.

Howe, James C. "Coast Guard Rescues of Cuban Migrants." *North-South: The Magazine of the Americas* 4, no. 2 (September–October 1994): 48.

Immigration and Naturalization Service (INS). *1991 Statistical Yearbook*. Washington: U.S. Government Printing Office, 1991.

Johnson, Clarence. "Smuggling Ship Puzzled Coast Guard." *San Francisco Chronicle*, May 25, 1993, A7.

Johnson, Dirk. "Children of 'Operation Pedro Pan' Recall Painful Separations from Parents." *New York Times*, April 22, 2000, A10.

Johnson, Roger N. "Bad News Revisited: The Portrayal of Violence, Conflict, and Suffering on Television News." *Peace and Conflict: Journal of Peace Psychology* 2, no. 3 (1996): 201–16.

Jones, Bob. "Haitian Migrant Interdiction—Chase Report." *Commandant's Bulletin*, January 25, 1982, 8–14.

Jordan, Mary. "A Risky Route to Freedom: Desperate Cubans Head for U.S. via Honduras." *Washington Post*, July 16, 2004, A1.

Kamen, Al, and Ruth Marcus. "Clinton to Continue Forcible Repatriation of Fleeing Haitians." *Washington Post*, January 15, 1993, A16.

Kaplan, Herbert R. "The Coast Guard and the Cuban Exodus." U.S. Coast Guard News Release 74-65, November 5, 1969, 2–3.

———. "The Coast Guard's Cuban Patrol." *Navy*, March 1965, 3–9.

Keefe, Patrick Radden. "The Snakehead: The Criminal Odyssey of Chinatown's Sister Ping." *New Yorker*, April 24, 2006.

———. *The Snakehead: An Epic Tale of the Chinatown Underworld and the American Dream*. Garden City, N.Y.: Doubleday, 2009.

Kleinberg, Howard. "Clinton Cuban Policy Wet and Dry." *The Seattle-Post Intelligencer*, September 22, 2000, B8.

Knott, Dick. "Workaday SAR: Coast Guard Miami." *Naval Aviation News*, April 1981, 18–23.

Kramek, Joseph. "The Crowded Deck." U.S. Naval Institute *Proceedings* 119 (December 1993): 48–53.

Kung, Cleo J. "Supporting the Snakeheads: Human Smuggling from China and the 1996 Amendment to the U.S. Statutory Definition of 'Refugee.'" *The Journal of Law & Criminology* 90, no. 4 (Summer 2000): 1271–1316.

Kudirka, Simas, and Larry Eichel, *For Those Still at Sea*. New York: Dial Press, 1978.

Kyle, David, and Rey Koslowski, eds. *Global Human Smuggling: Comparative Perspectives*. Baltimore, Md.: Johns Hopkins University Press, 2001.

Lacey, Marc, "For Cubans Fleeing to the U.S., The First Stop Is Often Mexico." *New York Times*, October 16, 2007, A1.

Larzelere, Alex. *The 1980 Cuban Boatlift: Castro's Ploy—America's Dilemma*. Washington, D.C.: National Defense University Press, 1988.

Legomsky, Stephen H. *Immigration and Refugee Law and Policy*, 3rd ed. New York: Foundation Press, 2002.

Lennox, Malissia. "Refugees, Racism, and Reparations: A Critique of the United States' Haitian Immigration Policy." *Stanford Law Review* 45 (February 1993): 687–724.

Leogrande, William M. "From Havana to Miami: U.S. Cuba Policy as a Two-Level Game." *Journal of Interamerican Studies and World Affairs* (1998): 67–86.

Leonard, John N. "The Coast Guard and Haitian Migrant Interdiction Operations in 2004." *Joint Center for Operational Analysis and Lessons Learned (JCOA-LL) Bulletin* 6, no. 4 (September 2004): 66–71.

Loescher, Gil, and John A. Scanlan. *Calculated Kindness: Refugees and America's Half-Open Door, 1945 to the Present*. London: Collier Macmillian Publishers, 1986.

Lohrmann, Reinhard. "Migrants, Refugees and Insecurity: Current Threats to Peace?" *International Migration* 38 (September 2000): 3–22.

Lopez, Ellas E. "Migrants say Cuba Slow to Issue Exit Visas." *Knight Ridder Tribune Business News*, December 17, 2006, 1.

Malone, Jim. "Boat-Filled Florida Straits a 'Zoo' for the Coast Guard." *Miami Herald*, April 26, 1980, 17A.

Mann, Jim. "Chinese Refugees Take to High Seas." *Los Angeles Times*, March 16, 1993.

Marcus, Ruth. "Clinton Besieged about Policy Shifts; Promises Not Broken, He Insists." *Washington Post*, January 15, 1993, A1.

Marx, Gary. "Cubans' Case Stirs Passions; Spotlight Intensifies on U.S. 'Wet Foot, Dry Foot' Policy." *Chicago Tribune*, March 6, 2006, 10.

Masud-Piloto, Felix Roberto. *From Welcomed Exiles to Illegal Immigrants: Cuban Migration to the U.S., 1959–1995*. Lanham, Md.: Rowman & Littlefield, 1996.

May, Robert E. *Manifest Destiny's Underworld: Filibustering in Antebellum America*. Chapel Hill: University Press of North Carolina, 2002.

McCready, Siobhan. "The Science of Saving Rafters." *Sea Frontiers* 40, no. 6 (1994):14.

Meade, James J. "'Vigilant' Revisited," U.S. Coast Guard Academy Alumni Association *Bulletin*, March–April 1972, 41–48.

Mercer, Pamela. "Miami Cubans Are Outraged at Treatment of 6 Refugees." *New York Times*, July 1, 1999, A14.

Mesa-Lago, Carmelo. "Cuba's Raft Exodus of 1994: Causes, Settlement, Effects, and Future." *North-South Agenda Papers*, no. 12 (April 1995): 1–29.

Mezies, Gordon. *1421: The Year China Discovered America*. New York: Morrow, 2003.

"Miami Protests Capture of 6 Cubans." *Seattle Times*, June 30, 1999, A3.

Miller, Alan F. "The *Olo Yumi* Incident." U.S. Naval Institute *Proceedings* 106 (October 1980): 51.

Miller, Jake. *The Plight of Haitian Refugees*. New York: Praeger, 1984.

Miranda, Carlos Ortiz. "Haiti and the United States during the 1980s and 1990s: Refugees, Immigration, and Foreign Policy." *San Diego Law Review* 32, no. 3 (1995): 673–744.

Mitchell, Christopher. "U.S. Policy toward Haitian Boat People, 1972–93." *Annals of the American Academy of Political and Social Science* 534(July 1994): 69–80.

Mohn, Michael A. "U.S. Caribbean Maritime Alien Migration Interdiction: A Perspective from an Enforcer." Unpublished paper, Brookings Institution, Washington, D.C., July 2008.

Moorehead, Caroline. *Human Cargo: A Journey among Refugees*. New York: Henry Holt, 2005.

Moreland, Bernard. "Stealing Passage to America." Master's thesis, Harvard University, 2000.

Morales, Waltraud Queiser. "After Fidel: What Future for U.S.-Cuba Relations?" *Military Review* (September–October 2007): 90–100.

Murray, Anne E. "Illegals Slip through the Cracks." New York Post, June 8, 1993.

Musalo, Karen, Jennifer Moore, and Richard A. Boswell. *Refugee Law and Policy: A Comparative and International Approach*. Durham, N.C.: Carolina Academic Press, 1995.

Nielsen, Richard. "We 'The Public': At Sea with the Anchors." *Policy Opinions*, September 2000, 64–67.

Newman, Maria. "Flight from Cuba: The Cubans; Cuba Patrolling Beaches to Keep Children Off Unseaworthy Rafts." *New York Times*, August 29, 1994, A1.

"No End to this Mistake." *Palm Beach Post* (West Palm Beach, Fla.), July 1, 1999, 2E.

Nordheimer, Jon. "Flight from Cuba: The Overview; U.S. Will Expand Patrols to Stop Cuban Refugees." *New York Times*, August 23, 1994, A1.

Norton, Michael. "Ferry Sinking Survivor: 'Sea Was Full of People'—Up to 1,700 May be Missing in Haitian Disaster." *Seattle Times*, February 19, 1993, A2.

"Of 800 to 1,200 Aboard Ferry, 285 Lived." *New York Times*, February 20, 1993, A1.

Offley, Ed, and Joel Connelly, "U.S., Canada Track Smugglers' Ships High-Tech Spies Follow Migrants from Canada." *Seattle Post-Intelligencer*, September 22, 1999, A1.

Ojito, Mirta A. *Finding Mañana: A Memoir of a Cuban Exodus*. New York: Penguin Press, 2005.

"174 Chinese Migrants Taken from Boat Seized by the U.S." *New York Times*, September 20, 1998, A1.

Operation Uphold Democracy: Joint After Action Report (JAAR). Norfolk, Va.: Director of Joint Training Command, United States Atlantic Command, 1995.

Parker, Gary. *Guarding the Coast: Alien Migrant Interdiction Operations at Sea*. Report 17-97. New London, Conn.: Center for Advanced Studies, United States Coast Guard Academy, 1997.

Parker, Robert C. "Did the USCG Use the Lessons Learned from the 1980 Mariel Boatlift from Cuba in Dealing with the Haitian Migration Crisis of 1991–92?" Paper, Naval War College, Newport, R.I., June 18, 1993.

Pastor, Robert A. "The Clinton Administration and the Americas: The Postwar Rhythm and Blues." *Journal of Interamerican Studies and World Affairs* 38, no. 4 (Winter 1996–1997): 99–129.

Patterson, Thomas E. "Bad News, Bad Governance." *Annals of the American Academy of Political and Social Science* 546 (July 1996): 97–108.

Pressley, Sue Anne. "Faster Boats Carry Cubans, Haitians to Florida," *Washington Post*, December 31, 1998, A2.

———. "Refugee Incident Spawns a Tempest: Miami in Uproar After Cubans' Arrest." *Washington Post*, July 3, 1999, A3.

Preston, Julia. "Prosecutors Say Defendant in Immigrant Smuggling Case Ran an Underground Empire." *New York Times*, May 25, 2005, B-1.

———. "Trial Starts with Details of Immigrant Smuggling." *New York Times*, May 17, 2005, B-1.

"Protestors Battle Police in Havana; Castro Warns U.S." *The New York Times*, August 6, 1994, A1.

Quigley, Kevin G. "Engagement or Containment: Preparing for a Post-Castro Cuba." Paper, Marine Corps War College, Marine Corps University, Quantico, Va., April 8, 2003.

Quisenberry, Anderson C. *Lopez's Expeditions to Cuba, 1850 and 1851.* Louisville, Ky.: John P. Morton & Company, 1906.

Reagan, Ronald. "Address Accepting the Presidential Nomination at the Republican Convention, Detroit, 1980," July 17, 1980. Available at The American Presidency Project, http://www.presidency.ucsb.edu/ws/index.php?pid=25970.

"Re-Examine U.S. Policy Administration Has Two Clear Choices," *Sun Sentinel* (Fort Lauderdale, Fla.), August 12, 1999, 20A.

Rey, Terry. "Vodou, Water, and Exile: Symbolizing Spirit and Pain in Port-au-Prince." In *Religion, Violence, Memory, and Place*, edited by Oren Baruch Stier and J. Shawn Landres, 198–213. Bloomington: Indiana University Press, 2006.

Reynolds, Nicholas E. *A Skillful Show of Strength: U.S. Marines in the Caribbean, 1991–1996.* Washington, D.C.: History and Museums Division, Headquarters, U.S. Marine Corps, 2003.

Richardo Luis, Roger. *Guantanamo: The Bay of Discord.* New York: Ocean Press, 1994.

Rivera, Mario Antonio. *Decision and Structure: U.S. Refugee Policy in the Mariel Crisis.* Lanham, Md.: University Press of America, 1991.

Robbins, Carla Anne. "Dateline Washington: Cuban-American Clout." *Foreign Policy*, Autumn 1992, 162–82.

Roig-Franzia, Manuel. "Smuggling of Cubans Surges in Mexico." *Washington Post*, August 4, 2007, A11.

Roorda, Eric Paul. *Cuba, America and the Sea: The Story of the Immigrant Boat* Analusia *and 500 Years of History Between Cuba and America.* Mystic, Conn.: Mystic Seaport, 2005.

Rosendahl, Bruce. "Awaiting Rafters." *Sea Frontiers* 40, no. 6 (1994): 8.

Rosendahl, Bruce R., Thomas N. Lee. "Roulette in the Straits of Florida." *Sea Frontiers* 39, no. 3 (May–June 1993): 8.

Ruksenas, Algis. *Day of Shame: The Truth about the Murderous Happings aboard the Cutter Vigilant during the Russian-American Confrontation off Martha's Vineyard.* New York: D. McKay Co., 1973.

Rumbaut, Ruben G. "Origins and Destinies: Immigration to the United States since World War II." *Sociological Forum* 9, no. 4 (December 1994): 583–621.

Sanchez, Rene. "For Stowaways, Perilous Passage as Human Cargo." *Washington Post*, January 17, 2000, A2.

Sanders, Jimy M. "The Refugees Who Came in from the Cold: Pawns of the Cold War in America." *Qualitative Sociology* 19, no. 4 (December 1996): 557–65.

Sartin, Jeffery S. "GITMO Revisited." *Wisconsin Medical Journal* 105, no. 5 (2006): 13–14.

Sawczyn, Read. "The United States Immigration Policy toward Cuba Violates Established Maritime Policy, It Does Not Curtail Illegal Immigration, and Thus Should Be Changed so that Cuban Immigrants Are Treated Similarly to Other

Immigrants." *Florida Journal of International Law* 13, no. 3 (Summer 2001): 341–60.

Scanlan, John A., and G. D. Loescher. "Mass Asylum and Human Rights in American Foreign Policy." *Political Science Quarterly* 97, no. 1 (Spring 1982): 39–56.

Scheina, Robert L. "The Cuban Exodus of 1980." U.S. Naval Institute *Proceedings* 106 (October 1980): 44–51.

Schmitt, Eric. "Flight from Cuba: The Military; Coast Guard and Navy Divert 70 Ships to Refugee Crisis off Florida." *New York Times*, August 26, 1994, A18.

Schulz, Donald E., and Gabriel Marcella. *Reconciling the Irreconcilable: The Troubled Outlook for U.S. Policy toward Haiti.* Carlisle Barracks, Pa.: U.S. Army War College, 1994.

Sengupta, Somini. "Crackdowns Have Smugglers Trying New Routes, Officials Say." *New York Times*, June 1, 1998, B6.

Silverstein, Judy L. "Memories of Mariel: 20 Years Later." *Reservist*, April–May 2000, 32–35. http://www.uscg.mil/reservist/mag2000/April-May2000.pdf.

Smagula, John W. "Redirecting Focus: Justifying the U.S. Embargo against Cuba and Resolving the Stalemate." *North Carolina Journal of International Law and Commercial Regulation* 21, no. 1 (Fall 1995): 66–109.

Smith, Jonathan C. "Foreign Policy for Sale? Interest Group Influence on President Clinton's Cuba Policy, August 1994." *Presidential Studies Quarterly* 28, no. 1 (Winter 1998): 207–20.

Smith, Paul J. "Chinese Migrant Trafficking: A Global Challenge." In *Human Smuggling: Chinese Migrant Trafficking and the Challenge to America's Immigration Tradition*, edited by Paul J. Smith, 1–22. Washington, D.C.: Center for Strategic & International Studies, 1997.

Smith, Wayne S. *Closest of Enemies: A Personal and Diplomatic Account of U.S.–Cuban Relations Since 1957.* New York: Norton, 1987.

Soroka, Stuart N. "Media, Public Opinion, and Foreign Policy." *Press & Politics* 8, no. 1 (Winter 2003): 27–48.

Stabile, Benedict L., and Robert L. Scheina. *U.S. Coast Guard Operations during the 1980 Cuban Exodus.* Washington, D.C.: U.S. Coast Guard Historian's Office, 1980.

Stepick, Alex. "Unintended Consequences: Rejecting Haitian Boat People and Destabilizing Duvalier." In *Western Hemisphere Immigration and United States Foreign Policy*, edited by Christopher Mitchell, 125–55. University Park: Penn State Press, 1992.

Suarez, Virgil. "The Culture of Leaving: Balsero Dreams." *Hopscotch: A Cultural Review* 2, no. 2 (2001): 2–13.

Suchlicki, Jaime. *Cuba: From Columbus to Castro and Beyond.* Washington, D.C.: Brasseys, 2002.

Sullivan, Mark P., and Maureen Taft-Morales. *Cuba: Issues for the 207th Congress.* Washington, D.C.: Congressional Research Service, Library of Congress, 2002.

Sundae, Scott. "19 Chinese Caught after Cargo Container Voyage Smuggling Trip across Pacific Took 2 Weeks." *Seattle Post-Intelligencer*, April 21, 1999, A1.

Suro, Roberto. "Smuggling Patrols Face Violence at Sea; Freighters Bearing Human Cargo Pose a Risky Test for Coast Guard." *Washington Post*, January 27, 2000, A1.

Thomas, Vincent C., Jr. "Search and Interdict." *Sea Power* 27, no. 9 (August 1984): 25–43.

Ting, Jan C. "The Door Stays Closed for Chinese." *Asiaweek*, September 9, 1994, 2.

Torres, Maria de los Angeles. "The Peter Pan Operation: The Cold War and the Politics of Refugee Children." Undated typescript located in the CIS Historical Reference Library, Washington, D.C.

Travis, Bill. "Operation Able Manner." *Coastline*, January 1993, 1–2.

Trebilcock, Craig T. "The Myth of Posse Comitatus," http://www.homelandsecurity.org/journal/articles/Trebilcock.htm, October 2000.

Triay, Victor Andres. *Fleeing Castro: Operation Peter Pan and the Cuban Children's Program*. Gainesville: University Press of Florida, 1999.

U.S. Coast Guard. *Record of Movements: Vessels of the United States Coast Guard, 1790–December 31, 1933*. Washington, D.C.: U.S. Coast Guard, N.d.

"U.S. Sets Up Sea Barricade to Halt Haiti Refugees." *Los Angeles Times*, January 17, 1993, A15.

Verhovek, Sam Howe. "Deadly Choice of Stowaways: Ship Containers." *New York Times*, January 12, 2000, A1.

Vest, Jason. "Haitians Flood U.S. Fleet—Thousands Are Rescued From Boats off Coast." *Seattle Times*, June 28, 1994, A3.

———. "In Windward Passage, Facing the Human Factor of Haitian Crisis." *Washington Post*, July 3, 1994, A17.

Waldman, Amy. "Smuggling Ship to Become a Reef Off Florida." *New York Times*, August 19, 2000, B3.

Waldschmidt, Dan. "Dangerous Voyage." *Commandant's Bulletin*, February 1996, 2–4.

———. "411 Haitians Rescued off South Florida," *Coastline*, May 1994, 1, 6.

———. "Haitian Interdiction Continues." *Commandant's Bulletin*, November 16, 1981, 8–15.

———. "Haitian Migrant Rescues Soars." *Coastline*, July 1994, 1, 4–6.

———. "Haitian Rescues Illustrate Importance of 'Able Manner.'" *Coastline*, February 1994, 1.

———. "Mercy Mission . . . Operation Able Manner." *Commandant's Bulletin*, October 1994, 2–5.

———. "Operation Able Vigil." *Commandant's Bulletin*, November 1994, 2–5.

Walker, Raymond J. "The Cuban Cruise of the Coast Guard." *The U.S. Coast Guard* 7 (January 1934): 7–9.

Wasem, Ruth Ellen. *CRS Report for Congress: Cuban Migration Policy and Issues*. Washington: D.C.: Library of Congress, Congressional Research Service, 2007.

———. *CRS Report for Congress: Haitian Migration: Statistical and Chronological Fact Sheet*. Washington, D.C.: Library of Congress, Congressional Research Service, 1993.

———. *CRS Report for Congress: Immigration Reform: Brief Synthesis of Issue*. Washington, D.C.: Library of Congress, Congressional Research Service, 2007.

———. *CRS Report for Congress: U.S. Immigration Policy on Asylum Seekers*. Washington, D.C.: Congressional Research Service, 2007.

———. *CRS Report for Congress: U.S. Immigration Policy on Haitian Migrants*. Washington: D.C.: Library of Congress, Congressional Research Service, 2005.

———. *CRS Report for Congress: U.S. Immigration Policy on Haitian Migrants*. Washington: D.C.: Library of Congress, Congressional Research Service, 2007.

Watson, Julie. "Mexico Is Returning Migrants to Cuba." *Orlando* (Fla.) *Sentinel*, December 5, 2008, A13.

Westerman, William. *Fly to Freedom: The Art of the* Golden Venture *Refugees*. New York: Museum of the Chinese in the Americas, 2001.

Wiesbecker, Allan. "Los Balseros: A Day in the Life of the Guard," July 16, 2003, http://www.aweisbecker.com/dsp/authors-corner/articles/los-balseros-a-day-in-the-life-of-the-guard/.

Willoughby, Malcolm F. *Rum War at Sea*. Washington, D.C.: Government Printing Office, 1964.

Woolwine, H. L. "Conditional Entrants—The New Refugees." *I and N Reporter*, October 1976, 21–23.

Woylych, Robert L. "The Cuban Refugee." *I and N Reporter*, October 1976, 15–19.

Zai Liang and Wenzhen Ye. "From Fujian to New York: Understanding the New Chinese Immigration." In *GlobalHuman Smuggling: Comparative Perspectives*, edited by David Kyle and Rey Koslowski, 187–215. Baltimore, Md.: Johns Hopkins University Press, 2001.

Zhang, Sheldon, and Ko-Lin Chin. "Enter the Dragon: Inside Chinese Human Smuggling Organizations." *Criminology* 40, no. 4 (November 2002): 737–66.

Zink, James R. "Race and Foreign Policy in Refugee Law: A Historical Perspective of the Haitian Refugee Crisis." *DePaul Law Review* 28 (1998): 559–617.

Zucker, Norman L., and Naomi F. Zucker. *Desperate Crossings: Seeking Refuge in America*. Armonk, N.Y.: M. E. Sharpe, 1996.

Index

Dennis L. Noble entered the enlisted force of the U.S. Coast Guard in 1957 and retired as a senior chief petty officer in 1978. Shore duty was on the East and West coasts and the Great Lakes. Sea duty took him six times to the Arctic, twice to the Antarctic, on International Ice Patrol, and to other locations between these extremes.

After retirement, Noble earned a Ph.D. in U.S. history from Purdue University. He is author of fourteen books, with his latest, *Captain "Hell Roaring" Mike Healy: From American Slave to Arctic Hero* published by the University Press of Florida. Noble lives in Sequim, Washington, with his wife, Loren, and a strange cat.

New Perspectives on Maritime History and Nautical Archaeology Series

Edited by James C. Bradford and Gene Allen Smith

Maritime Heritage of the Cayman Islands, by Roger C. Smith (1999)

The Three German Navies: Dissolution, Transition, and New Beginnings, 1945–1960, by Douglas C. Peifer (2002)

The Rescue of the Gale Runner: *Death, Heroism, and the U.S. Coast Guard*, by Dennis L. Noble (2002); first paperback edition, 2008

Brown Water Warfare: The U.S. Navy in Riverine Warfare and the Emergence of a Tactical Doctrine, 1775–1970, by R. Blake Dunnavent (2003)

Sea Power in the Medieval Mediterranean: The Catalan-Aragonese Fleet in the War of the Sicilian Vespers by Lawrence V. Mott (2003)

An Admiral for America: Sir Peter Warren, Vice Admiral of the Red, 1703–1752, by Julian Gwyn (2004)

Maritime History as World History, edited by Daniel Finamore (2004)

Counterpoint to Trafalgar: The Anglo-Russian Invasion of Naples, 1805–1806, by William Henry Flayhart III (first paperback edition, 2004)

Life and Death on the Greenland Patrol, 1942, by Thaddeus D. Novak, edited by P. J. Capelotti (2005)

X Marks the Spot: The Archaeology of Piracy, edited by Russell K. Skowronek and Charles R. Ewen (2006)

Industrializing American Shipbuilding: The Transformation of Ship Design and Construction, 1820–1920, by William H. Thiesen (2006)

Admiral Lord Keith and the Naval War Against Napoleon, by Kevin D. McCranie (2006)

Commodore John Rodgers: Paragon of the Early American Navy, by John H. Schroeder (2006)

Borderland Smuggling: Patriots, Loyalists, and Illicit Trade in the Northeast, 1783–1820, by Joshua M. Smith (2006)

Brutality on Trial: "Hellfire" Pedersen, "Fighting" Hansen, and the Seamen's Act of 1915, by E. Kay Gibson (2006)

Uriah Levy: Reformer of the Antebellum Navy, by Ira Dye (2006)

Crisis at Sea: The United States Navy in European Waters in World War I, by William N. Still Jr. (2006)

Chinese Junks on the Pacific: Views from a Different Deck, by Hans Konrad Van Tilburg (2007)

Eight Thousand Years of Maltese Maritime History: Trade, Piracy, and Naval Warfare in the Central Mediterranean, by Ayşe Devrim Atauz (2007)

Merchant Mariners at War: An Oral History of World War II, by George J. Billy and Christine M. Billy (2008)

The Steamboat Montana *and the Opening of the West: History, Excavation, and Architecture*, by Annalies Corbin and Bradley A. Rodgers (2008)

Attack Transport: USS Charles Carroll *in World War II*, by Kenneth H. Goldman (2008)

Diplomats in Blue: U.S. Naval Officers in China, 1922–1933, by William Reynolds Braisted (2009)

Sir Samuel Hood and the Battle of the Chesapeake, by Colin Pengelly (2009)

Voyages, The Age of Sail: Documents in Maritime History, Volume I, 1492–1865; Volume II: The Age of Engines, 1865–Present, edited by Joshua M. Smith and the National Maritime Historical Society (2009)

Voyages, the Age of Engines: Documents in Maritime History, Volume II, 1865–Present, edited by Joshua M. Smith and the National Maritime Historical Society (2009)

HMS Fowey *Lost . . . and Found!*, by Russell K. Skowronek and George R. Fischer (2009)

American Coastal Rescue Craft: A Design History of Coastal Rescue Craft Used by the United States Life-Saving Service and the United States Coast Guard, by William D. Wilkinson and Commander Timothy R. Dring, USNR (Ret.) (2009)

The Spanish Convoy of 1750: Heaven's Hammer and International Diplomacy, by James A. Lewis (2009)

The Development of Mobile Logistic Support in Anglo-American Naval Policy, 1900–1953, by Peter V. Nash (2009)

Captain "Hell Roaring" Mike Healy: From American Slave to Arctic Hero, by Dennis L. Noble and Truman R. Strobridge (2009)

Sovereignty at Sea: U.S. Merchant Ships and American Entry into World War I, by Rodney Carlisle (2009)

Commodore Abraham Whipple of the Continental Navy: Privateer, Patriot, Pioneer, by Sheldon S. Cohen (2010)

Lucky 73: USS Pampanito*'s Unlikely Rescue of Allied POWs in WWII*, by Aldona Sendzikas (2010)

Cruise of the Dashing Wave*: Rounding Cape Horn in 1860*, by Philip Hichborn, edited by William H. Thiesen (2010)

Seated by the Sea: The Maritime History of Portland, Maine, and Its Irish Longshoremen, by Michael C. Connolly (2010)

The Whaling Expedition of the Ulysses*, 1937–1938*, by Lt. (jg) Quentin R. Walsh, U.S. Coast Guard, edited and with an Introduction by P. J. Capelotti (2010)

Stalking the U-Boat: U. S. Naval Aviation in Europe During World War I, by Geoffrey L. Rossano (2010)

In Katrina's Wake: The U.S. Coast Guard and the Gulf Coast Hurricanes of 2005, by Donald L. Canney (2010)

A Civil War Gunboat in Pacific Waters: Life On Board USS Saginaw, by Hans K. Van Tilburg (2010)

The U.S. Coast Guard's War on Human Smuggling, by Dennis L. Noble (2011)